beth hillel congregation
LIBRARY
3220 big tree lane

Wilmette, Illinois 60091

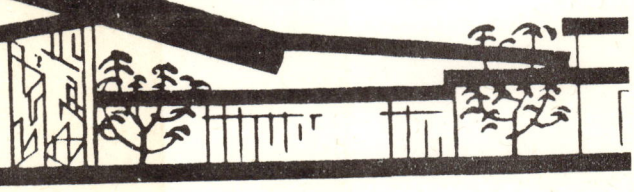

presented by

_____

_____

in memory of / honor of

_____

_____

WITHDRAWN

WITH FURY POURED OUT

A Torah Perspective on the Holocaust

1

WITH FURY POURED OUT

A Torah Perspective on the Holocaust

by
Rabbi Bernard Maza

KTAV PUBLISHING HOUSE, INC.
Hoboken, NJ
1986

Copyright © 1986
Bernard Maza

Library of Congress Cataloging-in-Publication Data

Maza, Bernard.
  With fury poured out.

  Bibliography: p.
  1. Holocaust (Jewish theology) 2. Holocaust, Jewish (1939-1945) I. Title.
BM645.H6M38 1986   926.3   86-15248
ISBN 0-88125-107-0

Manufactured in the United States of America

DEDICATION

This book is dedicated to my father, the Gaon Harav Eliyahu Mordecai Maza, of blessed memory, who in a life filled with sacrifice never lost an iota of his infinite faith in Hashem.

In 1938, at a time of great suffering for the Jewish people and at a time when all signs pointed to a darkening fate for millions of his Jewish brothers, he wrote in his classic book of faith, *Messiah is On His Way*, the following words:

> The time in which we are now living is an exceptional one in the history of our people. Nobody gives it a thought; nobody wants to understand what is now happening. Our belief is weak. Many Jews have lost hope during this long and bitter exile, in spite of the fact that it is just because of our hope that we have lived through all the bitter and difficult times we had. And though many Jews still believe and hope, their faith and their hope is not what it should be. For it is not true faith if you believe that Messiah will some day eventually come, but that in the meantime you suffer exile and pain and do not expect help or salvation. Such faith and hope is not true hope because it does not give any solace to the suffering. And this is what our Rabbis meant when they said that in the world to come Hashem will ask, "Did you expect salvation?" Even if you hoped Messiah would come but you thought who knows when that will be, that is not true faith and hope.
>
> We must believe and hope that suddenly, unexpectedly, Messiah may come. You are sitting in your store, you are going about your business, you are riding to work, every one is busy with his own activity, when suddenly there comes a blast of a Shofar, loud and long which is heard from one end of the world to the other and the Prophet Elijah runs up and calls out, "Messiah is on his way!" That is what every man must believe, that this could happen any minute.

So staunch was his faith. His teachings and examples of faith in Hashem while in the midst of the most difficult periods were a source of strength to the Jewish people of the East Side whom he served with love during the critical decades of the thirties, forties, and fifties.

In a time and place crucial to the struggle for the survival of Torah in America, he was an inspiration to all men.

RABBI MOSES FEINSTEIN	משה פיינשטיין
455 F. D. R. DRIVE	ר"מ תפארת ירושלים
New York, N. Y. 10002	בנוא יארק
ORegon 7-1222	בע"ה

בשמחה באתי בזה לכתוב כמה מילים בתור הסכמה לתלמידי וידידי הרה"ג מוהר"ר ד.ב.מזאה שליט"א, שזכה לכתוב ספר אודות החורבן ביוראפ והשרשה החדשה של תורה באמריקא ובארצינו הקדשה.

והנה אף שכרגיל אני נזהר שלא ליתן הסכמות על ספרי השקפה, מ"מ, בקשתי שנכדי הרה"ג מוהר"ר מרדכי סנדלר שליט"א יעיין היטב בכל פרק ופרק מספר זה, וכך עשה, והיה מוסר לי ראשי הפרקים, והייתי מביע דעתי אודותם ע"י נכדי להמחבר הנ"ל ששינה כמה דברים בעבורם.

והריני מברך להרה"ג המחבר שליט"א שיצליחהו השי"ת בספרו זה, ויזכה לחבר עוד ספרים חשובים לתפארת השם ותורתו.

ומאחר שקשה לפני לחתום, הריני שם חותמתי לראיה ביום כ"ג אייר תשמ"ה בנוא יארק.

HASKAMA TRANSLATION

It is with a feeling of happiness that I take this opportunity to write a few words in the nature of a Haskama for my Talmid and my dear friend Harav Hagaon Reb Dov Ber Maza who had the privilege to write a sefer about the destruction in Europe, and the new growth of Torah in America and in our Holy Land.

And though, customarily, I am careful not to give Haskamos for sforim about Hashkofa, nevertheless, I requested of my grandson Harav Hagaon Reb Mordecai Tendler to study carefully every chapter of this sefer. He did so and he transmitted to me the general content of each chapter and I expressed my opinion about them by way of my grandson to the author who changed a number of things because of my words.

I hereby bless the author that Hashem may bring to him success with this sefer and may he have the merits to publish more sforim of substance for the Glory of Hashem and His Torah.

And since it is difficult for me to sign my name, I hereby affix my seal as witness on this twenty-third day of Iyar 5745 in New York.

Rabbi Moshe Feinstein

CONTENTS

ACKNOWLEDGMENTS	xi
INTRODUCTION	xiii
Part I—The Question	1
1. The Question	3
2. "In the Beginning"	7
3. The Prophecy	11
Part II—Before the Sun Sets	13
4. Jews in Eastern Europe—Bright Sunshine	15
5. New Winds	23
6. Clouds	28
7. The Dark Horizon	34
8. Overhead the Blue Sky	48
9. Before the Sun Sets	51
10. Jews in the Soviet Union	53
11. Jews in the United States	75
12. Jews in Palestine	102
13. What of the Prophecy?	120
Part III—"With Fury Poured Out"	121
14. "Look Down from the Heavens"	123
15. The Six Million	128
Part IV—The Sun Rises	141
16. "And with the Consent of the Kings of Nations"	143
17. Freedom from Oppression	163
18. Sun Rising in the West	172
19. Delaying the Eastern Sunrise	184
20. Sun Rising in the East	201
21. Prophecy Fulfilled	225
22. The Answer	226
EPILOGUE	227
POSTSCRIPT	229
A LIVING TORAH	230
BIBLIOGRAPHY	231

ACKNOWLEDGMENTS

I express with humble gratitude my appreciation to the Rosh Yeshiva Hagaon Harav Moshe Feinstein, shlita, for his encouragement in the writing of this book. His warm interest in the works of his talmidim is an inspiration to all who have the privilege to call him Rebbe.

I extend my deep sense of gratitude to Rabbi Mordecai Tendler for his indispensable contribution to the publication of this work. Rabbi Tendler is a man of great wisdom and outstanding character, the grandson of our revered rosh yeshiva. Rabbi Tendler fulfills with devotion the Biblical description of the great disciple of Moshe Rabeinu, "The young Yehoshua bin Nun did not move from within the tent." He tirelessly ministers to the personal needs of the rosh yeshiva with dedication and love.

Because of the profound sensitivity of the thoughts discussed in this book, it was deemed wise that this material be published only with the consent of the rosh yeshiva. Each chapter was presented to Rabbi Tendler for discussion with the rosh yeshiva. Consent was given for publication.

I express with admiration my thanks to these major Jewish organizations and their directors for their share in making this book possible, not only for their kind cooperation in making available to me the material to research the history of the period studied, but also for their share in the history here recounted.

The organizations are: Torah Umesorah, Agudas Israel of America, Mizrachi Organization of America, The National Council of Young Israel, P'eylim, Tashbar, Chinuch Atzmai, and the American Joint Distribution Committee.

In my research through the vast files and archives of these organizations I was received warmly and helped generously by many people. To all of them I extend my personal thanks.

I acknowledge with gratitude the help of Rabbi Moshe Kolodny, the librarian of the Agudah, who guided me patiently through the archives. His help was indispensable for the thoroughness of the research that this sensitive theme demanded.

I extend my thanks to Dr. Arnold Streiter, professor of English literature at Brooklyn College, whose guidance was invaluable. Thanks also to Edith Hirshon and Lea Altusky, whose careful reading of the manuscript was of great help to me.

I acknowledge with appreciation the efforts of Eliyahu Alpert for his patient assistance in the preparation of this book and Shlomo Wertenteil who, when in Israel, helped with the research for the final chapter.

I acknowledge with special appreciation the patient and unselfish support of my beloved wife Malka, whose contributions in all aspects of publication made this book possible.

INTRODUCTION

The Torah (Exodus 33) relates the following dialogue between Hashem and Moshe.

Moshe said to Hashem, "Please let me see Your Glory."

Hashem said, "You cannot see My Face, for no man can see Me and live." And Hashem said, "Behold there is a place by Me, and you will stand upon the rock. And when My Glory passes by, I will place you in the cleft of the rock and I will cover you with My Hand until I have passed by. I will remove My Hand and you will see My Back and My Face you will not see."

This passage requires deeper understanding. For one of the Rambam's thirteen principles of faith is that Hashem is without a body. What then is the meaning of the words "My Face" and "My Back"?

The Chsam Sofer explains that Moshe asked Hashem for the understanding to comprehend the acts of Hashem. Hashem answered him, "You cannot see My Face." Mortal man cannot understand the acts of Hashem before the effects of His acts have come to pass. But, "I will show you My Back." You will be able to understand the ways of Hashem after He has passed by and the effects of His acts have become history.

Forty years ago six million Jews died in a holocaust unequalled in the thousands of years of the divine history of the Jewish people.

When we seek to understand the Holocaust and place it in the eternal design of Hashem for the Jewish people, we can look into history to the events that followed after the tragedy to see what has been revealed to us so far.

PART I

THE QUESTION

1

THE QUESTION

The apochryphal literature of the Holocaust records a debate that took place during the years of the destruction, on the eve of Yom Kippur in a synagogue in the ghetto.

When the Cantor began to chant the blessing Shehecheyonu, "Thou hast given us life," the silence was broken by wild screams from a dark corner at the edge of the tent.

"Lies, lies, it's all lies!"

The congregants began to knock on the wooden benches with their fists and they said, "Oy, oy, desecration and blasphemy! Sh! Quiet! On the eve of Kol Nidre?! Quiet!"

However, the man paid no attention to their protests. He raised his voice above their banging and quieted them.

The man was Reb Chaim, a righteous and holy man, who had led a pious and holy life for all of his sixty years, and who had never turned away from the ways of the Torah. In the last slaughter, all of his family had been taken away. By a miracle he had remained alive, and he could not explain why only he, the old man, had remained, while his young sons and daughters had been led to the death pits behind the city.

Only one Jew dared interrupt the words of Reb Chaim. A young man stepped forward. The worshippers made way for Leibele Brodsky who came to face his opponent.

Who in the city did not know Leibele Brodsky, the yeshiva student who had strayed from the Torah's ways. He had become a public desecrator of the Sabbath, a man who mocked the customs of Israel and all who observed them. But from the day the Nazis began their murders he had repented. All day he sat in his house and recited Psalms.

"Jews," said Leibele. "You know that I was a blasphemer, a mocker of Israel, a lost soul. And I tell you, yes, there is a G-d in heaven. Here we have seen fulfilled the words of the Prophets and their curses. All the curses have fallen upon us—not one is missing."

He opened the book he held in his hands, found the passage he sought, and read: "And it shall come to pass if you will not hearken to the voice of the Lord your G-d, to take care to fulfill all His commandments and His statutes which I command you this day, that all these curses shall come upon you and overtake you.... In the morning you will say who would but grant that it were evening, and in the evening you will say who would but grant that it were morning, from the dread of the heart which you will feel, and from the sight of your eyes which you will see."

Leibele raised his voice and said, "Behold our eyes have plainly seen the hand of G-d raised to punish His people who betrayed their mission and rejected Him and His Torah!"

Leibele looked to every side with an air of victory. The listeners had listened to the fiery words of the "new Tzadik" and now waited for the response of Reb Chaim who had stood silently with his eyes closed when Leibele was speaking.

Reb Chaim clapped his hands and began to speak in a soft voice as though from the depths.

"My teachers, you heard, G-d destroys His people from off the face of the earth because of their sins. Isn't it foolish to believe that? If this were a punishment from heaven because of our sins, why did all the Rabbis, the pure and holy Tzadikim who were full of Torah and good deeds, why did they die?"

For decades people with infinite faith in Hashem have asked this question along with Reb Chaim: "Why did they die?"

II

In order to begin to address the issue, let us introduce the subject with a deeper perception of "The Question."

The Torah tells us of the following events that took place before

THE QUESTION

the Exodus, and the ensuing dialogue between Hashem and Moshe.

Hashem heard the cries of the people of Israel and decided to take them out of their bondage. He called on Moshe and told him to go to Pharaoh and tell him that the G-d of Israel said to let His people go to the desert and celebrate a holiday to His Name. Pharaoh refused the request, saying to Moshe that the children of Israel want to sacrifice to their G-d because they are lazy. He thereupon ordered that their work be increased. He commanded that they no longer be given the straw to make the bricks and that they should themselves have to gather all the necessary quantities of straw. But the number of bricks that they had to provide each day would be maintained. When the Israelites could not meet that order, they were beaten by the slave masters who shouted, "Why did you not complete your quota of bricks as you did yesterday and the day before?"

When Moshe saw what had resulted from his mission he said to Hashem, "Why have you done harm to this people, why have you sent me? From the time that I came to Pharaoh to speak in Your Name, he has dealt harshly with this people, and You have not saved them."

And Hashem said to Moshe, "Now you will see what I shall do to Pharaoh, that because of My Strong Hand he will send them out."

In the sentences quoted, the Hebrew word for the question "why" differs. In one sentence the word is מדוע. In the other sentence it is למה. Targum Onkelos translates each of them differently. In the earlier posuk, "Why did you not complete your quota of bricks?" Onkelos translates מדוע as מא דין meaning "What is this?" In the posuk "Why did you do harm to this people?" Onkelos translates למה, why, as למא דין, which means "to what is this."

There is a clear distinction between these two questions. In a cause and effect relationship, the question "why" may be directed at the past cause or it may be directed at the future effect.

The question "Why did you not complete your quota of bricks?" is directed at the cause. What was the cause for your not completing your quota of bricks? The question of Moshe, "Why did You do harm to this people?" is directed at the effect. For what effect did You do harm to the people, for You have not saved Your people?

Moshe did not ask מדוע. He asked למה. He asked the purpose, he did not question the cause. Moshe knew that the question, why Hashem chooses a certain path to arrive at His goal, is not within the realm of man to question. Only Hashem knows His ways. And though it means that harm may befall the righteous, only Hashem knows why He chose that path.

It is within the realm of man to ask what effect is intended by Hashem when He chooses certain things to happen.

The martyrs of the Holocaust did not ask מדוע. In the midst of the Holocaust a song of pleading was on the lips of six million. They sang the plaintive words from the Psalms of David.

"My Lord, My Lord why did You leave me."

The word in the song for why is למה.

Therefore when we seek to understand the Holocaust, the question מדוע —what were the past causes that Hashem judged, and why did He permit the Satan to destroy six million of His children?—is not the question. It is not the subject of this study.

The question that we may ask is: למה —what purpose did Hashem intend to achieve as a result of the Holocaust? The answer to that question is revealed to man with the passage of time.

2

"IN THE BEGINNING"

The Torah begins with the history of creation. The first word in the Torah is "Breishit," which translated loosely means "In the beginning." That is a loose translation, for the literal translation is "In the first."

Rashi questions the irregularity of this grammatical expression. He quotes the Midrash that explains the word to mean "For the sake of the first"—for the Torah that is called "The first of His Ways" and for the people of Israel who are called "The first of His harvest." Rashi explains that here the Torah teaches that the world was created for the Torah and for the people of Israel.

Hashem created the world to bless man with a life of peace and happiness. The guide to the life of peace and happiness is the Torah. The people of Israel are to be the bearers of the Torah, chosen by Hashem to be the carriers of the Torah to the world.

The destiny of the people of Israel is therefore determined by the effect of their experiences on their loyalty to the Torah. When Hashem's blessings are used by the people of Israel to live by the Torah, Hashem fills their cup with blessings. When the Almighty deems that not blessings but tragedy would increase their dedication to the Torah, tragedy befalls them.

This message of the interrelationship of the destiny of the Jewish people and the fortunes of the Torah is the underlying theme of all of Biblical history.

The Jewish people were slaves in Egypt and they were freed from their slavery. The Torah explains the reason for their slavery and for their freedom.

Moshe said to the people of Israel (Deuteronomy 4):

> And He took you out from the iron furnace of Egypt to be unto Him a people of His inheritance.

Rashi explains the "iron furnace" as "a furnace in which one refines gold."

Rashi herein explains that the Jewish people suffered the bondage of Egypt because that experience refined their character to reach the level to be "a people of His inheritance." The slavery of Egypt prepared them to be a great nation that would be ready to receive and follow the Torah.

And Hashem told Moshe (Exodus 3) that the freedom from Egypt will come because

> when you take the people out of Egypt they will serve Hashem on this mountain.

The people of Israel became a free nation because they were to accept the Torah at Mount Sinai. Slavery and freedom were dictated by their effect upon the dedication of the people of Israel to the Torah. This principle determines the Jewish experience through all the centuries of the history of the Eternal People.

II

The Talmud (Gitin 56) tells of an event that occurred during the Roman siege of Jerusalem. Rabbi Yochanon Ben Zakkai saw the end of the war approaching and he knew that the destruction of the Holy Temple and Jerusalem was imminent. He determined to meet the Roman general Vespasian and plead before him. However, the Zealots inside Jerusalem permitted no one to go through the lines to leave the city. Rabbi Yochanon's pupils announced that their master had died. They received permission to bury him outside the walls of Jerusalem. His students carried him in a coffin into the Roman camp where he emerged and bowed before Vespasian. He greeted Vespasian with the words "Peace be unto you, O King." Vespasian said, "But I am not king." Rabbi Yochanon answered, "In truth you are a king for otherwise Jerusalem would not fall into your hands as the prophet Isaiah had said, 'The Temple will fall before a Ruler.' "

Just then a messenger came from Rome saying, "Arise, the king has died and the leaders of Rome have selected you to be at their head." Vespasian then said to Rabbi Yochanon, "Ask anything of me and I will grant it." Rabbi Yochanon said, "Give me Yavneh and its wise men."

Rabbi Yochanon knew that the Jewish people were headed for a long and bitter exile. How would they survive their dispersion? How could they remain alive as a people without a land? His solution was "Give me Yavneh and its wise men." He wanted the right to establish a school at Yavneh where its students and scholars would keep the Torah alive. He knew that only the Torah, the heritage of the Jewish people, could maintain the Jewish people through the exile.

The wisdom of Rabbi Yochanon ben Zakkai saved the Jewish people—Yavneh became their source of spiritual unity.

Soon afterwards a period arose when the Romans forbade the study and teaching of the Torah. The Talmud (Brachos 61) relates that in spite of this, Rabbi Akiva continued to teach. When Rabbi Akiva was asked, "Are you not afraid of the Romans?" he answered, "Let me give you an example. There was once a fox who was walking on the bank of the river and he saw fish running here and there. He said to the fish, 'Why are you running?' They said to him, 'We are afraid of the nets that are spread out to catch us.' The fox said to them, 'Why don't you come up to the bank and live together with me?' They said to him, 'If in the place which is our life we are afraid, in the place which is our death we are surely afraid.' "

"So it is with us," said Rabbi Akiva. "If we are afraid when we are studying Torah about which it is written, 'It is our life and the length of our days,' when we would stop learning we must surely be afraid."

The Jewish people never faltered in their commitment to Torah, and their tenacious adherence to the Torah kept them alive as a people through all the years of their exile. They were persecuted in the countries in which they were allowed to live and chased from other countries. The centers of Jewish population passed from one country to another as the Jews wandered among the nations. But through all their suffering they lived on as a people.

Their history of persecution brought them the name "the wandering Jews." Their miraculous ability to endure and live on as a people earned them the title "the eternal people."

The history of the Jewish people was living testimony to the prophecy of Zecharia that the Jewish people will live,

> Not by armies, not by strength, but by My Spirit saith the Lord of Hosts.

In the light of this knowledge of the dependence of the Jewish people on the life-giving powers of the Torah, let us examine the fateful events of the twentieth century and endeavor to gain some understanding of the period before, during, and after the Holocaust.

3

THE PROPHECY

King Solomon said in Ecclesiastes, "And the sun rises and the sun sets." The Talmud (Kidushin 72) interprets this in the following manner. "The tzaddik, the great man, does not die until there is created a tzaddik like him, as it is written, 'The sun rises and the sun sets.' Before the sun of Eli dimmed the sun of Samuel shone, as it is written, "The candle of G-d had not yet dimmed and Samuel sat, etc.' "

The Talmud thus explains the words of King Solomon as a prophetic analysis of Jewish history. The tzaddik, the great righteous man, represents the light of Torah. The eternity of the Jewish people depends upon the uninterrupted presence of the light of Torah shining from some central source. There must and always will be, says King Solomon, a source from which Torah will glow and light the way for all the Jewish people. Before this light dims, somewhere will be born another light that will replace it and maintain the unending glow of the light of Torah.

The prophecy of King Solomon is a remarkable fact of Jewish history. There was never a moment in Jewish history in which the sunshine of Torah dimmed. There was always a center where Torah shone with brilliance to give light to the entire Jewish people.

The historian Grayzel, in *A History of the Jews*, notes with awe this fact of Jewish history.

> One of the most remarkable facts in the history of the Jews is that they have never been without a central leadership. No sooner was one important Jewish community destroyed or

fallen into decay, than another came into being. Even before the one center realized that it was destined to give up the leadership of the scattered Jewish people, the next was developing the ability to resume where the former was leaving off.

In the thousands of years of Jewish dispersion, Torah leadership did not remain in one place. The light of Torah rose in one community after another, passing from one corner of the earth to the other. As the twentieth century dawned, the sun of Torah shone brilliantly from the shtetl and the ghetto of Eastern Europe.

PART

BEFORE THE SUN SETS

4

JEWS IN EASTERN EUROPE—BRIGHT SUNSHINE

As the twentieth century dawned, the Torah center of the world was Eastern Europe. In the small town, or shtetl, where the great mass of East European Jewry lived, Torah placed its stamp on everything and everyone. Their way of life was completely Torah-centered. The shtetl way of life was the response of the Jews of Eastern Europe to the problem they faced as a nation in exile.

The problem as they saw it was this: They believed that Judaism had meaning and had the capacity for survival only if it were based on Torah. They believed that if the Jewish people abandoned the Torah they would be extinct after a generation or two. The Torah was their life in terms of the present and the future.

They believed too, that a man is greatly influenced by his environment. A man cannot be exposed to alien ideas and values and not be influenced by them. How then could Judaism survive in exile?

Their solution to the problem of Jewish survival was to concentrate mightily on protecting their Torah way of life. Torah must be preserved not only from alien influences but even from neutral influences. Anything unrelated to Torah must be regarded as a diversion from the single life-giving fountain of Torah and shut out of their environment.

They believed that the study of the Torah must be the most important concern of Jewish living. The Torah covers a broad range of human activity: philosophy, prayer, holidays, customs and ceremonies, social relationships, civil law, business relationships, ethics, morals, and character. Every sphere of human activity is spelled out in minute detail in the Torah and commentaries. The Jews of Eastern Europe believed in Torah as the one total source of all values and the complete guide to the true way of life.

The result was that the Jewish people in all the shtetlach were bound together by the powerful bonds of a common belief. Their way of life, their philosophy, and their attitudes towards their environment were strikingly similar.

In *In Those Days* Mendele Mocher Sforim writes about this remarkable uniformity of Jews all over the world.

> Is there another nation in the world that all the ways of life of its people, from the time that they come into the world until their last breath, go according to one text as ours does? Bringing up children, their education, their studying, the ways of prayer, the time for every song, the text of every liturgical poem, are all in one manner, definite and distinct. Even the food and drink are the same. Has such a thing ever been, or heard of, that at one specific hour on Friday evening for example, all of them on the face of the earth will be eating fish and noodles. On Saturday, they will all be eating liver with onions and eggs and radishes. At the time that one person opens his mouth and sings "kol mekadesh" or shouts with a loud voice "Chai V'kayim" in Aspamia, immediately this tune and this voice are heard in Argentina at the other end of the world. We are a pile of ants, the individual is just like the whole group.

There were of course arguments and often even bitter controversies in the life of the shtetl. There may have been a different emphasis in the approach to prayer, a difference of opinion as to the wisdom of some customs adopted by a group, different opinions about the authority of a rabbi or a leader, arguments about positions of honor and seating in the synagogue. Sometimes the argument over the selection of a rabbi almost tore the shtetl apart. The celebrated disputes between the Chasidim and the Misnagdim created tremendous conflict within the Jewish community. But it was all within the framework of an agreed upon philosophy: the supremacy of Torah and the exclusion of all other influences irrelevant to Torah.

The Jew kept himself purposely apart and distinct from the

non-Jew. His language was different. Even his clothing was different. He wanted always to remind himself of his distinction as a man of Torah. Only economics brought the Jew together with the non-Jew and the relationship was kept on a strictly business basis.

In the shtetl people worked very hard to make a living, but the activity that was significant was the spiritual. Everyone recognized the primacy of "davening" or praying, and "learning," which meant studying Torah. Spiritual activity was the central and most meaningful activity of every member of the community. Torah learning was conducted on different levels of complexity. Some merely read from the Holy Books and recited "Tehilim" or Psalms. Some studied the simpler passages of Talmudic text, and some studied more difficult passages. Some participated in group learning under the direction of a lecturer, others studied by themselves. But, in one way or another, Torah study was an activity shared by all. Torah belonged to everyone.

The shtetl had several institutions set up to conduct davening and learning. There was the great synagogue of the shtetl, which was generally used for services on the Sabbath and holidays. Then there was the bais medrash, in which daily services took place and where the Torah study of the shtetl was held. In most shtetlach there was also the shtibel, the place of davening for the followers of hasidic rabbis. There were usually more than one bais medrash and more than one shtibel to serve the needs of the various elements of the community.

In the book *Ratne*, Yudel Kanishter describes religious life in the shtetl in those days.

> The Bais Medrash was never empty even for a moment, people were either davening or learning. It was a beautiful picture to see in those days, in the end of the nineteenth and the beginning of the twentieth century. In every Bais Medrash elderly people, young men and boys, sat around the long table with holy books of Torah open before them, and they learned and studied and they swayed and sang with such a sentimental tune that everyone just thrilled, and the learners were carried away to wide magic worlds.
>
> The Jews sat in the Bais Medrash. Even those who were busy all day trying to make a living, tore themselves away for a few

hours and learned. They shook off from themselves the gray dust of the earth and transplanted themselves to the great world of the heavens.

People began to daven in the bais medrash at the break of dawn. Many people had to leave early to go to the marketplace or to other pressing business that had to be conducted very early. Services were conducted one after the other and were attended by the people whose work schedule was most suited to that hour. Businessmen who were not rushed, storekeepers whose wives were minding the store, and students davened at later hours and at a more leisurely pace.

As the sun set, the bais medrash was again filled with people coming to daven late afternoon and evening services. Services followed one after the other for the people who came in from their affairs at different intervals. Between late afternoon and evening services, the people would remain in the bais medrash and learn.

The men of the shtetl spent their day in the bais medrash, coming to learn and to daven. Now and then they would relax over a glass of tea and exchange views on politics and the affairs of the day. Thus, the bais medrash served not only as the spiritual center but, incidentally, as the social center of the shtetl.

The Cheder

The dominant activity of the children of the shtetl was education. All children learned, and the place in which they learned was the "cheder." During the early days of the old czarist regime the Jewish children were not compelled to go to the government schools. The cheder was set up by an individual who fancied himself a teacher and established a school in his home. In one room, he set up a long table and around it were long wooden benches. The "melamed" or teacher sat at the head of the table and the students sat on the benches all around the table. The child would begin studying at the cheder at around the age of three or four to learn the "alef-beit" or alphabet. The young children would stay in the cheder each day until evening, when they would be led home by the "behelfer" or assistant to the melamed.

The child advanced from one cheder to the next. From the melamed who taught him reading he would advance to the melamed who taught him davening and Chumash, or Bible. Then he would advance to Gemorah. He would study with the Gemorah melamed for several years until he was able to study independently and understand the Gemorah without explanation by the teacher. At the age of twelve or thirteen the boy was ready to leave the cheder.

The cheder was the only accepted institution of education for the child. Any attempt to introduce other forms of education, even by the government, were like blows to the heart of every member of the shtetl and were resisted in every way.

In *In Those Days* Mendele Mocher Sforim describes a time in the life of the shtetl when the government tried to introduce compulsory secular education.

> When Shloimele came home he heard, upon entering, shouts and cries like cries for a death. Immediately he saw his mother wringing her hands and pouring out her soul in cries. David and Eidel, her two young sons, stood far away in the corner watching their mother cry. They opened their mouths and also cried. Leah, his older sister, sat on the stool dejected and sad, with her head lowered. At once his eyes filled with tears and he began to cry. "Cry, Shloimele, cry," his mother said to him in a prayerful voice as she put her hands on his head. "May our prayers be answered by our Father in Heaven. May He hear the cries of the children who haven't sinned and have mercy upon us. Oy, the children of Israel are being led to 'schools' and what will become of us."
>
> They all agreed to decree a day of fasting. The people of the town stood in prayer, fasted and said Psalms in the synagogue, and women went to the cemetery and poured out rivers of tears.
>
> Even the children of the cheder fasted. The "fast day of the schools" was the first time in Shloimele's life that he fasted.
>
> The passing days, however, proved the panic to be unnecessary. Children were not forced to go to "school" and all was as before. The children remained in their cheder and nothing was changed. In some cities they did put up schools for children, but they had very few students.

The boy received his early education in the cheder. When he was ready to leave the cheder he had various alternatives. He could continue his learning in the shtetl, where he would either learn by himself in the bais medrash or study with a teacher. He could begin an occupation and in his spare time join one of the many learning groups of the shtetl. Or he could go on to the yeshiva, the higher school of learning, in some nearby shtetl.

The Yeshiva

Boys came from many shtetlach to study in the yeshiva. They usually were accepted tuition-free and were supported by the community in which the yeshiva was located. The students of the yeshiva were supported by a system called "eating days." They were assigned to different homes for each of the days of the week, where they were provided with meals. Their meals were as good as the heart and means of their hosts. Most days their meals were quite modest, for their hosts were usually people of very modest means.

They sat in the yeshiva and learned day and night, devoting themselves to studying Torah.

The education of the "yeshiva bochur" is described by Chaim N. Bialik in his classic poem "The Mathmid."

> In the Yeshiva reigns a sacred silence
> Which he, the youth, is first to break,
> For there, in the dark corner, wait for him
> Faithful friends, his stand, his candle and his Talmud.
> As if the moments could not move too swiftly
> That lie between him and his trusted friends,
> He hastens to his place and takes his stand,
> And like a pillar stands from morn till night
> Granite is yielding clay compared to him,
> A Jewish boy unto the Torah vowed.

When the boy graduated the yeshiva he did not leave Torah learning behind. Sometimes he was able to continue to spend his day studying Torah in the bais medrash of his own shtetl. In most cases he found work, davened, learned, and settled into the pattern of the shtetl.

The Sabbath

The Sabbath in the shtetl was a day completely apart. On that day the busy, bustling shtetl came to a complete halt. As the Sabbath approached, all work was set aside by everyone; almost no one violated the Shabbos rest. The synagogues were filled. Everyone wore his Sabbath clothing and ate the special Sabbath foods.

The gentile knew that no business was conducted on that day and he rarely came to the Jewish quarters of the shtetl.

The Sabbath and holiday celebrations provided all the change and excitement that the shtetl sought. Participation was whole-hearted and shared by all. The peace of the Sabbath spread itself over the streets of the shtetl.

In the book of the shtetl Biala, the Sabbath is described in the following way:

> On a Sabbath or holiday, business came to a complete halt. The presence of G-d spread its wings over the streets and every business was closed and locked. The Jews who for six days of the week were seen in their stores, were now seen going to and from their davening with their Talis under their coats.

The synagogue, the bais medrash, the cheder, the yeshiva, the Sabbath and the holidays, these were the hallmarks of shtetl society. There was no activity, social, communal, or leisure, that took place anywhere but in the bais medrash. There was no cultural activity unrelated to Torah.

The only form of learning that was permitted was Torah learning—all other learning was actively discouraged. Any book not directly related to Torah was considered "treife," or unclean. Intense pressure was exerted to prevent the reading of material that was outside the framework of Torah. The literary works of the great Yiddish and Hebrew writers were not acceptable to the people of the shtetl.

There were no libraries other than the library of the bais medrash and its "Sforim," or Torah-books. There were no lectures on any other topics but Torah. There were "maggidim," or lecturers, in those days who were renowned for their ability to draw and hold audiences, but their subject matter was Torah.

There were no political organizations, no discussion groups, no reading rooms, no non-Torah classes. It was a society completely Torah-centered with a philosophy of exclusion of all non-Torah activities and ideas.

Thus generations blended. The Torah way of life was continued by children who walked in the footsteps of their parents.

This was Eastern Europe as the nineteenth century drew to a close.

5

NEW WINDS

At the end of the nineteenth century and in the early years of the twentieth century, new winds began to blow in Eastern Europe and the beginning of change began to be felt. Three significant trends began to develop and they gained a foothold in the shtetl. These trends were secularism, Zionism, and socialism.

Secularism

Until this period almost no one would dare to read anything but Torah and its related literature. If anyone even dared to read other material, he would do so in the most secretive manner. And woe to the young man who was caught. The book would be immediately destroyed and the young man would suffer terrible shame. The culprit would probably be thrown out of the shtibel, not to return until everyone was sure that such a crime would never be repeated.

But at the turn of the century new winds blew. Some young people began to read "treife" books. At first, the young man who dared to read the "treife" reading matter would do so only in secret. But if he were caught the young man would not humbly repent and pledge never to read such books again. Now the young man would defiantly hold on to his books. The determination of the young man to read forbidden material was not so easily overcome. He was curious about the new culture, and his curiosity was not to be denied.

Gradually the reading began to take place more and more openly. The resistance of the youth who were reading the "treife" material was stiffening and spreading. The less courageous were beginning to take heart from the courage of their friends, and they too began reading forbidden books. Even the most Torah-committed of the youth were becoming attracted to the new culture. Frequently they were torn by conflict and guilt feelings, but many left their Torah study for the new world of "enlightenment."

In the book *The Last*, Yakir Varshavsky describes the period of the beginning of the rebellion of the youth against the old order. He tells about the young man, Moshe Revele, who was seen by his young friend Abele secretly reading "treife" material. Abele told the leaders of the town what he had seen, and Moshe Revele was thrown out of the shtibel in disgrace, like the young men before him who had dared to read such books.

But unlike those who came before him, Moshe Revele did not humbly accept his fate. He was determined to influence other young people to join him. His efforts were successful and gradually the literary revolution spread, eventually engulfing the leading lights of the shtibel youth, even his friend Abele.

> In time Avigdor and Avraham Shmuel, the lights of the shtibel, were also attracted by Moshe Revele into the group of the enlightened. Avigdor didn't know how it happened but all at once he noticed that he had moved into another world and was not the same person he was before. The passion for learning had stopped and the worldly books attracted him like a magnet. He still tried to fight, suffered inner pangs, tried to return to the straight path. At night he couldn't sleep from the inner doubts that tormented him. Many times he cried like a little child, unable to find a choice between the two worlds, each one pulling in another direction. He felt that he was lost, every day getting further away from his father's world and going over to a new one. In the afternoon he didn't go back to the shtibel but instead he went to the fields behind the shtibel and there he lost himself in the Hebrew language books. They gradually made a revolution in his mind.
>
> With Avraham Shmuel it went easier, without great strain and inner pain. In place of the sharp analyses of the Talmud commentaries, he began to delve into the discoveries of algebra and geometry. He secretly learned Polish.
>
> Abele also joined the group and became Moshe Revele's stu-

dent. His job was to stand guard to see that no one caught the secret "enlightened" students, and that no one would throw them out of the shtibel or look at them with an evil eye.

The youth were being drawn to new interests. Their curiosity was attracting them to hitherto unknown subjects. Torah was still the major subject of study. But non-Torah readings were beginning to challenge Torah for the attention of the youth, and it was a challenge that was not easily squelched.

At the same time that the new curiosity of the youth was rearing its head, there were movements arising that intensified the interests of the youth in non-Torah activities. These organized movements were the political parties of Zionism and socialism.

These movements began to grow in the early part of the twentieth century. The growth of these movements, along with the newly arising secular curiosity of the youth, merged in an increasingly powerful drive to change the direction of the shtetl society.

Zionism

In 1897 the World Zionist Congress met in Basle, Switzerland and established the World Zionist Organization.

The aim of Zionism was to weld the Jewish people into a nation that would be united in a land of their own. It aimed to promote activity that would bring about the rebirth of the land of Israel. Zionism believed that the ideal of building the land was the bond that would keep the Jewish people in exile united as a nation until the land of Israel was reborn.

To some Zionists, Torah remained the central purpose of Judaism. Zionism to them was the means of achieving the highest form of Torah living. Only in Israel could Jews truly fulfill the Torah in every respect, removed from the distractions and troubles of the exile.

To most Zionists, however, Torah was not related to their Zionist ideal. Nationalism was their goal for the Jewish people— to them Torah was unnecessary as a unifying force and was not accepted as an ideal. Some considered Torah irrelevant to the Jewish future, and many considered it a hindrance to the Jewish future. The Jewish people were to be kept alive by a land.

This program for national unity, which was based upon the

common striving for the rebirth of Israel, meant a complete reshaping of the psychology, philosophy, and social interests of every Jew.

Many changes would have to occur. Instead of waiting and praying for the Messiah to come and redeem him, the Jew had to be convinced that he must actively pursue his own redemption. Instead of believing that a common Jewish culture and practice was the mainstay of Judaism, he was to be convinced that the land was the tie binding the Jewish nation together. He had to be changed from a passive and insulated person to an active and involved person. The Zionist program envisaged Hebrew as the language of the land, and a language program thus had to be instituted. A program had to be initiated that would capture and reshape the heart of the Jew.

Aims of such scope and magnitude required the establishment of a program of equal magnitude. A whole people had to be convinced, inspired, activated, and educated. Local organizations had to be formed, schools had to be founded, libraries had to be collected, books and periodicals and newspapers had to be published. The program was staggering to the imagination and seemingly impossible to realize. But the Zionist ideal had become a great dream to many. They were prepared to do everything to foster its growth. And this program brought the Zionists into direct conflict with the established shtetl way of life.

Socialism

At about the same time, another movement was also headed for a confrontation with the shtetl way of life. This movement was socialism. In 1897 a conference in Vilna founded the Bund, which was to be the leading Jewish socialist party for half a century.

Revolutionary ferment was brewing in the Russian empire. The forces leading to revolution were intensified by the Russo-Japanese War, which had been extremely unpopular and totally unsuccessful. Many Jews dreamed of socialism and revolution, longed for a better world, and saw the socialist movement as the solution. They were inspired by socialism and were prepared to make any sacrifice to advance it.

The aims were to create an organization of the Jewish proletariat that would be part of the general revolutionary movement in

Russia and at the same time represent the specific demands of the Jewish workers and population.

This attitude was directly opposed to the shtetl way of life. The shtetl believed that the Jew should isolate himself from the outside world. The socialists believed in total involvement of the Jew in the outside world. The shtetl was committed to political isolation from the affairs of state. The socialists were committed to active political involvement in the affairs of state.

Socialism, in the mind of the socialists, superseded Torah. Socialism had its own ideals, its own system of thought and values, and its own program of action. Socialism was a universal ideal that meant shaping the world to its plan. Socialism was pervasive and demanding. It left no room for Torah.

The Jewish socialist did not want to deny his Jewishness. He was absolutely committed to his identity as a Jew; however, he sought to build his Jewishness on new foundations.

His approach was the development of "Jewish Culture." It meant giving life, vitality, and prestige to a specifically Jewish language. The language of the masses was Yiddish, and therefore Yiddish was to be the carrier of the new Jewish culture. The development of the Yiddish language and literature was the basis of Jewish culture. Books, newspapers, periodicals, every form of expression including art, music, and drama made up this Jewish culture. The common language and literature was to be the bond that would keep the Jewish people united. All this meant that a great program of educational and cultural activity had to be carried on. It meant building an appreciation of socialism and Yiddish literature among the Jewish people. Organizations had to be established, literature had to be published, cultural activities of every conceivable type had to be planned, people had to be convinced.

Thus, three powerful movements, secularism, Zionism, and socialism, arose at the turn of the century, and they threatened the entire structure of Torah-dominated shtetl living. All of them converged in their efforts to divert the shtetl from concentrating upon Torah. They sought to break down the barriers that the shtetl had erected against other ideals and ideas.

The shtetl did not easily yield to these movements, but it began to feel their presence.

6

CLOUDS

The Torah life of the shtetl, which had so successfully vanquished all challenges up to the twentieth century, could not destroy these new challenges.

True, these movements did not immediately overwhelm the shtetl. At first they encountered very successful resistance. The challengers were on the defensive and made only limited progress. But this time they gained a foothold and gradually, inexorably, grew.

The New Culture

Y. Feigenbaum writes in *Biala* about the changing cultural life of his shtetl.

> At the beginning of this century there was practically no cultural activity in our shtetl. The followers of the Biala rabbis and of the Chassidic movements had deeply rooted themselves in the city and they gave the main tone to Jewish life, which was based on strong religious traditions. Every attempt to weaken the established life-pattern was considered as actual heresy and any method of resisting change was considered proper.
>
> There was a group of young boys who studied Hebrew and Russian. This group arranged to receive books from Mezritch. Among the books that came to Biala was the book "Love of Zion" by Mapu which played a pioneering role in the Haskala movement in Russia. The book went from hand to hand and was

read in the inner sanctums in greatest secrecy. At the end one boy was caught suddenly with the "treife" book in his hand. The "catcher," a fanatic Chassid, was so excited by his discovery that he ran around in the shtetl with the book and began to shout wildly, "Help! Fire, the Jewish faith is in danger and we have to put out the fire!"

But time does its work. Even in the dark Biala ghetto there began to appear signs of new cultural progress in Jewish life. The religious groups continued their powerful resistance, but the challengers grew stronger and stronger. A great part of the cultural progress was due to the Jewish "gymnazisten," students who came from Russia to study in the Russian Government Gymnasium. They established contact with the Jewish youth and influenced them to be interested in worldly education. The Biala fanatics were powerless against these "gymnazisten" because they couldn't throw their parents out of the shtibel.

In the years 1904 to 1906 the cultural and national renaissance began to be felt in the shtetlach, and even the little shtetl Ratne felt the coming of a new era. Signs of a new life were beginning to be noticeable. During the year 1905 a library was formed, consisting of a few hundred books. Discussions were held in private homes that became cultural centers for young men.

In 1910 in the shtetl Melave a library was formed in a private home. The library immediately became the home and school for some of the youth.

In the shtetl Ratne the new library had a great influence on the shtetl youth. Yaakov Radak gives the following account.

> I still remember the Friday evenings in the small, crowded room where the young boys and girls had come to hear the big-city news and lectures. I still remember the Chassidic intensity with which we repeated the so-called "Torah" of the speakers and discussed every party ideology and program.
>
> Saturday afternoon in the library there were meetings and discussions. The library also had a dramatics section. The first production they put on was "The Jewish Child." It was very successful and the people had a lot of pleasure. We were prepared to put on more productions of the same type when the

religious people began to scream, "Jewish boys and girls are becoming Purim players in middle of the year, may G-d help us."

In the book *The Jews of Lithuania* M. S. Slansky traces the career of a librarian in Slobodka.

In mid 1894 my father, a cantor, moved to Slobodka. My father gave me to the best melamed in the city. The son of the melamed used to secretly give me Hebrew books and at night I swallowed them like water. The books gave me great pleasure. I wanted to do a favor for my friends, the students of the Cheder, and give them the pleasure of reading the books. In my mind the idea of making a library was born. At that time my father had just completed building his home and I had enough boards, nails, and locks, to make a closet and a cover for my "library." Twice a week I smuggled out my library to a place where there was a Succah. There the conspirators, my readers, were gathered. I stood upon the box of books and held a lecture for the children about the importance of reading books. Afterwards I gave everyone a book according to his taste. But once it happened that a father of one of the children caught his son reading a story book. First the father slapped him hard on his cheeks. Then when he found out that I was the leader, he came to my father with a complaint. My father also did not hold back any slaps. With my flaming cheeks and red eyes, I led my father, followed by other fathers of my readers, to the place where I uncovered my "treasure." Thus ended my first attempt at being a Jewish librarian in Slobodka.

Several years later when I was a student at the Yeshiva, I tried again to place books before my friends. One time I was caught by the supervisor of the Yeshiva. I received from him a proper beating. After that I gave my father a promise that I would be good.

But one day in 1903 the Satan again persuaded me to read "treife" books and I tried to become a librarian again. At that time there was a meeting for the founding of the first Zionist organization among the Yeshiva boys and I began to provide these "treife" books for the Yeshiva boys.

At the end of 1906 I went to America and returned early in 1910. In Slobodka was now to be found a large group of Jewish intelligentsia. So I called them together and proposed the idea of a library. My plan was accepted and we immediately began to carry it out.

The library was open every day except Friday and Sabbath. We had no lack of readers. Besides the inhabitants of the town there also came, secretly, the Yeshiva boys.

The city of Kovne in Lithuania was a center for the young people who pointed to Torah and for those who turned to "culture." In the book *The Jews of Lithuania*, this is how life in Kovne is described in those years.

In Kovne there were two bridges. One bridge led to Slobodka, to Torah, to traditional Judaism, to the Yeshivos which played so important a role in Lithuania. A second bridge, over the Neimann, led to the Alexeter Mountains. Upon this bridge walked the "new youth" which was devoted to new ideas, Yiddish and Hebrew literature, and culture. Two bridges, leading in different directions, but between them there was an inner bond, the bond of nation, of national Jewish heritage. In the hearts of the young Jews following the new Jewish worldly ways there was no less of a religious flame than in the hearts of the students in the Yeshiva of Slobodka. They both held on to that old, old shout of Shma Yisrael, Hear O Israel, learn the new program. Hear the new ways.

Political Parties and Organizations

In the early years of the twentieth century some of the Jewish youth were drawn into the revolutionary movement. Young Bundist organizations were formed in many shtetlach, but the parents fiercely resisted the Bundist movement. They warned their children against the "Tzitzilisten," and in most shtetlach the Bundists had only limited success.

Yudel Kanishter writes about Ratne,

We had, at that time, already heard about the "Tzitzilisten" in the world who want to change the world and, G-d forbid, overthrow the Czar. We also heard about Jewish Zionists who want to force the Messiah to come and bring the Jews to Israel.

The shtetl, however, laughed at them because according to the Jewish law you are not allowed to go against the government. On the contrary you are supposed to pray to G-d for its peace. And also you are not supposed to force the Redemption to come.

In 1905 a Jewish revolutionary group was formed in Rakishak, spreading proclamations and organizing demonstrations against the czar. The Jewish revolutionaries learned to handle revolvers on the Sabbath in the Rakishak woods.

The story is told that a man named Velvele and his two sons spied upon the revolutionaries, and because of them some of the revolutionaries were sent to Siberia. The revolutionary group decreed the death sentence against Velvele and his sons. One Simchat Torah holiday in the morning, when the spies were in the bais medrash, they were shot at, but because the attackers did not want to hurt innocent people in the bais medrash they only slightly wounded the spies. The boys who made the attack fled from Russia. Some were caught and sent to Siberia.

Though the new winds had made an impression, they had not radically changed the life of the shtetl. Most of the children continued in the cheder and the yeshiva. No political parties and organizations of any significant numbers were established. The Sabbath remained undisturbed. The youth still filled the synagogues and the bais medrash.

N. Nachumovitch writes about Rakishak:

> Until the First World War life continued in one pattern, without great changes. Everything passed on from generation to generation. The children inherited from their parents their customs, their riches, their family status, their good name, and their seat in the synagogue. The Rabbi was the spiritual leader of the shtetl. Not only did he answer questions of Jewish law, he was also the authority in community affairs. Defying the Rabbi was considered the greatest sin.
>
> The whole shtetl concentrated in and around the Bais Medrash. There, people davened and said Psalms. The revolutionaries in 1905 held their first meetings in the synagogue. When the revolutionaries wanted to shoot the Jewish spy, they did it Simchat Torah in the synagogue.

On the surface life in the shtetl seemed to continue as before. But underneath the surface of the seemingly stable shtetl society there was a new feeling of unrest that had been blown in by the new winds.

As B. Varshavsky writes about Melave;

> In the shtetl, in the Bais Medrash, they still sat day and night and learned. But the Satan had already then gained control over segments of the youth. The process of going away to new paths was most painful and most difficult for the Chassidic boys. The next generation, my generation, found "getting spoiled" much easier.

The clouds had not darkened the sun; the sun of Torah shone with a steady brightness. But the winds, which had blown in small clouds, were now gathering strength.

In the period starting with the First World War, these winds began to grow in intensity and great clouds began to form, threatening to darken the sun.

7

THE DARK HORIZON

As a result of the events of the First World War, the Russian Empire, home to about six million Jews, was divided from the outside and overthrown from the inside. The Czarist regime was replaced by the Bolsheviks and independent nations were separated from the Russian Empire. The six million Jews were now almost evenly divided between the new Soviet Russia and the other nations of Eastern Europe.

In the newly independent nations of Poland and Lithuania, approximately three million Jews lived very much as before. Their life in the shtetl was relatively undisturbed by the great national changes. However, the new ideas, which had remained under the surface of shtetl society, began to grow and rise to the surface. No longer were they invisible—they arose in every aspect of shtetl society, they challenged every shtetl institution, they defied customs and tradition.

The old order did not accept the change easily. They felt that the very fiber of Jewish life was being threatened and that everything sacred and holy was being scorned. They used every method of resistance to try to overcome the challenge to the Torah way of life. However, all their efforts failed. The growth of the new way of life could not be denied.

Schools

At about the time of the First World War the first schools began to appear in the shtetl. In Ratne, which was one of the first shtetlach to have a school, a modest school was established in

1912–1913. A young teacher came to the shtetl, rented a large well-lit room, furnished it with school benches, and opened a Hebrew school. He didn't have many students at first, but it was a start. In 1913–1914 another and larger school was begun in Ratne with three teachers.

The school became a major battleground for the opposing forces. All the different groups saw the school as a crucial instrument in their struggle for influence.

The first attempts to change the educational system came in the form of the "cheder metukan" or the improved cheder. It was not anti-Torah but an attempt to adapt the cheder to new conditions. The major emphasis of the cheder metukan was still Torah, but it expanded its program to include other subjects. It also introduced educational methods and provided educational facilities that were more in tune with the new ideas.

In *Pinkas Mlava*, Dr. Z. Yunis describes the cheder metukan.

> He was a Rabbi with a completely new appearance; no beard, no kapote. In the house of one of the Chassidim he opened his so-called Cheder Metukan. According to its external appearance his Cheder was a modern school. There were classes, students sat on benches two together like in a real school. Except for worldly learning, everything was taught in Hebrew. Most of the Jews in the shtetl called it "heresy." "Why send him to that school, convert him yourself," they would say to the parents who had the nerve to send their children to that Cheder. They were thrown from the shtibel, they lost friends, their lives were made bitter.
>
> In the upper grades children spoke Hebrew among themselves. There was a bell which sounded the beginning and end of every lecture according to a time schedule. There were periods of song and gymnastics, then new to the Jewish children. For Chanukah and Purim the children performed for the parents.

The cheder metukan was only the beginning of change. Schools began to appear representing all the different factions. Among the religious groups there were many who believed in Zionism and in the value of worldly knowledge. They founded schools that added Zionism and secular subjects to the basic religious program. The non-religious groups also established schools, with the goals of Zionism and socialism and without a religious program. Most shtetlach soon had several schools alongside the cheder.

In the book of the shtetl Zshetl, the story is told of the opening of the school in 1919.

> The leaders of the drama group and library met and decided to open a school in Zshetl. It wasn't clear to them what character the school should have. But upon one thing they were all united—the old one was not good.

In *Kletzk* Y. Frankel tells about the Tarbut School that opened in Kletzk in 1924 with five grades and 160 students.

> At first it was decided to open only the lowest grades and to build gradually. However, many parents who had older children insisted that their needs also be provided for and we were unable to refuse. Students streamed to us from the other schools. Those who came from the Polish government schools had extensive knowledge of general subjects and of the Polish language, but were ignorant of Jewish learning. And on the other hand there were the students of the Cheder and the religious schools who had a wealth of knowledge of Bible and Talmud, but had difficulty with modern Hebrew and were weak in scientific knowledge.
>
> Another problem arose, namely, covering the head during the learning. We knew that this seemingly trivial question was the cause of sharp conflict in other places. We knew that among the parents there were religious people from the Mizrachi who required that the head be covered during all lessons. Except for the learning of Bible and Talmud we opposed this request. We saw in it an example of the denial of the religious freedom of the parents of the non-religious children. We decided that the children would have the right to make their own choice. At the beginning, there were some who sat in class with caps upon their heads. But with the passage of time they mixed with the group and accepted the practice of the majority. And so we came out of this problem peacefully and were not again disturbed by it.

In addition to the Jewish schools established by the Jewish community, there were government schools that were heavily attended by Jewish children.

When once in the time of Mendele Mocher Sforim the prospect of children being led to public schools brought tears of grief, now even religious Jews sent their children to the government gymnasium. The threat of the severest punishment was shrugged off. The rabbis fought the new schools only to find that their words went unheeded—sometimes they were attacked in return. With their attacks upon the new schools they succeeded only in diminishing their own influence and losing the support of their congregants.

Z. Zamir relates what happened when the Polish gymnasium was opened in Zambrow in 1918.

> The opening of the Gymnasium was a very important event even among the Jews but it aroused arguments and fights and practically split the community into two parts. The Gymnasium was opened in a nice building surrounded with a beautiful yard and trees. Many Jewish children registered there, even though under no circumstances would the Gymnasium free them from writing on the Sabbath. The Rabbi, who was a zealot and who guarded Judaism with all his strength, organized a group of laymen to oppose the attendance of Jewish children in the Gymnasium where the Sabbath was violated.
>
> There were many parents who feared the opposition of the Rabbi. They were afraid that the Rabbi would excommunicate them so they removed their children from the Gymnasium. However, many people did not give in. They maintained that their children's learning in the Gymnasium did not remove them from Judasim and that they would not be converted. A great and bitter dispute arose. The Rabbi threatened to excommunicate one of the leaders of the Gymnasium, and all the members of the family who were up to then among the staunchest supporters of the Rabbi, rose against him. He was forced to move from the Bais Medrash which was his fortress and the place of his greatest influence, to the other Bais Medrash in the shtetl.
>
> The people who were intent on preserving the old order soon began to realize that adaptations to the new conditions had to be

made. They established new schools that had a program of secular studies, albeit a minimum, and whose method and organization were more in line with the new ideas. Horev schools for boys and Bais Yaakov schools for girls were founded to help the cheder meet the challenge of the schools of the new culture.

Thus there arose, besides the cheder, six networks of Jewish schools. Horev, Bais Yaakov, and Yavneh were religious schools. Tarbut, Cysho, and Shul-kult were non-religious schools.

The Horev and Bais Yaakov schools were the schools of the Agudah. They concentrated on Torah study, and in most schools a program of general studies was added to their curriculum.

The Yavneh school was the school of the Mizrachi Religious Zionist Organization. Their program included Torah study, nationalistic Zionism, and general or social knowledge.

The Tarbut schools were Zionist schools. Their program was secular and Zionism was the nucleus of the curriculum. The students were taught the history and geography of Palestine, principles and development of Zionism, and Hebrew language and literature.

The schools of Cysho, the Central Yiddish School Organization, and the Shul-kult of the Labor Zionists were secular with a socialist frame of reference. The emphasis in Jewish studies was upon Yiddish language and literature.

The secular schools, especially the Tarbut schools, grew rapidly. In the year 1925–1926 the Tarbut school network consisted of 176 schools. In 1926–1927 there were 204 and in 1927–1928 there were 234. In 1931–1932 there were 242 schools, with a student population of over 25,000.

In 1937 the educational picture in Eastern Europe was as follows: The Tarbut network consisted of 269 schools with 44,780 students. The Cysho schools consisted of 169 institutions with 16,486 students. The Shul-kult schools of the Labor Zionists had 2,343 students. The religious schools of Yavneh, Horev, and Bais Yaakov, and the great yeshivot of Poland had a combined student population of 116,000 in 820 institutions.

No longer did all children attend institutions of Torah study. In the span of approximately one generation, Jewish education had changed greatly. A large percentage of the children were receiving an education in which Torah was not the primary learning.

Organizations

At the same time that the educational scene was changing, another important development was taking place that was equally significant in its effect upon the Torah character of the shtetl.

During this period organizations grew at a phenomenal rate. The Zionist and Bundist organizations began to establish themselves in the shtetlach. In 1924 there were already 70 active organizaitons of Tzukunft, the Bundist youth organization, with over three thousand members. In 1929 there were 171 organizations with over ten thousand members. At first, members came from the Jewish culture schools, later from the government schools. Soon even the children from the cheder began to join.

Every group had its own program and its own activities. They initiated the establishment of schools, dramatic and literary clubs, libraries, and sports organizations.

In *Melave* the new ways are described.

> The First World War shook Poland. Youth immediately felt the change. A scout organization was formed. From the scouts there eventually came the Hashomer Hatzair.
>
> It all started with gymnastics, hikes, nice uniforms with colored bands and emblems. "Children are playing soldier," they used to say.
>
> Every Sabbath they marched into shul, true to the scout order of "G-d and Fatherland." The marching, the trumpeting, the banging, were a wild new experience. As long as these were just parades, fathers and mothers looked and kept quiet, even enjoying it. The first conflict with the parents came when we began to go into the woods, in the villages of the gentiles. The parents were afraid maybe something might happen that they did not want. So, we ran away from home.

The following is told in *Ratne* about an event that took place in the shtetl in the year 1929.

> The Hashomer had organized a march which was planned to last several days. What fights and screams there arose between the parents and the children, especially the girls. The parents railed against the Hashomer and its leaders! How could they

permit girls to go away from their homes to wander in the villages and along the roads with boys, for several days! Many parents kept their children at home and did not let them out. Other children did manage to tear themselves away from their homes and went on the march.

A very popular organization that began to come up at this time was the sports club, usually called Maccabee.

In Zambrow, in the year 1916, a Maccabee sports group was formed. It was an immediate success and many boys joined. The Maccabee parades through the streets of the shtetl, with all the boys in uniform marching in rhythm and singing, made such an impression on the Polish peasants that they shouted, "Jewish Army, Jewish Army!"

In Opte, one of the boys refused to accept the fact that Opte would not have a football team while all the nearby shtetlach already had several sports clubs. It was not easy to get the team started. He realized that in order to receive the necessary financial support an organization would have to be formed. He formed a successful organization and named it Maccabee. The team was able to get white and blue uniforms, special shoes and socks, and a reserve of other supplies for a football team.

In Rakishak the Maccabee received the enthusiastic support of the youth.

> There was not a city or a shtetl where there was not a Maccabee group. Where all these sport organizations and good gymnasts suddenly all came from was a wonder.
>
> The shtetl was not very large, but relatively, the Maccabee was a very large organization. The youth of Rakishak were physically very strong. The football team was very good. . . . All the activities of the Maccabees were conducted in Hebrew.

Another organization that began serious activity during this period was the dramatics group. Dramatics was a major part of the program of the new culture.

Shlomo Friling describes the advent of the dramatic society in Frampol.

THE DARK HORIZON

As I remember, in the year 1921–1922 Frampol was frozen in a stillness and stagnation which was in sharp contrast to the vibrant social and political life which was rising in the Jewish street in Poland. At that time, there was no party life in Frampol. The shtetl slept as though there were no changes in the land. The children learned in the Cheder, the youth in the Bais Medrash, and the older generation lived its life in the world of Torah and strictly observed the traditional Jewish way of life.

Suddenly rumors spread that somewhere in the shtetl there were heretics, "Shabbath-goyim." Some time passed and the activities of these young people were discovered. "They are playing theatre." And as though that was not enough, the income from the presentations went for Zionist causes. The shtetl was in an uproar.

Making a dramatics circle in the shtetl was a delicate step. The initiators knew that they were putting themselves into sharp conflict with the parents, the Rabbi, and with the religious Jews, and that they would disturb the entire settled way of life of the shtetl, which had such deep roots. But time had its effect. The first performance was presented.

Purim 1924 we prepared our own Zionist Purim "shpiel" and instead of the traditional Purim presentation we prepared something about Israel. We visited homes during the traditional Purim feast. In the homes of the simple people we were greeted with surprise, but at the same time with sympathy and understanding. In the strict Chassidic homes, they didn't want to hear us and even showed us the door. There were many parents who did not want to accept the fact that their children were going in "bad ways."

The conflict between father-mother and their sons and daughters started. In some families children did not come home to sleep for two weeks or didn't eat at the same table with their parents.

After the success of the Purim play we started a regular dramatics group. In the winter evenings we were up until 11–12 at night, learning our roles. There were rumors that the Chassidim were going to come Saturday night to prevent the performance from taking place. We decided to set up a strong guard, both sides prepared for a confrontation. But the performance was carried out peacefully.

However, Sunday morning in the shtetl there was an uproar when some of the performers came to the Bais Medrash for services. One of them was thrown out of the Bais Medrash. For three months he didn't come home. That's what the life of the youth was like in the shtetl at that time.

Thus drama groups arose in the shtetl over the opposition of the parents, the rabbi, and the religious community.

New Centers

Increasingly the bais medrash was being replaced as the focal point for the youth. The many functions of the bais medrash were being moved to other settings.

In every shtetl there was now a library, very often the center of literary and social activity.

In *Zambrow* the history of the library is told.

The library acquired its own building, bought Hebrew and Polish books, and the number of readers from all the parties increased. Many conflicts arose among the readers for control of the library, which was the center of interest of a great portion of the youth. The Bund considered itself the rightful owner and spread its wings over it. The youth of the Labor Zionists, who were on the outside, tried to capture it. After stormy meetings it was decided to make it a community non-partisan library.

In *Vishkov* the writer tells what happened when the Labor Zionists obtained their new quarters.

Soon there was a library with socialist books and brochures. Courses were given in reading and writing. Discussions on political and literary themes were held. We also had a buffet where you could drink a glass of tea and have a bite of something. Vishkover youth began to stream into the local headquarters thirsting for worldly knowledge and eager to keep informed of the political events of the world and of the Jewish street. Every evening the local was full.

Somtimes the new center was the school. In *Melave* Dr. Z. Yunis relates:

The gymnasium was the center of Jewish cultural activity and social events. The Hashomer Hatzair met there, the women's organization Viza, the dramatic group, all Jewish performances and assemblies, meetings of all political parties, social events, bazaars for Jewish National Fund, and so on, were held in its rooms.

The search for a new center to replace the bais medrash sometimes brought the youth to very unusual places. In the book *Vishkov* the writer tells where the youth of that shtetl found their social center.

Vishkov did not have many places for social activity where the local residents could relax after a day's work. The Jewish youth, which was tearing itself away to a new life, used the bridge as a place for taking walks. That was the meeting place of the youth. There the young people all engaged in discussions and conversations, and sang songs. But in Vishkov there was also another place where you could breathe the free air. That place was the railroad station. The beautiful memories of our shtetl center around the railroad station. There the boys and girls met. At the bridge everyone felt informal, as though they were at home. But the walk to the railroad station had a more intellectual character and required a proper carriage. At the railroad station our young dreams had the power to tear us away from the routine character of our lives. It filled our lives with dreams of a beautiful future. We cannot say that our shtetl had any expectations of better times for its youth. The old generation was nailed to its place, incapable of moving. The youth, which had already left the cheder and the Bais Medrash and had a broader view of life, felt all closed up in the shtetl. That is why they tried to tear themselves away from the small-town atmosphere. So the walks to the railroad station served as a means of going away, even if only for a few hours, from the daily shtetl depression. There, in the free air, we looked through a window to the great world.

In *Lita* Y. Gurman relates,

The Bais Medrash, which was for generations the center of all community activities, lost its central position. The social life of the youth moved over to the party local. The youth became party conscious. There were many different Zionist parties, from the Religious Zionist Mizrachi to the Zionist Socialist Hashomer Hatzair or Hachalutz. Each organization had its own local and its "propaganda apparatus." Only a small group called "Tifereth Bachurim," which met a few times a week to learn Bible and Talmud, continued to meet in the Bais Medrash.

A deep awareness of this trend that was drawing the youth away from the bais medrash is reflected in the Torah journal *Kerem Bais Shmuel* published in 1933. A report is given about the founding of an organization named "Machzikei Hatorah" or "Strengthening the Torah," which aimed to intensify Torah study among the youth.

> Our youth decided to establish this organization when they saw that the religious youth began a little bit at a time to leave the halls of the Bais Medrash and to stray from the right path. On one side, the frightful economic situation pressed upon them, may G-d have mercy, and it was not within their means to remain constantly within the doors of Torah. And on the other side, the stream of heresy drowned them with a flood of free-thinking newspapers full of vice. At one time in the years before the World War, the benches in the Bais Medrash in every city and town were full from corner to corner and the echo of the voice of Torah reached distant places. And now! The benches of the Bais Medrash are empty, the sound of Torah is stopped, a terrible stillness hangs over the Bais Medrash, the house of learning. At this critical time the boys still remaining in the Bais Medrash could no longer control their beating souls and their awakened hearts. They arose to establish this organization, which will be a defense for all that is dear to us, our holy Torah, and thus they hope to return the Torah to its glory.

The trend could not be denied. The youth center of the shtetl moved from the bais medrash.

The Sabbath

The Sabbath in the shtetl was for generations an undisturbed day of rest. And in 1939 the streets of the shtetl were hardly changed. But, though the change had not yet greatly affected the street, the Sabbath in the home had changed.

In the book *A Guest for a Night*, which is a description of life in the shtetl after the First World War, S. Y. Agnon presents this scene of the Sabbath at home.

> We said before that the sons and daughters of the inn-keeper don't come at mealtime. I didn't mean to say that they are careful not to join their parents on Sabbath evenings at the meal. But rather, sometimes they come and sometimes they don't. Anyway, they don't come together and they don't come to hear Kiddush, and usually they come in the middle of the meal. And when they come, they come and eat like on all other days.
>
> Babitshke comes from wherever she comes, throws down her cap from her head, rolls off her coat and puts it wherever she puts it, passes her left hand through her hair, and takes a chair, sits down, grabs her food, and eats. Sometimes her father raises his eyes and looks at her. But more than he looks at her, he looks at her things that she had thrown here and there, and he closes his eyes again, touches his prayer book and keeps silent or starts again to sing Sabbath songs.
>
> Dulik and Lulik come, their father raises his eyes and looks to see if their heads are covered. If they sit with their heads uncovered during the week he doesn't care, but at the Sabbath meal he is strict. One time Dulik forgot and didn't cover his head and his father scolded him. Dulik said to him, "Are you still a cap merchant that you are looking to get me a cap?" His father got up, took Dulik's cap and put his two thumbs, bent, into the cap and pressed it on Dulik's head in anger until Dulik screamed, "Oy."

Though most of the youth went along with the public observance of the Sabbath, many of them did not have their hearts in it. They were unenthusiastic, their participation was perfunctory, and frequently they openly violated the Sabbath.

In *Vishkov* Y. Granat tells about the Jewish Workers Sports Club "Stern" and its attitude towards the Sabbath of the shtetl.

> We played only on the Sabbath because at that time we were free. The local Sabbath observers reacted very sharply and they

announced an excommunication. In the Bais Medrash an announcement was made that every Sabbath violator would, after death, be buried behind the partition.

One Sabbath day, while swimming in the river, someone drowned. Since he was a Sabbath violator, the Burial Society decided that he would be buried behind the partition. The entire youth of the shtetl, from right to left, organized themselves and did not want to permit this disgrace to take place. Police were brought out from Paviat, and under a strong guard the decision of the Society was carried out. He was buried behind the partition. But this was the first and last case in Vishkov.

The Sabbath observers in Vishkov organized a group that attempted to prevent the desecration of the Sabbath, but with poor results.

Sabbath after the meal, the Sabbath observers gathered near the bridge and tried to prevent the youth from going on walks. They also found out that the boys played football at the horse-meadow. They went there with the Rabbi and tried to stop them. The players laughed at them.

In Zambrow the rabbi tried with all his heart to combat the spreading violation of the Sabbath.

The Rabbi conducted a bitter struggle against the movie house which was open on the Sabbath. They wanted to beat him up. They blocked his way and for more than a week did not let him go into his own house. The Rabbi did not get frightened, pronounced excommunication on all who went to the movies on the Sabbath, and the Rabbi won the battle. When the Rabbi found out that the barbers were working late into the Sabbath, he went one Friday evening at candle-lighting time to the barber shop, sat down on a chair and said, "Give me a haircut." The barber shop immediately emptied out. He did the same thing every Friday evening until the barbers decided to close their stores at sundown according to the Sabbath law. This way he also prevented the owner of the movie house from opening Saturday night before the permitted time.

THE DARK HORIZON

Another chapter in the tragic frustration of the rabbi in his desperate attempt to control Sabbath violation is told in the book of the shtetl Zambrow.

> For more than fifty years he used to sit and look through the window of his house and see Jewish children going to the cheder, and men going to the synagogue. He saw the young people being led to their wedding and the older people to their eternal rest. He knew the fathers and the grandfathers, the grandsons and the great-grandsons. However, once in the morning of a snowy Sabbath he looked through the window of his city and did not recognize his city of Zambrow anymore. He saw, woe to the eyes that saw it, a bus full of Jewish riders from the surrounding shtetlach passing through Zambrow on the Sabbath. He remained frozen to the window of his house. And all the old people outside who were going to the synagogue remained standing glued to their spot and stuck in the snow up to their knees.
>
> The Rabbi began to storm in the Bais Medrash, in the market place, at meetings. He cried and pleaded, "Zambrow should not permit the bus full of Jewish riders to go through its streets on the Sabbath." This is how it ended. Gradually the youth of Zambrow also began to ride in that bus to Byalistok, to Shneyadov, to Lomza, and to the other cities nearby. Even the old men of the city who at first were all shaken up by the Sabbath desecration began to get used to it. The Rabbi stopped looking out of his window. For more than fifty years he looked out, but now he stopped.

The rabbi of Zambrow was a picture of sadness. He had fought heroically to hold back the tide of secularism, but he was afraid that he had lost the struggle. The youth were leaving the Torah and the future was dim.

8

OVERHEAD THE BLUE SKY

The book *Polish Jews—A Pictorial Record* by Roman Vishniac is a collection of pictures of Jewish life in Poland in 1938. Abraham Joshua Heschel states in the preface:

> These thirty-one photographs were selected not merely because of their aesthetic value, but because they make up together one great portrait of a life abjectly poor in its material condition, and in its spiritual condition exaltedly religious.

The book vividly portrays Heschel's observation. The pictures show graphically the material and the spiritual character of the Polish Jews. They are pictures of normal everyday life, and the religious flavor comes through in all of them. There is a picture of children learning, of a Jew walking through the streets carrying his books, of a fish seller, of people eating supper, and of people sitting idly in the synagogue court. Every picture shows people who have upon them the signs of the religious character of the Jews of Poland. The men and women have their heads covered. The men have earlocks and are wearing tzitzis. In a picture of a crowded street in the Jewish section of Warsaw, nearly all the people are obviously religious Jews, except for a few young people. In 1938 the image of Jewish life in Poland was one of Torah observance.

Many of the youth were drifting away. But Jewish life in Poland was still predominantly Torah-observant. The synagogues were full, the yeshivot for young and old were vigorous, and the Sabbath was a day of rest.

The majority of the Jewish children were receiving a comprehensive Torah education in the schools of Horev, Yavneh, and Bais Yaakov, and in the cheder of the shetetl.

When the bais medrash began to show signs of weakening, the leaders of Torah Jewry encouraged the young people to attend advanced yeshivot rather than continue their studies in the local bais medrash. In the period between the two World Wars, many new yeshivot were established and the old yeshivot were expanded. The bais medrash, as a center for the youth, was replaced by the yeshiva.

The yeshivot of Eastern Europe were world-famous. The roshei yeshiva, the rabbis who headed these yeshivot, were held in awe and their names reverberated all through the Jewish world.

In the book *Toldot Hachinuch B'dorot Haacharonim*, Dr. Zvi Scharfstein describes at length the great yeshivot of Eastern Europe and their world-renowned leaders. He describes the dedication of the yeshiva student and concludes,

> Our great will for spiritual survival and our love for Torah were never revealed with greater brilliance than in the period between the two World Wars. At the time when the pillars of the economic and political world trembled and the foundations shook, when young people were leaving the life of their fathers and scorning their traditions and following ideas of revolution and destruction of the old, when our people in the Poland of those days were being persecuted and the people who ruled over them were oppressing them, in those days our young men lived with the Torah and their voices, the voice of Jacob, spilled over into the streets of the cities and the shtetlach with their sweet song of learning, and their hearts were devoted to the eternity of the Jewish people.

The prominent librarian of Yeshiva University, Rabbi Berish Mandelbaum, lived in Zamosch, Poland, until the war. In an interview in 1984 Rabbi Mandelbaum described life in Poland before the World War.

> The synagogues were packed. Even the Zionists who declared themselves as not being religious were in the synagogues every Shabbat and Yom Tov. The Bundists stayed away, and some of

the young Zionists. But everyone else was in the synagogue. In Warsaw, which had a Jewish population of 350,000, there were over 300 synagogues and they were all filled. In my little town of Zamosch there were ten synagogues, bursting with worshippers. And the Bais Medrash was busy in the afternoon and in the evening when the worshippers would come to learn.

The Sabbath was a day of undisturbed rest. In Warsaw not a store was open on the Sabbath, though it was said that a store was open on the edge of the city. In the shtetl Zamosch, who ever heard of a store open on Shabbos!

In the book of the shtetl Biala, N.Y. Feigenbaum writes,

> Despite all the changes in religious life, the religious Jews continued to rule the shtetl on the Sabbath and the holidays until the outbreak of the Second World War. Time had naturally made its mark and caused many cracks in religious life. The revolutionary years of the Czarist period, the years of the First World War and the spirit of freedom between the two World Wars, had had their influence. But after all the blows which the religious life had received, the atmosphere of Sabbath in the street had hardly changed. All stores were closed except for two drug stores, a colonial business, and two barber shops. You did not see a Jew with a cigarette in his mouth on the Sabbath.

Great changes were taking place in Eastern Europe. But if one looked, not ahead to the next generation, but only directly overhead at the present generation, he saw a bright blue sky with the sunshine of Torah shining above.

Such was the situation in Eastern Europe in 1939.

9

BEFORE THE SUN SETS

In 1939 the future of Torah Judaism in Eastern Europe was bleak. The leaders of Torah Jewry were alarmed, and helpless, as events relentlessly moved Eastern European Jewry toward decline.

The Chofetz Chaim, who was a leader of Jewry in the era between the two World Wars, wrote in the book *Chizuk Haemunah* in 1930.

> The sanctity of the Holy Torah is declining from day to day at a frightening pace. The new generation is growing up without Torah and faith. They are becoming wayward children who deny Hashem and His Torah. And if, G-d forbid, this situation continues much longer who knows to what condition we will fall. The mind compels one to believe that it will not be long before our righteous Messiah will come.
>
> Let us hasten the Redemption by sincere repentance. Let us prepare ourslevs with Torah and good deeds.

The historian Rabbi Chaim Dov Rabinowitz in *Divrei Ymei Yisrael* writes about Eastern European Jewry before the Second World War.

> We may ask what would have been with Jewish life in Europe if the Jewish people would have been following the same road until today? What would be the lot of Judaism if the secular parties would have continued their activity in the manner in which they were working? What would have happened if the

great leaning towards assimilation, even in the large Jewish centers like Warsaw and Lemberg, would have continued until today without change? It seems certain that the foundations of Judaism would have shaken.

King Solomon said, "The sun rises and the sun sets," and the Talmud explained his words as a prophecy of the history of the Torah. "The sun rises" and then "The sun sets."

The Torah will begin to rise in a new place before the sun sets in the center from which it is passing.

In 1939 the sun of Torah shone brilliantly in Eastern Europe. But it was heading for the sunset. What was to be the new center of Torah? Where would the sun rise? Where was the prophecy of King Solomon to be realized in this period of Jewish history?

The Jewish people in their exile in the twentieth century were scattered to the four corners of the earth. Three other countries were the major centers of the Jewish people: the Soviet Union, the United States, and Palestine.

The Soviet Union and the United States were especially important because of the numbers of Jews living there; and Palestine because of its special place in the hearts of the Jewish people in the past, present, and future.

Was the sun of Torah rising in any of these places?

10

JEWS IN THE SOVIET UNION

While the Jews in the nations separated from Russia were tenaciously fighting to hold on to their Torah-centered life, the Jews in the new Russia were being overwhelmed in their fight for their old life. In the years from 1917 to 1939 the life of the Jews in Russia was completely transformed. Almost no remnant of their former life-style remained. The shtetl became a thing of the past, and the Torah life that characterized the shtetl Jew was non-existent.

The new winds of culture and ideology that had so serious an effect on the Jews of Poland were irresistible in Russia. Russia was the center of the new ideology. The whole national apparatus was involved in creating a climate of acceptance of the new and rejection of the old. A basic tenet of the new doctrine was the decadence of religion, and many of the Jewish youth came to accept this doctrine.

The decline of religion was hastened by a campaign of religious persecution that began soon after the Revolution.

Religious Persecution

In 1918 the Commissariat for Jewish National Affairs was established. The Commissariat declared its purpose as follows:

> In view of the fact that the Jews are failing to fulfill the spirit of the Revolution and do not grasp it in its full significance it is necessary to arouse in the Jews a greater spirit of revolution. Therefore the Commissariat is to wage a campaign of education to this end and is to establish the rule of the Proletariat in the Jewish street.

The Commissariat progressed along the road to the "dictatorship of the proletariat in the Jewish street" in the following manner. In October 1918 the committee of the Commissariat resolved to liquidate the "kehila," the organized Jewish communities of Russia. These kehilot had, for hundreds of years, conducted the affairs of the Jewish communities. They provided the budget for the religious, social, and welfare needs of the Jewish people. They paid the salary of the rabbi, provided the budget for old-age homes and hospitals, and supported the educational institutions. These kehilot were ordered liquidated by the order of the Commissariat, which said:

> This committee resolves that there is no further place in our lives for the Jewish institutions which conducted their affairs until this time, or for the kehilot whose officers were chosen by secret elections. In this period of great struggle there is no room for compromise with bourgeoisie. All these types of institutions are harmful to the interests of the mass of Jews. After the victory of the proletariat in the October Revolution, the Jewish working class takes power into its own hands, and proclaims their dictatorship in the Jewish street.
> We call to all Jewish workers to unite behind the Commissariat and secure this dictatorship.

In June 1919 this order went into effect. All the kehilot were ordered liquidated and all their possessions were to be turned over to the local commissariat. This was followed by orders that liquidated all parties and societies in the Jewish community.

In the summer of 1919, there was established by the Interior Ministry of Kiev "The Committee for the Liquidation of Jewish Affairs," which was to be the central committee for the liquidation of all Jewish parties and societies.

It issued the following proclamation:

> Taking into consideration the opposition of the Zionist and Clerical Parties to the teachings of the Soviet government, and their orientation to the victory of international imperialism over the Soviet government, and recognizing that the work of these parties is not in accord with the goals of the government and is harmful to its defense and security and also to the poor

class, the Interior Ministry proposes, according to the recommendations of the Committee for Liquidation of Jewish Affairs of the Ministry of the Interior and with the agreement of the Jewish section of the Communist Party in the Ukraine and the Central Committee of the Communist Party, that an end should be put to all the activities of the Committees and local chapters of the Zionist Organization and the Clerical Organization and to warn them that if they do not obey these orders their leaders will be brought to trial before the Revolutionary Tribunal.

The kehilot, the political parties, and the social institutions of the Jewish people of Russia were forbidden.

Thus the preliminary steps were taken in the effort to separate Jews from Judaism. The work began in earnest after 1919 with the establishment of the Yevsektsia, the Jewish Sections of the Communist Party.

The Yevsektsia

The Yevsektsia was established by the Communist Party to intensify the work of the party in the Jewish street. The Yevsektsia was composed of a handful of Communists and a large number of former Bundists and Socialists who flocked to the party after the Revolution and after the final victory of the Bolsheviks.

The Yevsektsia was not a legal body set up to promulgate laws or to execute decrees. The purpose for which it was organized was not to force, persecute, or intimidate. It was intended to be the organ through which Communism was to be presented to the "Jewish Street." But the young Jews of the Yevsektsia were consumed with hate for the religious Jews and their institutions. They pushed their campaign with a passion and a fury. The Yevsektsia ushered in an era of persecution of religious Jewry in Russia.

At first the Yevsektsia members did not dare to use brute force. They wanted to portray themselves as the representatives of the masses. They therefore tried to build a climate of support among the people. They placed the war against religion on an ideological plane.

Ordinary propaganda in the press and from speakers' platforms was not sufficient to build this climate of support for attacks against the religious Jews. The Yevsektsia began to stage "public trials" of Jewish religious institutions.

The cheder, the yeshiva, the Jewish faith, specific commandments of the Torah, all these institutions and practices were placed on public trial.

Representatives of religious Jewry were called upon to defend these institutions against charges made by the Yevsektsia, which conducted the trial and handed down the verdict.

This was the method of the Yevsektsia during the first half of the 1920s. Countless trials were held during those years. In most cases the Yevsektsia declared the religious side the losers, closing many institutions and declaring many religious acts hostile to the Revolution.

In the year 1921 the Yevsektsia held a trial against the Jewish faith in the city of Kiev. The following is the description of that trial as it appears in the book *In the Era of the Revolution.*

> A few days before the trial, announcements were made in the newspapers inviting all Jewish Communists, the masses of Jewish workers, and all Jews to come to the trial.
>
> The trial began with the chairman announcing that the trial against the Jewish religion is now open. The first "accused" to appear before the three judges was an old woman dressed in the fashion of an old Jewess. The chairman turned to her and asked, "Why do you destroy your children by sending them to Yeshivot and to Cheder, places where they teach them foolishness? Why don't you send your children to the Communist schools where the children are educated in the spirit of Communism and are free from ancient laws like religious nationalism?"
>
> The "accused" answered, "What do you think, Comrades, judges, that I come from the low class, like tailors, and shoemakers? I come from Rabbis. I can't stuff my children with that Communism of yours."
>
> The chairman ordered the "counter-revolutionary" woman removed from the hall.
>
> Then a "Rabbi" entered the court with a long beard dressed in the style of the old rabbis. The chairman asked, "Why do you Rabbis establish Yeshivos and Cheders and synagogues where

the Jewish youth is misled with foolish religious and chauvinistic ideas?"

The Rabbi answered that the Rabbis do this so that the poor masses should sink into ignorance, be content with little, and remain enslaved to their bourgeois masters.

Then there appeared before the judges the third "accused." A bourgeois Jew with a big stomach, dressed extravagantly, ornamented with gold. The "bourgeois" declared that the Jewish bourgeoisie is interested in the survival and the spread of religion and its institutions so that they could enslave the masses and destroy their will to fight against their oppressors.

After listening to this testimony the prosecutor appeared and delivered a speech in which he explained that the Jewish religion, like all religions, is a means of economic oppression in the hands of the rich class and that the religious and nationalistic institutions serve this purpose. Therefore, the proletariat desires to liquidate religion and its institutions. The prosecutor demanded the death penalty against the Jewish religion.

The well-known leader Moshe Rosenblatt, who was in the audience, asked permission to speak. Since the trial was also a debate, the chairman gave him permission to speak. The Jewish leader arose and declared, "You Red judges! Ten years ago the Black Hundred of the Czar recreated the 'blood libels' and placed on trial the unfortunate sacrificial lamb Beiles. The Black judges slandered the Jewish religion, the Talmud, and everything that is Jewish. Now, you Red judges repeat all those slanders against the Jewish religion and against the Jewish heritage, like true enemies of the Jewish people and real anti-Semites."

The audience responded to this speech with stormy applause. The chairman shouted an order to place Rosenblatt under arrest. The judges left the hall and entered a second room to "deliberate." After a few minutes they returned to the hall. A deathly stillness hung over the hall. They announced their verdict. "The Jewish religion is sentenced to death!" Great excitement broke out in the audience. The chairman then closed the trial.

The majority of the Jews were not frightened by these trials. On the holidays which immediately followed, the synagogues were filled with worshippers.

Decline of Torah Education

In 1918 *Izvestia* announced this proclamation of the Ministry of Culture:

> The National Committee in its meeting of August 24, 1918 declared that all institutions of religious education are forbidden to all those who have not reached the age of 18.

This resolution was later incorporated into Soviet law. A government directive permitted religious learning in the home, on condition that there be no more than three children taking part.

The Yevsektsia was determined to destroy the cheder. But it did not at first pursue the destruction of the cheder with the full force of the law. It tried to create a climate of support among the masses for its measures against the cheder and therefore until 1922 concentrated on the public trial.

One of the earliest of these trials took place in the city of Vitebsk. In December 1920 a special committee was appointed by the Jewish Commissariat in the city of Vitebsk whose function it was to investigate the cheders in the city in preparation for the trial.

In the beginning of January 1921 announcements were made in the city that the trial would take place in the theatre on January 8. Admission cards were required in order to attend the trial. The Yevsektsia sent 400 cards to its friends and 250 to the "synagogue committee," which was invited to participate in the trial as defenders of the cheder. The synagogue committee replied that they would not officially accept the invitation, since they did not recognize the authority of the Yevsektsia to conduct such a trial. However, they would participate as private individuals. The committee reluctantly accepted the unequal division of admission cards, in spite of the fact that Vitebsk was a city in which the vast majority of Jews were religious and only a very small percentage were sympathetic to the Yevsektsia.

One of the leaders of the Yevsektsia, the head of the Jewish Commissariat in Vitebsk, L. Abram, writes in his memoirs:

> This trial was supposed to start at seven in the evening, but at four the area around the theatre was crowded with about

eight thousand people. When I came to the theatre the crowd was already gathered. Everyone was screaming that they would not allow the trial against the Cheder.

I managed to get into the building, which was so full you could choke. In the midst of all the shouting and confusion, a delegation appeared in the name of ten thousand Jews who demanded that they be permitted to enter the hall or that the trial be postponed. Of course we were not frightened by this delegation. We knew that this group of snuff-smellers was not capable of fighting. But we saw that in the midst of all this confusion and shouting it would be impossible to conduct the trial. Besides, for some reason the electricity went out that evening in the theatre. The confusion and the darkness convinced us to postpone the trial.

The trial was set for the twelfth of January. The interest in the trial grew. We moved the trial to another building. This time we mobilized sufficient force to guard the building inside and outside. Admission was carefully checked. Again there were attempts at fighting, but those who tried it were placed in a suitable place for a few days for disturbing the trial.

The trial was supposed to be a debate about the educational standards of the cheder and not about religion, but the Yevsektsia used the occasion as an opportunity to wage a campaign against religion.

It began by declaring that neither the melamed nor the program of the cheder met the requirements of modern pedagogy. They described the melamed as stupid, incompetent, and cruel. They said also that from a hygienic point of view, the cheder did not fulfill the necessary requirements.

But when one of the health experts of the Yevsektsia suggested that the solution would be to place the cheder under the supervision and support of the government, and when this was supported by the defenders of the cheder, the Yevsektsia broadened the condemnation of the cheder.

The Yevsektsia declared that religion serves the bourgeoisie and they need the cheder to dull the understanding of the masses.

After the debate and the speeches, the judges retired for "deliberation." A recess of forty minutes was announced. After an hour the judges returned, looking fatigued, as though they had worked very hard to reach their verdict. The judgment was announced: all the slanders against the cheder and against the religion were reviewed, and they were declared servants of the bourgeoisie. The verdict was to immediately close every cheder.

Similar trials were held by the Yevsektsia all over Russia. Similar sentences were passed against thousands of Russian cheders.

Public trials and debates regularly took place during the entire first half of the decade of the 1920s. But they were not held as frequently as in 1921; the Yevesktsia did not consider them necessary any longer. The people already knew the purpose and manner of the trials. And in most cases the religious side recognized the futility of their defense and refused to participate.

During the years 1922 and 1923, committees for the liquidation of the cheders were set up in every city and town by the Jewish Commissariat and the Yevsektsia. These committees worked with the local governments and helped them close the cheders.

New types of trials were begun, not public ideological trials but actual criminal trials. The melamed was tried and punished for the crime of teaching religion to Jewish children.

During these two years, thousands of cheders were closed. And even though the Soviet schools had no place for all the children turned out of their cheders, the Yevsektsia remained determined to close them.

The religious education of the children went underground. In many towns classes were secretly continued in the bais medrash.

D. Persky, who visited Minsk in the year 1930, describes an underground cheder:

> In Minsk I wanted to see the secret Cheders. From some old woman I found out that in a room in one of the synagogues in the downtown part of the city, the Shamash (sexton) lives and he secretly teaches Torah to little children. I came to the Yard which was known to me from my youth. I looked quickly in the windows. I saw six children sitting around a table and the Shamash was explaining to them a passage from the Bible. I was happy that I found what I was looking for. I opened the door and behold, I saw an empty room. The Shamash was sitting and patching his garment. In a second room his wife was lying on her bed holding a baby. I turned to the Shamash and asked

him if there is a Cheder here. "G-d forbid," he answered me tremblingly. "Who needs a Cheder in these days? And besides it is forbidden to have a Cheder."

After a lengthy conversation he arose with a cry, "Oh, you are the son of Rivka. I knew you as a child when you came here for services."

Suddenly all the six children appeared before me. They had become experts in hiding. The Shamash showed me their hiding places and said, "This one was hiding in a coop under the oven, this one behind the oven, and the other in a pile of rags. They are used to it. In the middle of the learning, if they hear a footstep they immediately disappear." His wife hides the books under her pillow. And she added, "That's the way we learn Torah today in the free Russia."

Another means of continuing the Torah education of the children was to divide them into groups of three or fewer, which was permitted under Soviet law. The children went to the Soviet schools during the regular hours and studied Torah during the evening or in the early morning.

But even though Soviet law permitted this type of learning, the Yevsektsia crushed it as well. It used its power ruthlessly and disregarded the legalities.

A communist describes the condition of religious education in a shtetl in the mid-twenties in the following manner.

> The Cheders have been liquidated. But the teachers are still going into the homes and giving lessons. For fear of the government, the Melamed takes his wife with him when he goes to teach. He goes into the house to teach and she stands guard in front of the house. In the street they already know what it means when the Melamed's wife is standing in front of the house. A child enjoys a joke, tells the woman that he is going to tell the police what is happening. She immediately runs away with her husband, holding the holy books in their hands, while the children stand and laugh at the trick. Thus the Melamed is turned into a laughingstock in the eyes of the young people.

The religious education of the Jewish children decreased from year to year. The persecution by the Yevsektsia and the poverty of the masses who could not afford private teaching discouraged parents from providing a religious education for their children.

During the early period of Soviet rule, Torah learning was still widespread and intensive, not only among the children but also among the young men. The young men of Russia were steeped in Torah learning—ignorance of Torah was considered shameful for even the ordinary young man. Yeshivot were numerous and they provided the opportunity for Torah learning to the young men of the Russian shtetl.

In addition to the local yeshivot, Russia boasted of many of the most famous yeshivot and many of the greatest Torah scholars in the world. To these yeshivot young men came from all corners of the nation and the world. The Yevsektsia's desire to destroy Torah education knew no bounds. It aimed to destroy all its institutions, from the smallest cheder and its melamed to the most famous yeshiva and its revered dean.

They persecuted the rabbis and slandered the institutions. They declared that the yeshivot were poisoning the masses and demanded that the yeshivot be closed. Some of the great yeshivot and their rabbis succeeded in receiving permission to leave Russia, others escaped from Russia, still others were persecuted and harassed until they closed down. The great yeshivot of Mir, Slobodka, and Chofetz Chaim left legally. The rabbis and students of the Yeshiva Novorodack managed to escape across the borders after years of persecution and periodic imprisonment of their rabbis. The Lubavitcher Yeshiva remained in Russia and heroically managed to survive many years of persecution. Courageous efforts were made by many rabbis in many towns to keep their yeshivot functioning, but the great widespread Torah learning of the young men of Russia declined and was no more.

The education of the girls of the religious Russian families suffered even more than that of the boys. Whenever possible, boys were sent away to yeshivot. Girls were not sent away from home but had no local religious institutions for their education. Since education was compulsory, they could not be at home during school hours, lest they be reported to the police.

Most parents, even the most religious, had no alternative but to send their daughter to the Russian school. No religious education of any consequence was available to supplement their secular education. Thus, in most families, the daughters drew away from their parents. Most attended classes on the Sabbath. Some of the girls sat in class but did not write, others found excuses for not attending classes on the Sabbath. The girls engaged in a constant struggle against the school to maintain their religion and their ties with their parents. In most cases the struggle was lost.

Liquidation of the Synagogue

The Soviet government guaranteed the freedom of religious worship. Synagogues were legally approved, but the Jewish Commissariat and Yevsektsia found a way to liquidate them.

According to the law, all synagogues were to become the property of the local workers' councils, which in turn permitted the use of these buildings for religious worship.

In light of the law the Jewish Commissariat issued the following directive:

> According to the directive regarding the elimination of illiteracy among the masses, the cultural ministry of the Commissariat has the right to make use for this purpose of all public buildings like synagogues, clubs, and even private homes and other suitable places such as factories. In this manner it is possible to make use, for this purpose, of the Bais Medrash.
>
> It is well to take into account the possibilities of this in the struggle against the foolish beliefs of religion and clericalism.

This call was the signal for the Yevsektsia to begin its activities against the synagogue. It found reasons to need the local synagogues for educational purposes for the workers.

At first the Yevsektsia found it necessary to make the need for the synagogue sound convincing. It staged mass meetings of workers, who declared that they needed the synagogue, or arranged to have the cultural ministry request the use of the building for its needs.

The religious people fought desperately to preserve their synagogues. Many times they would appeal to the government against the Yevsektsia; the Russian government was the judge between the religious Jew and the Yevsektsia Jew. Sometimes the religious Jews were able to keep their synagogue, but more often the power of the Yevsektsia could not be overcome.

In 1923 a group of Communists in Moscow tried to have the Great Synagogue of Moscow turned over to them for purposes of "culture." A petition signed by the worshippers was presented to the Justice Ministry protesting the attempt to take over the synagogue:

> There is no doubt in our mind that those eight people who are requesting from the Soviet in Moscow that the synagogue be given to them as a club are trying to steal from thousands of believers their right to fulfil their religious needs. The great majority of religious people will see great danger in this. It will remind them of the frightful events of past years. The law of the Soviet Union guarantees to all its citizens freedom of religion and worship. We therefore are certain that the Justice Commissariat, whose function it is to protect the laws, will give its decision to the leadership of the Soviet in Moscow that the closing of the Synagogue in Moscow violates freedom of religion and worship as guaranteed by the law.
>
> We also see it as our obligation, while we are protecting our own synagogue, to bring to the attention of the government the fact that many synagogues are being closed by local authorities. The Jewish community of Moscow receives masses of requests to protect synagogues from the harassment of local authorities. It is known to us that synagogues in many cities have been closed. We, the representatives of the Jewish community and the Synagogue in Moscow, have decided to raise our voices to protect the Jewish religion.

The synagogue remained in the hands of the worshippers, but it was one of few that escaped the clutches of the Yevsektsia.

The religious Jew sometimes engaged the forces of the Yevsektsia in physical combat in fighting the attempted takeovers. Blood flowed in the synagogues as the Yevsektsia violently enforced its confiscations.

In the winter of 1921, the Section of Jewish Culture in Vitebsk requested from the Jewish Commissariat in the city that several synagogues be turned over to it for use as a school and for other cultural activities. The Section of Jewish Culture claimed that it needed to find homes for poor children who were suffering terribly from the cold in the poor, unheated homes of their parents.

The synagogues requested were a group of five buildings centered around a courtyard. A special committee of the Jewish Commissariat inspected the synagogues and found them suitable for the requested purpose of the cultural section. The request was approved by the executive committee. The notice was then sent to the Synagogue Committee and they were informed that they must remove their possessions within three days. The Synagogue Committee refused to obey the demand. They were given a second warning and an extension of two days; they refused again. The Commissariat itself had to remove all the religious articles from the synagogues, along with the worshippers.

The work was not easy—the city stormed against the Yevsektsia, and there were mass meetings and protests. But the Yevsektsia was determined to go through with its decision regardless of the reaction.

The religious Jews held sit-ins in the synagogue from dawn until late at night, holding prayers and protest meetings against the Commissariat. The Commissariat finally succeeded in locking the Jews out of the synagogue.

The Jews gathered in the courtyard in their prayer shawls and refused to leave the yard from early morning until late at night. The Commissariat then mobilized fifteen men to empty the courtyard. As soon as the group appeared in the yard and commanded the religious Jews to leave, the excited crowd attacked them with rocks and mud. The group could not overpower the crowd and retreated to the Commissariat. That day any Communist walking the street was pelted with rocks and mud. The Commissariat then brought in an army unit of twenty horsemen who emptied the courtyard and scattered the people.

In this way thousands of synagogues were closed. Resistance was heroic, but to no avail. A letter from the city of Muzir in 1929, quoted in *Yahadut B'Russia Hasovietit*, by A. A. Gershuni, states:

> From all the Yeshivot and synagogues there is now not a memory. Everything is confiscated. This week the two last remaining synagogues were taken over and turned into clubs. Our pain is great, but even greater is our shame. For whose hands have committed all this? It is the hands of our own sons and daughters, Pioneers, Yevsektsia, Communists, and Komso-

mol. There is no place to put the holy Torah Scrolls which were removed from the synagogues. The community is weary and shrouded in sadness.

All-out War Against Religion

The Yevsektsia was not content with closing down schools and synagogues. It also harassed the rabbis and all other religious functionaries and tried to prevent the religious masses from fulfilling religious duties.

The rabbi's life was made miserable by a system of "declassing." A declassed person not only lost his political rights but was even stripped of fundamental human rights. A declassed person could not get a job in a government office or factory, he could not enter a secondary school, he could not live in a government-owned apartment, and he did not receive a ration card for food. These rights were removed from him and from his entire family. Children could receive the rights denied to the declassed father only if they announced publicly in the newspapers that they broke all ties with their parents. Many children of rabbis could not bear the suffering and hardship and they separated themselves from their declassed father.

Thus the life of the rabbi was terribly discouraging. Many rabbis found the situation unbearable and were forced to leave their positions.

The Yevsektsia found ways to harass the religious Jews in their personal observance of religion. They slandered and declassed the "shochet" who slaughtered the animals for kosher meat. They heaped abuse and vilification on the "mohel" who circumcised the Jewish children. If a child died near the age of circumcision, they would blame the mohel and the act of circumcision for his death. The mohel would be brought to trial, at which time the ritual of circumcision would be called barbaric and murderous. Any member of the Communist Party or any person who held a government or public position, if he circumcised his child, would be banished from the party and removed from his position. He would be placed under suspicion as a counterrevolutionary. The act of circumcision became very perilous.

The Yevsektsia campaigned actively to prevent the Sabbath

from being the rest day of the workers. In most cases it succeeded in having the rest day set for Sunday. Thus the religious Jew was faced with the choice of not working in the factory or not keeping the Sabbath.

During the holidays the Yevsektsia was very active in disturbing the holiday atmosphere of the religious Jews, especially on the most holy day of the year, Yom Kippur.

A report from the city of Vitebsk tells the following:

> September 22, 1920 was Yom Kippur. The Yevsektsia planned an "Anti-Yom Kippur" celebration. All the Communist comrades participated. This included all members of the Bund, the Communist Youth, the Bundist Youth, and unaffiliated workers, altogether about one thousand people. They gathered in Freedom Circle at the time that the religious Jews were going to the synagogue during the High Holy Day. They stood there armed with hammer and sickle. The band began to play and the parade began, headed for the Great Synagogue. From there they went to the forest to chop wood for the railroad. This demonstration was like a bombshell on the heads of the Jewish community. But what could they do? The "Anti-Yom Kippur" celebration became popular in every town in Russia.

These demonstrations were widespread all over Russia in those years. In many places fights broke out, blood was spilled, and many people were put into prison. The sport of disturbing and harassing the synagogue prayers was very popular.

The notorious leader of the Yevsektsia, Esther Frumkin, writes:

> Minsk, the evening of Yom Kippur, the synagogue is full of Jews, stillness in the streets, not a living soul. Suddenly loud voices are heard, from the club of the Commissariat Youth. The noise begins to draw closer and closer. It is now in Freedom Circle. The youth is demonstrating. Thousands of people are walking, carrying flags and lighted torches. Above the heads of the demonstrators wave figures made of cardboard. The figures are of a priest and a rabbi. The priest and the rabbi are embracing. The youth are marching and singing, "Down with the rabbis and the priests." Song and laughter and loud voices

crash into the synagogue. There the people are standing, weeping, and fearing G-d.

The campaign against the Jewish religion exceeded by far the bounds of official government policy. The zeal of the Yevsektsia members far exceeded the zeal of their non-Jewish comrades in their activities against religion.

Esther Frumkin proudly writes in her pamphlet, "Down With the Rabbis":

> From this pamphlet every Russian comrade can see that the struggle against religion and the war against the influence of the rabbis is conducted in the Jewish section in no smaller measure, and on the contrary, with greater force and determination and with more consistency than in the non-Jewish section.

By 1928 the situation was rapidly deteriorating, but not yet hopelessly lost. In spite of the new trends that had captured much of the youth, and in spite of the persecution by the Yevsektsia, the religious Jew still held grimly to his Torah way of life.

The American Jewish writer M. Chanin, who knew prerevolutionary Russia well, visited Russia in 1928 and wrote:

> I wanted to see the Sabbath day in a shtetl. I wanted to see how much the spiritual life of the Jews had changed in the shtetl. I had already seen the condition of the large cities. On the Sabbath the stores were open, Russians and Jews putting out displays in the cooperatives if they had anything to sell. The Jewish customers are young people. Many people are walking in the streets on Sabbath, but dressed in week-day clothing. The atmosphere of the Sabbath of the past is not felt. When I visited the synagogue I saw old people or middle-aged people. I also saw some young men but not many.
>
> The shtetl is different. The Sabbath is felt here like in the "good old days." In the home Sabbath candlesticks are on the table. The table is arranged in a Sabbath manner. It all looks like there was no revolution in Jewish life in Russia.
>
> However, that was only in the home. In the street you feel a

week-day atmosphere. The marketplace, the place where stores used to be closed on Sabbath, is now different. Now there is no distinction apparent between Sabbath and weekday.

The cooperative stores are open on the Sabbath. The farmers of the village come on the Sabbath to buy and sell and the shtetl looks like it does on the weekdays.

In the synagogue there are many people praying. But when they walk out you don't see the peace of Sabbath on their faces. The slow step of the group walking together is gone. Now they walk through the streets quickly. You can see from their hurried walk that they are not happy with the atmosphere of the street, which is not in keeping with their Sabbath.

The New Line

The religious Jews were able to hold on to some vestige of their way of life up to 1929. But in 1929 a new official policy towards religion was adopted, far tougher and more effective than the unofficial Yevsektsia policy.

Until 1929 the law of the land was equality for religious and antireligious activity. Though the Yevsektsia distorted it, the official government policy served as a restraint upon the Yevsektsia. It had to adjust its campaign to the limitation of its power. But in 1929 the Stalin government adopted a policy of inequality. They limited freedom of religion to freedom of worship, and they permitted unlimited freedom of antireligious activity.

The new law, adopted in April 1929, made it illegal for religious organizations to participate in any cultural or social activity except for actual religious services. Only services within the walls of the religious institutions were allowed without a special permit. Religious activity and services were forbidden in all public places. No religious group could collect funds or hold meetings anywhere but within the building of worship. Charitable societies, benevolent societies, cooperatives, youth groups, libraries, hospitals, youth festivals, and outings were all forbidden to religious organizations. The teaching of religion was forbidden except by special permission, which required application to the Ministry of the Interior.

These new controls over religious activity were the signal for a new government policy to destroy the influence of religion in Russia. No longer did the Yevsektsia lead in antireligious activity. Now the government placed its full force behind the antireligious campaign. Yeshivot, which were in some small measure able to resist the Yevsektsia, could not resist the government and the secret police. Synagogues, which managed to stay open in the 1920s, could no longer avoid the relentless pursuit of the government authorities, who found reasons to close their doors, or who closed them down without reason. In most of the towns of Russia not a single synagogue escaped.

A favorite target of the new line was the rabbi. The authorities wanted to force rabbis to leave their positions and levied special taxes on them, more than they could pay, to accomplish this.

A campaign of accusations was mounted against rabbis. They were accused not only of secret, illegal, religious activity, but more seriously, of economic crimes and counterrevolutionary activity.

In the city of Zembin in 1929 the rabbi was accused of hoarding coins and he was exiled from his city. Similar charges were made against many rabbis. The rabbi of Pohust was convicted of stealing the clock from the synagogue.

By the beginning of the 1930s almost all the rabbis of the shtetlach of Russia had been removed from their positions. Some rabbis still occupied positions in the cities, but their situation was desperate. They were the target of constant abuse and suspicion, and people were encouraged to spy upon them and upon anyone who engaged in religious activity. Spying became so widespread that people began to fear their neighbors. An example of the state of abuse to which the rabbis had fallen is told by D. Persky in the name of the rabbi of Oozda. He relates that the children of the shtetl would chase the rabbi in the street, pull his coat, and scream at him, "Oh, there is no G-d, there is no G-d!"

Decline of the Shtetl

The established way of life of the shtetl was an important factor in maintaining the vitality of religion among the Jewish inhabitants. It was a powerful factor in preventing assimilation. Its intense tradition even withstood the attacks of the Yevsektsia and the new winds of ideology. As long as the shtetl survived, religious life still held on.

But the shtetl was not master of its own destiny. Its stability fluctuated with the economic development of the Soviet Union.

The years of upheaval in the era of the Bolshevik Revolution created chaotic conditions in the country. The measures taken to liquidate the bourgeoisie and all aspects of private capital brought hunger to the land.

At the Communist Convention in 1921 Lenin called for a slowdown in the liquidation of small private capital.

> We have gone too far with our nationalization of business and industry, with the destruction of private business. Was this a mistake? Of course.
>
> We often repeat that Capitalism is bad and Socialism is good. True, Capitalism compared to Socialism is surely bad. But in comparison to Medieval ways, it is good. As long as we cannot go over directly from small production to Socialism, Capitalism during that time is unavoidable. To try to eliminate private capital completely would be not only folly but also suicide of the Party.
>
> It would be folly because such a policy is economically impractical. It would be suicide because parties which would try to achieve this would be bankrupt.

With the ushering in of the new economic policy, small business, which was the backbone of the shtetl, began to revive. The marketplace was lively, the stores were opened. The people were very poor, but compared with the years of militant communism, conditions were much improved. Economic conditions were better and opportunities for employment were improved for everyone.

But the new economic policy did not last very long. In 1924 the government retreated from it and began to harass private capital. Taxes on the small merchant were increased. The establishment of cooperatives and government shops limited the little merchants' opportunities for success. Work was not to be found—there was not much industry in the shtetl. The craftsmen did not have the money to equip themselves with the necessary instruments.

An article describing the plight of the shtetl appeared in *Emes*, July 16, 1924.

The condition of the Jews especially in the shtetlach of Ukraine is frightful. As a result of the development of the cooperative and government business, the shtetl population has been pushed out of its last economic position. The poverty in the shtetl is reaching colossal proportions.

Conditions continued to deteriorate. The years 1925 to 1929 were extremely difficult for the shtetl inhabitants. A report by A. A. Veitzbett in 1931 stated:

The number of people who took licenses for business in the Ukraine in 1925–1926 was 125,913 and in 1927–1928 only 106,227. In 1928–1929 the tempo of people leaving private business increased. It is anticipated that by the year 1929 fifty percent of the above group will be counted among the declassed. About the other half, there is no doubt that they are candidates for declassification in the very near future.

M. Kiefer, in the *Jewish Shtetl in Ukraine*, writes:

The majority of the youth of the shtetl is unemployed. And those who work for tradesmen are ruthlessly exploited. When their apprenticeship ends they become unemployed. Near the shtetl there are industries, factories, mills, etc. But the Jewish youth is not taken into them. In Romanov from 259 young people, 215 are unemployed and without skills [60 percent]. In Baronivka from 237, there are 105 unemployed [44.3 percent]. In Vinograd 160 are unemployed out of 236 [68 percent]. In Talne from about 1000, over 600 are unemployed. In Cheshtshevette from 303, there are 130 unemployed. In the reports from Chudnov and Yozepov it is reported that almost all the youth are unemployed.

The shtetl offered no hope, only poverty and stagnation. But, in 1929, opportunities elsewhere were also severely restricted. The stream from the shtetl to the city was constant but it did not reach flood proportions.

The year 1929 was a year of great change in the lives of the Jewish masses. That was the year of the great Russian industrialization, and the growth in industry during this period was phenomenal.

In 1913, 59.4% of the entire production of Russia was agricultural products and 40.6 percent industrial. In 1939 industrial production was 78 percent and agricultural products 22 percent.

The great national industrialization created jobs in industry and multiplied the number of government functionaries administering the giant nationalized industrial apparatus. The Jews of Russia found opportunities open to them in the cities. The Jews were happy to find work in industry and even more eager to obtain positions in government employ. The numbers of Jewish youth engaged in study increased rapidly. In 1927–1928 in all of Soviet Russia there were 23,405 Jewish students; in 1935 there were 61,384. Students in secondary schools included 20.4 Jews per thousand compared with 2.8 for White Russians and 2.0 for Ukrainians.

Some 420,000 Jews worked for the government in 1934—33 percent of the total Jews employed. Another 300,000 (23.6 percent) were industrial workers, and in the liberal professions there were 100,000 (7.8 percent).

The Jews streamed to the city to fill the jobs in government and industry. As a result, the population of the shtetlach dropped sharply. About 600,000 Jews emigrated from the shtetlach to the big cities from 1920 to 1940. In 1939, 42 percent of the entire Jewish population was concentrated in six large Russian cities—Moscow, Leningrad, Odessa, Kiev, Kharkhov, and Dnepropetrosvk.

By the latter part of the 1930s the Jewish population was living and working in the big city. The shtetl was virtually gone, and with it the shtetl way of life. The Jews who had gone into government employ quickly reconciled themselves to a way of life not in harmony with their old Jewish tradition. Even the Jews working in the factories in the large Russian cities drifted away from the old ways. There was very little Jewish education, very few religious institutions, hardly any religious leaders. Gone too was the social climate that reminded Jews of their past tradition.

Chairman Kalinin, the Communist most sympathetic to the Jewish people and their way of life, said in a speech:

> When I was asked in one of the factories of Moscow why are there so many Jews now in Moscow, I answered that if I were a Rabbi among the Jews, an old Rabbi with influence whose heart and soul feel the pain of the Jewish nation, I would

excommunicate every Jew who comes to Moscow to occupy a Soviet position because they are lost to the Jewish people forever. In Moscow the blood of the Jew and the blood of the Russian join and they are lost to Judaism, if not the second generation, then the third.

With the decline of the shtetl came the fall of the last guardian of the Jewish spirit in Russia. The Jew who came to the big city joined his spirit with the spirit of the Russian and was lost to Judaism.

This was the fate of Russian Jewry. There were three million Jews in a land that had once been the center of Torah. But the sun of Torah did not shine there anymore. The sun had set in Soviet Russia.

11

JEWS IN THE UNITED STATES

Until the 1880s America was only a small outpost of world-dispersed Jewry. Most of the Jews of the world lived in Europe. The first Jewish settlement in the United States was by the Spanish-Portuguese, who came as early as 1654. But they came only a few at a time, and during the Revolutionary War period their number was estimated at 3000. This slow immigration continued until their estimated number rose to 15,000 in 1840.

The influx of Spanish Jews was followed and overshadowed by the much larger immigration of German Jews, who began to come to the United States in 1815. During this immigration, approximately 200,000 Jews came to the United States and the Jewish population in 1880 grew to about 250,000.

The German Jews who came to the United States were mostly poor or middle-class workers. They were hardworking and very ambitious, and they spared no effort in their attempts to climb the ladder of economic success.

Many of them started out as peddlers. They invested their small capital in a pack of merchandise, which they carried with them along the road. When they made a little profit they invested it in a horse and buggy. When they accumulated enough they would open a store in a place that had struck their fancy when they travelled on their peddling route.

For many of them this path led to a good deal of success. By 1880 they were very well established in the economic life of the United States, successfully settled in many cities. Significant centers of Jewish population existed in such cities as New York, Chicago, and Cincinnati.

The German Jews who came to the United States believed intensely in America and wanted to be absorbed into its society, to become "Americans." They wanted their children to receive the finest American education. They idealized the public school as an institution of American democracy. They admired the colleges of America as institutions for professional development. They wanted to be part of America and to adopt the American life-style completely.

They established synagogues and Hebrew schools. But their synagogues were intended only as a means to retain their Jewish identity, not to serve as the all-encompassing social-cultural institution. Their Hebrew schools were intended only to keep the children aware of their Jewish identity, not to educate them in a distinct Jewish way of life.

Concerning the role of religious education for their children, a leading rabbi of the German Jewish community, Rabbi J. M. Weiss, is thus quoted in the Report of Education in the United States in the year 1870:

> It is our opinion that the education of the children is the responsibility of the government, and their religious education is the responsibility of the parent. Secular studies belong in the public schools and the religion of Israel in the Sabbath schools.

And the editor of the section about the Jews, J. J. Noah, writes:

> Separate schools are not as desirable in the United States as they used to be because the Jews of the United States are very proud of their citizenship. And even though they want to educate their children in their spirit, they do not want to interfere with the progress of free education. They want to receive the education in the public schools where there are no restrictions, and which are free for all religions.

The same report gives the following information about the condition of Jewish education in various cities. In Chicago, the Jewish population numbered about 10,000. Ninety percent of the children attended public schools. Most of the children who received a Jewish education attended the Sabbath school, which had an enrollment of 600 students.

In St. Louis the estimated number of Jewish children attending the public schools was 1,120. There were three Sabbath schools in the city, which enrolled 398 students.

In Cincinnati there were three Hebrew schools. One held classes twice a week, on Saturday and Sunday, and had 180 students. The others conducted classes one day a week, one school attended by 150 students and the other by 60 students.

At about the same period in New York there were several congregational schools that taught on Sundays, and one congregational school that taught twice a week.

The German Jews wanted their expression of Jewish identity to be not distinctly and separately Jewish, but rather a synthesis of a Jewish and American identity. Therefore, they took their cultural and social life out of the synagogue. To provide for their social and cultural needs in the manner in which they desired, they organized the Young Men's Hebrew Association. The YMHA conducted activities that were not religious in nature, but rather cultural and social, and that united for them the Jewish and American ways of life.

They also emphasized philanthropic and charitable work as a major form of their Jewish expression. They formed the Bnai Brith, which engaged in extensive cultural and charitable activities. They aided Jewish causes in the United States and overseas. They supported homes for orphans and the aged and relief organizations.

For the German Jews, the synagogue was not the central social and cultural institution in their lives and the Hebrew school was not the central educational institution in their children's lives. Thus America in 1880 was, relative to the world Jewish population, numerically small and spiritually insignificant.

The Golden Land

In 1881 there began a new chapter in the history of the Jewish settlement of the United States. The United States became the land to which streams of Jews from the great population centers of Eastern Europe began to flow. The streams became rivers and oceans until the number of Jews coming to the United States rose into the millions.

This immigration began with the pogroms that shook 160

cities and towns in Russia, and it continued unabated as the Jews wearied of the persecution and the poverty that stifled them in Eastern Europe. America was open to them and they came. They emigrated to the "Golden Land," the "Land of Liberty," the "Land of Opportunity."

The Jewish population in the United States rose from 250,000 in 1880 to 3,500,000 in 1920. Over two million Jews entered the United States during that period. Most of them came from the Russian Empire and from Rumania and Austria-Hungary. By 1928 the Jewish population of the United States had risen to 4,200,000. Over 3,100,000 of them were of Eastern European birth or descent. By 1933 the Jewish population of the United States exceeded 4,500,000.

The Jews came mostly from the shtetlach of Eastern Europe. But they came with different feelings about the life they were leaving behind and different attitudes towards the life they were entering.

Many of the Jews came with the hope that they would be able to maintain the Torah-centered shtetl way of life in America. They knew that the America to which they were coming was almost barren of the religious institutions the shtetl possessed in such abundance. Eastern Europe was filled with schools of Torah learning for young and old, and America had hardly any. In Eastern Europe, Shabbos was an accepted day of rest for all Jews. In America it was an accepted day of work for most Jews.

These religious Jews coming to America knew that it would be an uphill struggle to reestablish the "Old Home" in America. But they were determined to make no compromises. They would make every necessary sacrifice to plant a true religious life in America.

Many other religious Jews came to America with the thought of adjusting to America while holding on to as much of their religious life as they could. They were fascinated by the great American opportunity and wanted their children to receive the kind of education that would equip them to meet the American challenge. They did not want to forsake their religion. But, unlike the other group, they wanted to develop a religious life-style that would also be conducive to "Americanization."

And many other Jews who came to America were quite ready to leave the religious life of Eastern Europe behind them. They were not at all disturbed by the religious problems posed by life in America. So what if one had to work on the Sabbath in order to find employment? What did it matter that the opportunities for a Torah education for their children were very limited? Their main interests were making a living and helping their children make a good adjustment to America. That was all that mattered.

Of these varied groups, only the last found it relatively easy to adjust to the new life in America. For the religious Jews, life in America presented enormous problems.

Keeping the Sabbath was very difficult—it was very hard to rise above poverty without violating the Sabbath. Finding a job usually depended upon working on the Sabbath.

Establishing the institutions for a Torah environment was very expensive when the Jews were hard-pressed to maintain their own existence. It was a staggering task for them to establish the institutions required to fill their religious needs.

The problems of trying to bring up their children in a traditional manner were overwhelming. The language of the parents was Yiddish; the language of the children was English. The parents were European; the children were proud "Americans." For the same reasons, it was very difficult to attract the children to the synagogue.

Besides all these problems there was the inescapable fact that the father had no time for his children. Making a living in America was very hard. Laboring all day in a sweat shop or as a peddler sapped his strength and demanded all his time. He was not able to give his children the attention they needed if he was to instill in them love for his values and traditions.

Thus, the European religious Jew who came to America faced a terrible struggle. And the developing life of American Jewry reflected this struggle.

The Cheder

The school that first arose to serve the children of the new immigrants was the cheder. This was a school set up by a private individual who would proclaim himself a melamed, or teacher. He would hold classes in his apartment or some other equally shabby place. The melamed was often a poor, unsuccessful man who could find no other means of livelihood. He was quite likely also to be unlearned. The Hebrew school was often dirty and dingy and the teacher equally so.

J. Buchalter, writing in *Hatzfirah* in 1898 describes a private cheder in New York:

> The teachers in whose care the parents placed their children were of the older generation, from Russia and Poland (the new land had unfortunately not yet produced pedagogues in Hebrew studies). These teachers would teach the children three or four hours a day, that is from four in the afternoon until seven or eight in the evening. The children would come to the Cheder tired and weary after having been in the public school from morning until three in the afternoon. In these few hours the teacher would lecture to twenty or thirty assorted children, all vastly different in their level of learning. Seeing the teacher try to teach all of them at the same time is like watching a tragic comedy. While one is reading Hebrew, a second one is loudly translating a sentence from the Bible, a third is chanting the Haftorah, and the fourth is reciting the Mincha service. In the meantime the others were talking to each other and trading toys. The noise builds and becomes so loud that everyone passing by says, "This must be a Hebrew School."
>
> And what is the teacher doing during all this? The teacher is trying desperately to quiet them. When he sees that he is unable to quiet them he becomes terrible angry, and he lets go with a volley of curses that the evil angels of America could not understand (curses are in Russian or Polish). At the same time he keeps his hands busy, one child he slaps on the cheek, another he pulls by the lobe of the ear, and his hands leave their mark all over.

Another description of the cheder of New York is given by J. Kahana in the *Hatoran*, Volume 3, Chapter 1.

> My first contact with Hebrew education was on Madison Street on the East Side of New York. I was walking along the street, and as I passed a stable, my eyes fell upon a sign hanging above the gate, upon which was written the word "Cheder."
>
> I heard children's voices coming from a room above the

stable. I went up a crooked staircase and through a dark hall. There I saw a Melamed doing his holy work. On the table next to him was a strap which he would now and then lash against the back of an unruly child. The Siddur lay open in front of a student who was seated next to him and who repeated after him, word by word. Then he would call a second child to him, and then a third, and so on. He would spend five to ten minutes with each one. As soon as the child finished his lessons he would be set free. The number of children in the Cheder was about twenty-five and all of them were playing and shouting and screaming—little children and Bar-Mitzvah boys all together. In the middle of everything two women entered the room and the Melamed stopped his work and wrote letters for them to their relatives in Europe and received a quarter for his fee.

This was the picture of the Cheder that existed in those days. Most of them were in rooms above stables or over dance halls, in attics and in dark synagogues located in old ramshackle buildings. The overwhelming majority of the teachers were ignorant boors. And all their learning consisted of reading, a few blessings, and Bar-Mitzvah.

The child who was thus taught his Jewish studies was the same child who earlier in the day had studied in the public school. There he was taught by a trained, cultured teacher, in a big, spacious building, well organized and smoothly functioning. His experiences in the public school contrasted sharply with his experiences in the Hebrew school, and surely his respect for Jewish learning was not enhanced by the comparison.

Hutchins Hapgood in *The Spirit of the Ghetto*, published in 1902, writes,

> With his entrance into the public schools the little fellow runs plumb against a system of education and a set of influences which are at total variance with those traditional to his race and to his home life. The religious element is entirely lacking. The educational system of the public schools is heterogeneous and worldly. The boy becomes acquainted in the school reader with fragments of writings on subjects, with a little mathematics, a little history. His instruction, in the interests of liberal

nonsectarianism, is entirely secular. English becomes his most familiar language. He achieves a growing comprehension and sympathy with the independent, free, rather skeptical spirit of the American boy. The orthodox Jewish influences still at work upon him are rapidly weakened. Compelled by law to go to the American public school, the boy can attend Chaider only before the public school opens in the morning or after it closes in the afternoon. At such times the Hebrew teacher, who dresses in a long black coat, outlandish tall hat, and commonly speaks no English, visits the boy at home or the boy goes to a neighborhood Chaider.

Contempt for the Chaider's teaching comes the more easily because the boy rarely understands his Hebrew lessons to the full. His real language is English, the teacher's is commonly Yiddish and the language to be learned is Hebrew.

The orthodox parents begin to see that the boy in order to get along in the new world must receive a Gentile training. Instead of hoping to make a rabbi of him, they reluctantly consent to his becoming an American businessman, or still better, an American doctor or lawyer.

The desperate condition of Jewish education in the early years of the Eastern European Jewish immigration is described in *Hatzfirah* by J. Buchalter in 1889.

> To our great distress, we see the victims of American Jewish education increasing from day to day. Children who grow up in the homes of fine, humble, sincere members of the older generation are growing up without Torah or manners. Our hair would stand on end if we could visualize the frightening picture of our children as they are growing up in America. We see our children scorning and deriding everything that is sacred, desecrating the Sabbath and Holy Days in public and doing every vile thing contrary to all morality and manners.

The Talmud Torah

The Jews of America realized that they were failing terribly in their educational program. They knew that neither they nor their children respected the cheder, and they began to devote themselves to improving the situation. They established community educational institutions known as Talmud Torahs.

In their efforts to improve Jewish education they did not reevaluate their goals, assigning to the Talmud Torah the same role and function they had assigned to the cheder. They continued to consider Jewish education as an after-hours supplement to public school and accepted the place of Jewish education as secondary to the education of their children as Americans. They continued to place the primary responsibility for education on the public schools. Jewish education would be taught after school for a number of hours per week.

The curricular goals of the Talmud Torah and congregational school were the same as those they had hoped they could attain from the cheder. They surely did not expect that their children would become Torah scholars, versed in Talmud and in the other sacred books of Judaism. They did not expect them to develop a thirst for higher Jewish learning or a great commitment to maximum religious observance. They hoped that the Jewish education they gave their children would make them aware of their heritage and continue their bond with the Jewish people. They hoped that the children could get whatever could be gotten from the study of Jewish subject matter for a number of hours per week after school. They were convinced that the cheder was failing, and they were determined to replace it with schools that would achieve the maximum within this framework.

The Talmud Torah was a more respectable school. It had a better physical plant, often its own building, and better-trained teachers, new textbooks, a more organized curriculum, better supervision, and community support. The numbers of hours spent in the Talmud Torah and in the schools of the Jewish congregations varied from one school to another. In most of the Tulmud Torahs, classes were held one and a half hours per day, five days a week, for seven and a half hours per week. The congregational school usually held classes five hours per week, two or three days a week. The children came to the Hebrew school after they completed their school day at the public schools.

The community Talmud Torah gained greater respect from parents, children, and community. Community campaigns were conducted for Jewish education and bureaus were organized to set standards for curriculum, teachers, and hours of instruction.

Textbooks were published and Jewish teachers' training schools were founded. Jewish education became a serious endeavor of the Jewish community.

Community Hebrew schools increased steadily in enrollment and in community financial support. Jewish education continued on an upward trend until the end of the 1920s. But with the advent of the 1930s the trend stopped and began to reverse—the number of children enrolled ceased to increase, and enthusiasm for Jewish education began to wane.

Z. Scharfstein, in *The History of Jewish Education in Modern Times*, Volume II, writes:

> The drive for education came from the new immigrant and the weakening of the spirit and life of Judaism came from the new American born generation, which was bereft of tradition and stricken with disinterest. The earlier neglect of Jewish education had its effect on the life of the present. Tens of thousands of "new" Jews entered adult Jewish life yearly. They were Jews in name, Jews who in their youth looked down upon their "green" parents. When they grew up they married and built homes, homes that were empty of all Jewish content. They did not participate in the life of their people, did not attend a synagogue except on the High Holidays. These people saw no need to educate their children in a Hebrew School. Only because of their parents or grandparents did they send their son to Talmud Torah or to a Congregational School. And as soon as the child learned to read the prayers mechanically, and immediately after the Bar Mitzvah ceremony when the boy delivered his speech which the teacher wrote for him, the boy left the Hebrew School. His Jewish education was ended.

The decline in Jewish education was given impetus by the move to the suburbs. The young Jewish families left the poor, crowded ghetto and moved to the new, clean, uncrowded sections of the city. But leaving the ghetto meant also leaving a neighborhood filled with Jewish life, with institutions built with heart and sweat, to enter a neighborhood empty of Jewish life and Jewish institutions. A new effort had to be made to regain some of the Jewish life left back in the ghetto.

The rebuilding problem was made all the more difficult and

complicated by the depression that hit the nation during the thirties. Financial support for maintenance of old, or building of new institutions was not forthcoming. The number of children in attendance decreased.

Z. Scharfstein gives the following picture of Jewish education in that period. In 1935 the number of children in the United States receiving a Jewish education of any kind was estimated at 200,000, though many of the children not in attendance during that specific year had briefly attended Hebrew school at some period of time. The number of years that each child attended was estimated as follows: 40 percent attended less than one year, 80 percent did not complete two years, and only 7 or 8 percent stayed in Hebrew school four or five years.

Various reasons were given for the children leaving Hebrew school. Among them were the following: 26 percent said that they were now too old to continue, 19 percent were dissatisfied with the school, 16 percent claimed that the distance to the Hebrew school was too great, 14 percent transferred or took a private tutor, 10 percent gave poor health as the reason for leaving, and 15 percent listed various other reasons.

Obviously a lack of enthusiasm or interest for the Hebrew studies was an important factor in all of these considerations for leaving Hebrew school.

The after-school Hebrew schools of America, which even in their finest hour held out no promise of greatness for the Jewish future, promised even less in the 1930s.

The Yeshiva

While the overwhelming majority of America's Jews confined Jewish education to an after-school supplementary role, others had different aims and aspirations and tried to give a different direction to Jewish education.

They too believed that Jewish children should learn to be Americans, learn the language, and develop all the skills necessary to succeed in America. But they refused to accept as inevitable that the major part of the day be spent studying those subjects, and that those skills need be developed in the public schools. They believed that a portion of the day should be devoted to those subjects, that at least an equal portion should be given to

Torah subjects, and that all education should occur in the Jewish school, where Torah studies would be given primacy in time and respect.

They realized the great difficulties they faced in establishing such schools. But they did not turn away from the problem and dedicated themselves to the founding of such schools, known as yeshivot. The yeshiva had a dual program: Torah studies as well as a program of secular education. The aim of the yeshiva was to develop Torah scholars, some of whom would choose to be rabbis and others would be learned Jews prepared to compete successfully to meet the American challenge.

The first attempt to organize a yeshiva came in 1886, with the founding of the Yeshiva Eitz Chaim. One of the founders of the Yeshiva, A. M. Dushkin, writes in *Jewish Education in New York City:*

> We rented a room on East Broadway. We did not have enough money to buy books of Talmud, so we bought one book for ninety cents and divided it into three parts and gave one of the parts to each of three teachers. We went from door to door asking for contributions of five and ten cents. We also put charity boxes into the homes of some individuals and into the synagogues, and then we came to empty the charity boxes of the contributions that some good people had contributed to our Yeshiva.

The struggle was very hard since the people who interested themselves in the yeshivot were mostly poor. They received hardly any support from the wealthy Jews who for the most part did not welcome this kind of school on the American scene. But in spite of the hardships, yeshivot were founded and grew.

The growth of yeshivot was a slow and painful process. Even as the years went on and the yeshivot continued their steady though slow progress, American Jews did not show any signs of flocking to them, either to offer financial help or to enroll their children. But progress continued, and by the end of the 1930s the number of students enrolled in yeshivot in the United States rose to about 5,000 attending classes that ranged from kindergarten to rabbinical studies.

The total estimated number of Jewish children in the United States between the ages of six and fourteen was then about 725,000. The total number of Jewish children enrolled in yeshivot was thus less than 1 percent of the total eligible population.

The Synagogue

In the shtetl in Eastern Europe everything was very predictable. In the course of hundreds of years of history Jews had established their traditions, their customs, and their institutions. Central among these institutions was the synagogue, whose function was very clear. There the Jew came to pray and to study Torah. Everyone came to pray and everyone engaged in some level of Torah study. The synagogue was open and active from very early in the morning to deep into the night. Everyone knew that the synagogue was the place for religious expression, and religious expression was the dominant interest of the Jews of the shtetl.

The Jews who came to America, religious and non-religious alike, felt in common the need for a synagogue. But their ideas of the function of the synagogue varied according to their attitudes about their life in America.

The religious Jews wanted their synagogue to be like the one in the shtetl, a place to pray and study.

The non-religious Jews also wanted a synagogue. They too carried a strong awareness of their Jewish identity and intense feelings of belonging to a Jewish people. They wanted to retain that identification. They had attachments to the shtetl they left behind, friends and family who were still there and "landsmen," people who came to America from the same city and town.

They wanted to keep their identification with the Jewish people and their association with their fellow Jews, in life and after death. Dying as Jews was very important to them—they wanted to be buried in a Jewish cemetery. They needed an organization that would fill these purposes; that organization was the synagogue.

The religious Torah-centered Jew and the non-religious, association-minded Jew felt the need to join together in founding and maintaining the synagogue. They were mostly poor, they were alone, they felt a kinship with each other as Jews, and they needed all the strength they could gather. They joined together, the religious and the non-religious, the European and the Americanized.

Thus the synagogue in America was not a place exclusively devoted to prayer and Torah study; other activities often overshadowed them. Acquisition of property for the cemetery was a very important goal of the organization. "Business" became a major aspect of the synagogue activity.

This development in the synagogue of America is described in the journal *Degel Israel* in May 1927:

> A famous synagogue in New York recently announced in the newspapers that it now has three cemeteries and therefore hopes that all Jewish people will become members of their synagogue.
>
> When a synagogue boasts about cemeteries, it is not a good omen. Most of the time they also bury traditional Judaism. The synagogue of the Jewish people is a house of learning and the synagogue used to offer courses for adults. There used to be many groups studying the sacred Jewish culture. The Torah and the cemetery have little in common. The cemetery is for death, and the Torah is life.

And again in December 1927, the same journal declares:

> The synagogue lacks the spirit of Torah, and at the meetings of our synagogues they do not discuss Jewish subjects which deal with the rebuilding of Israel, with Jewish education, with Sabbath observance, Kashruth, and such subjects. All they discuss is property. Not property to purchase in Israel, to revive the Jewish people and the Jewish spirit, just property to bury dead Jews, brothers and sisters. You can often see on the walls of our synagogues big signs which tell you, not about the strengthening of Jewish religious activity, but rather, "We have purchased a lot of property and we can bury a lot of members."

The non-religious Jew was deeply concerned with the business of the synagogue and became very much involved in it. Very often non-religious Jews rose to positions of leadership in the synagogue. It was quite common for the president of the synagogue to be a Jew who did not observe the Sabbath.

In the *Jewish Light* of March 2, 1923, the writer Rabbi C. Y. Moseson declares:

> It is the work of the devil that a custom has spread in this land that even in the most religious synagogues where the majority of the members and worshippers are Sabbath observant, they insist on selecting as president a Sabbath desecrator. Sometimes they do this for financial reasons, other times because they want a "strong" president and among the Sabbath observing Jews they cannot find a man with so much arrogance and with such a loud mouth. It is hard to find a synagogue where the president should be a true Sabbath observer.

At first attempts were made to draw a line between the "business" and the religious activity of the synagogue. Attempts were made to limit the field of authority of the non-religious president to the "business" of the synagogue and to appoint trustees who would conduct the religious activities. However, these attempts at division of authority soon broke down. The line of demarcation was not always clear. And the presidents accepted no limits upon their area of activity.

In the *Jewish Light* of March 16, 1923, Rabbi C. Y. Moseson writes:

> It is told that when the custom began to select Sabbath desecrators as presidents and leaders, it was with the condition that they should only direct the business of the synagogue. It was felt that in regard to the business affairs of the synagogue the Sabbath desecrators were more expert than the Sabbath observers. In their own businesses they are more successful than the Sabbath observers. Therefore, in almost every synagogue Sabbath observant trustees were elected and were given the full authority over the sacred activities of the synagogue. These functions included standing near the Holy Torah as the honors are assigned, choosing a Rabbi, giving the Rabbis who collect for the institutions of Torah and charity the opportunity to make appeals, choosing the man to lead the congregation in the services, and so on. Lately it has developed in the orthodox synagogues that the Sabbath desecrating leaders are not content with wielding the hammer at meetings and with conduct-

ing only the business affairs of the synagogue. They have become the "whole Boss" even at the Sabbath services and at every religious occasion. It has now come to pass that the Sabbath desecrating president stands proudly at the Holy Torah and points with the Silver Pointer in his hands when the Reader reads the passages about observing the Sabbath and that he who desecrates the Sabbath shall die. And if this is not enough for the Sabbath desecrating leaders they have also become speakers and sermonizers. One Sabbath desecrating president once became so heated and worked up in the middle of one of his Sabbath sermons that the pencils and fountain pens, which are forbidden to be carried on the Sabbath, jumped out of his vest pocket and scattered all over the Holy platform. The congregants smiled a little, the president gathered the pencils together and continued his sermon about preserving Judaism.

Thus the synagogue of America came to be a place that was not characterized by dedication to prayer and Torah. "Business" was very important, and the synagogue was controlled by people to whom "business" came before Torah and prayer. The policies of the synagogue were based upon "business" considerations first and religious activity and religious laws second.

Rabbi Eliyahu Mordecai Maza, in the book *Ahavas Hatorah*, describes the synagogue of America in the 1930s and compares the synagogues of New York with the synagogue of the shtetl:

> I still remember, and we all remember, how it was in the synagogue in the old home between the afternoon and evening services. At one table people sat and studied the Mishnah, at another table people studied Ein Yaakov or the Shulchan Aruch, at another table people were studying the Talmud, and other men sat and studied by themselves in the Bais Medrash until the evening services and then they studied again. Here in many synagogues there are just barely enough people for a minyan for afternoon services. And no one thinks about learning Torah.
>
> In the large synagogues where many worshippers come, the Mincha (afternoon) services are repeated many times. Then the

Maariv (evening) services are conducted while it is still very early, and everybody goes away. Nobody thinks about studying Torah. The leaders of the synagogues are pleased, the Mincha services were conducted so many times, so many people had come to worship. But the Torah cries out, she weeps and mourns, "My children have forsaken me, they are not concerned about me." Ignorance increases, nobody cares about Torah study, nobody knows the Jewish Law, no one knows the seriousness of a sin, no one knows what may or may not be done. Our youth runs from the synagogue and no one is concerned. When the young man comes to the synagogue he does not feel the sanctity that was felt in the European synagogue. Our synagogues are for "business," only to make money. One feels as though he entered a large department store without merchandise. Torah is not heard. Mishna and Kadish are heard sometimes, but that is all.

There is no sanctity at a meeting. It is not like a gathering that took place in Europe, where the Rabbi would sit at the head of the assembled and at his side would sit the learned men of the community and people spoke for the cause of Torah. It goes without saying that no one thought to deviate from the Jewish law. Everyone sat with a holy attitude and spoke serious words with holiness. Sanctity was felt in every corner.

It is different at a meeting here. The Rabbi is not invited, because at every meeting the Rabbi is discussed and criticized. And who listens to the "Code of Jewish Law!" Who cares what the "Code of Jewish Law" says, he is not a member of the synagogue! And if there might be someone who would take seriously the statements of the "Code of Jewish Law," there is no one who knows what is written in it. No one studies Torah. If at a meeting there is a man who is a Torah-scholar from the old country, he is shouted down by the ignorant people. The talk at the meetings is vulgar. The people joke and laugh. They discuss the synagogue from a business standpoint and whether it pays to have a Rabbi or not. It is as though they were discussing whether or not it pays to take an article of merchandise into a store. They decide that this brother should be accepted, this brother should be thrown out. In the middle they fight and scream at each other and at the end of the meeting they meet their landsmen, they sit down to a game of cards for money, and they drink and enjoy themselves. This is what takes place at a meeting. Such meetings can not make the people feel the holiness of the synagogue. Such meetings can not attract our youth. Many people devote a great deal of time and energy to maintain the synagogue but they forget that a synagogue without Torah has no value. Where are the leaders who understand this? Where are the members who would demand from their leaders that they should give them true Torah for their money and that the voice of Torah should always be heard in the synagogue?

The Rabbi

The changed role of the synagogue in America seriously affected the position of the rabbi. Religious expression in the synagogues became secondary. There were so many other important issues to be discussed and the rabbi was not considered an authority on the business matters of the synagogue. His advice was not sought. The leaders of the synagogue, who were non-religious, frequently viewed some religious practices as interfering with synagogue business and believed that these practices and traditions should be set aside. The rabbi was thus placed in sharp conflict with the synagogue leadership. The rabbi was usually powerless to oppose them. He found himself shunted aside, helpless, left without influence even in religious matters.

In the *Degel Israel* of February 1927, the editor Rabbi S. L. Horowitz decries the situation and writes:

> How holy and pure was the atmosphere of the synagogue in Europe. And how much more important is it in America where the street and the home and the environment are secular, materialistic, strange, and confused. At a time when in all these places there is no sign of the awareness of G-d's presence, at a time when we feel assimilation eating up everything precious and close to us, destroying the homes of the people of Israel, bringing the spirit of impurity into the recesses of the heart and soul, and when Sabbath and Holy Days are desecrated in the most blatant way, at such a time the purest and most holy place should be the synagogue. But to our great sorrow, even this holy place is desecrated when we give the leadership of the

synagogue to people who must always be warned not to tamper with holiness.

The time has come for us to proclaim again and again that it is forbidden to place at the head of the synagogue a person who is an ignorant boor, who despises the bearers of the banner of Torah, who has no love or respect for the Rabbis of Israel, and who has no humility before a Torah scholar.

And the time has come for all the Rabbis of America to unite with one heart and soul and to declare open warfare upon all those who scorn holiness and who step with arrogant foot upon the Rabbis of Israel.

The rabbi who was thus left without authority was often also left without a voice. He turned away from conflict with the synagogue leadership. He knew that the leaders of the synagogue did not welcome his religious authority; his influence in all matters was very weak—in the synagogue scheme he was almost unnecessary. The pittance that was his salary was seen by many to be an expensive luxury. He recognized that he was at the mercy of the synagogue leadership, his tenure at the whim of the president.

In the *Yiddisher Veg Veizer* of March 1917, C. Y. Mosnitzky writes:

> In the shtetl when the Rabbi noticed a wrongdoing in his community he called an assembly and he did not rest until he accomplished his purpose. Who knows better than you, the Rabbis, how great was the power of the Rabbi! Why was your strength there greater than your strength here? Why is the strength of one Rabbi in a shtetl in the old home greater than the strength of all the Rabbis of America put together?
>
> The answer is that the Rabbi in the shtetl spoke without the slightest fear of the president or the members. He spoke not with half a mouth but with clear words. He pointed out every failing, and the more the Rabbi did to improve the congregation the more he was loved by the masses. Every community sought ways to improve the condition of the Rabbi. He never feared that he would be given notice to leave. His work was appreciated and he was successful.
>
> It is quite different here in America. Here the Rabbi must

speak half words. His contract here is for two or three years. And if he should touch the sensibilities of the president he gets a first warning. He must overlook many evils because his bread is in danger.

Should the Rabbi, however, persist in his strong words of admonition and say, "You are violating the Sabbath," then he receives a sign from above and he is told, "You know this is America and it can't be helped." And should the Rabbi insist on speaking about the Sabbath and the Holy days he will receive a second warning not to speak about Sabbath desecration again. But if the Rabbi is sincere and he continues to talk about it, then he can be sure that diplomatic relations will be cut off and he will be handed his passport. Or he will not be elected to a second term.

The position of the European Torah scholar rabbi was further weakened by the eagerness of the Jews to become Americanized. The members of the synagogue looked down upon the Yiddish-speaking Rabbi with the old-fashioned European ways. They wanted the synagogue to help them fulfill their aspirations to be Americanized. The rabbi did not fill these needs for them, and so the rabbi could not establish a firm position with his synagogue.

The July 1928 issue of *Degel Israel* gives a report of the just-concluded Rabbinical Convention:

> Those were deep, tragic, and terrible moments when the renowned Rabbis, members of the "Degel" and "Knesset Rabbinical Organizations," who occupied rabbinical positions in Europe with great honor, described the desperate plight of the orthodox Rabbis in America, their loneliness, and their humiliation. These words which came from the depths of their hearts cut the Jewish heart as with knives, and they cried out for a solution to the terrible degradation of the Rabbinate of America.

Parents and Children

The great number of Eastern European Jews who came to America were trying desperately to hold on to their Torah way of life, but most of them found their struggle harsh and lonely, especially in their own homes. Their children rejected their way of life.

The relationship between parents and children brought loneliness and heartbreak to the old Jew who saw his beloved world breaking and crumbling around him.

Sometimes the parents and children managed to live their own separate lives, avoiding conflict and confrontation, as in the following story told by Abraham Shiner in the *Yiddisher Veg Veizer* of September 1916.

> Reb Fishel Cohen, or as he was known in the old home, Reb Fishel Mitkovke, lives in America with his old wife Devorah now many years, and they are still not satisfied with the Golden Land.
>
> They came here because of the children. The children had come from Russia many years before them and then brought them to America. If not for the children Reb Fishel and Devorah would not have come here to America, really not.
>
> Reb Fishel was a Torah scholar, a really great one, he enjoyed Torah. He had plenty of time and plenty of books. He sat day and night and studied Torah. He did not want to go to the children in America. "I want to see them. My heart aches with loneliness for them," he would say to his wife Devorah. "I am a father, you know. But for elderly people America is no place. Jews there are not religious. I hear that they even desecrate the Sabbath."
>
> And when he would write to the children and ask them whether they are religious there in America, do they at least pray, the children would never answer the questions.
>
> "It looks like Judaism is not the most important thing to them. So why should we go to America? To see with our own eyes what our hearts won't believe?"
>
> But Reb Fishel still had a little bit of hope. His youngest son, he was a brilliant Torah scholar. He studied in the Telser Yeshiva until the age of seventeen. His Rabbi had predicted a great future for him. . . . In America he is probably not as religious. . . . Even at home in the last few years he was not as religious as before. But still, such a Torah scholar. He could not have gone away completely.

One day Reb Fishel received a letter from his son, the scholar, in which he wrote, "I just began my practice as a doctor, and I am doing very well. The other children are also making a good living. And it is now time that you came. In Russia the troubles are getting worse and a Jew should not put himself in peril for no reason. And if you are worried about Judaism, Jews are Jews all over. There are synagogues, and whoever wants to be a Jew can be a Jew even in America."

So they went to America. And now many years have gone by since they came to America, and they still cannot get used to things. Everything is so different. The synagogues, the Reverends. . . . Well why talk about others? What about his own children? The old Reb Fishel cannot get used to the thought that the elder son who, though a simple young man at home, was nevertheless a G-d fearing Jew, now carries around his newspapers on the Sabbath and the Holy Days. "So cold blooded, it doesn't bother him at all."

The other son sits in his candy store on the Sabbath and Holidays. The daughter goes to work in the shop. She sews, real sewing, on the Sabbath. Her husband, not religious at all.

He never had to live with his children even a day. His young son the doctor took care of that. He had taken rooms for them even before they had come, and they went straight from the boat to their apartment.

He hardly knew what went on in his children's homes. His wife Devorah took care of that. She went to the children often, more than he did. She wanted to find out everything. And she did. She found out such things that her hair almost stood up under her wig, and her heart pounded. "It is a miracle from Heaven that he doesn't know," she thought to herself. "If he would know, his poor health would just give out." And she loves the old man so. Who else does she have in the world, but him. Here she is alone, and lost . . . her own children like strangers. And she bustles around, poor old lady, hiding things and covering up.

On the Sabbath after lunch, when he decides that he wants to go see the children, she runs ahead. All out of breath, gasping, she dashes into the house calling, "Zalman, put away your cigarette, father is coming. Chayke, quick stop cooking. Malke, Golde, away from the machine, father is coming!"

Sometimes the parents, with deadened feelings, accepted their tragic situation, as related in the *Yiddisher Veg Veizer* of March 1917.

The fine Jewish gentleman gets up Sabbath morning and goes off to the synagogue. He leaves his daughter at the piano and his son doing his "lessons." Other parents watch their children go off to business or to work. They have convinced themselves that they cannot expect, in America, that children should go to the synagogue with their father. And they tell themselves they have to be thankful that the young people are tolerant of their old parents and let them live their Jewish life.

Sometimes the parents even adjusted their own religious life to the conditions of their family life, as told by Rabbi Moseson in the *Jewish Light* of June 29, 1923.

You can find religious parents who observe the Sabbath in every particular, and are so loyal and faithful to their beloved Sabbath-desecrating children, that they don't leave their houses to go to the synagogue Sabbath morning until they first wake up their children to go to work. And the poor devoted father stands pleadingly at the bed of the son warning him that he may, G-d forbid, be late for work. And the religious mother hurries around the kitchen preparing the lunch that her beloved child can take to work. And when they come home from the synagogue they wait patiently until the son comes home from work, to eat their Sabbath meal.

But sometimes the parent never learned to accept his situation. This story is told by Rabbi S. L. Horowitz in the *Yiddisher Veg Veizer* of September 1916.

Bere Reb Ures did absolutely not want to leave his old shtetl and "drag his old bones" to a strange land, to America.

His youngest son showered him with letters pleading with him that he should come to America soon. He wanted very, very deeply to go to his son. But he was frightened of this strange America so far away, at the bottom of the world, and where there were found thousands of Jews who are, so they say, public desecrators of the Sabbath, and who eat non-kosher food.

And how painful it would be to leave his good and beloved shtetl, where he was born and brought up, where he spent his whole life. How could he leave his good friends like Itza Yaakov the Melamed, and Avram Mashe's, and Moshe Tzipi Yente's, and other such dear friends.

But one day just when he had come from the funeral of his best friend, Moshe Tzipi Yente's, the mailman brought him a letter. He was able to tell from the stamps that the letter came from a distance, all the way from America. With trembling hands he opened the letter and began to read. "My dear father, I feel very much alone in America. I cannot nor do I want to go back to Europe. Having lived for a while in the free land of America, I could never live in the oppressive land of Russia. I love America very much, as I have written to you many times. But I feel very lonely. And whom do I have in the whole world? My brothers are dead, I have no sisters, my dear mother whom I will never forget is dead. All I have in the world is only you, my dear father. And if you will refuse to come to me, my life has no meaning.

And think, what will you have in my house? You will eat, drink, and sleep comfortably. There is a synagogue not far from my house. There they pray and study all the time. All the landsmen are anxious to see you. The day that you come will be a happy day in my house and for all your friends. My children are very anxious to see you. They always complain that everyone has a grandfather and they do not. Father! Have pity on yourself and on me and come to America. Your son, Chaim.

The funeral of his best friend together with the touching letter from his only son, made a deep impression upon him, and he decided to go to America. And he immediately sent a letter to his son which he wrote with tears in his eyes, and informed him that he was going to join him. He ended his letter with the following words, "Just as Jacob our father cried out to his son Joseph, 'I did not dare hope to live to see you and G-d gave me the life to see your children,' I will be with you in a few weeks. . . ."

Now it was Saturday morning before dawn. Everyone in the house is sleeping soundly, and Bere Reb Ures holds open his Bible, looks into the commentaries, and he does not understand a word. The words all mix together, his head throbs, he is terribly nervous, restless. He remembers those wonderful years when he lived in his litle shtetl, in his own old, little house. Then he also used to get up before dawn on the Sabbath morning to review the Biblical portion and to study all the commentaries. But those were different times. And as he thinks, he lets out a deep sigh. He remembers those sweet, holy moments of his life. He remembers how much joy he felt when he arrived in America and was united with his only son and his old, good friends from the old home. But he also remembers how his son's children, his grandchildren, chattered to him in a strange tongue and they kept calling him the strange name "grandpa." Ah, how he would like to talk to his grandchildren, teach them the holiness of Judaism. But neither does he understand them, nor can they understand him. . . .

And suddenly he hears a sigh coming from someone asleep. He recognizes that sigh, it comes from his son. And he remembers something which had completely shaken him and had cut him like a knife in his heart. He remembers how his son had asked him to please wake him very early Saturday morning because he must go to work. . . .

His son had told him with tears in his eyes, how he finally had to give up. And now if he would not work on the Sabbath, he and his children would perish from hunger. This is truly a matter of life and death, he argued to his father.

Reb Bere laughed at this. G-d takes care of everyone and surely does He take care of someone who observes the Holy Sabbath. The tragedy is that we lack the faith in G-d.

His son tried to obey him. But when hunger made itself felt in the house, he could no longer control himself and he went to work on the Sabbath.

He remembered how his son had urgently pleaded with him to awaken him because it was a new job and if he would be late he could lose the job. He must awaken him. His bread, his livelihood . . . his wife and children. . . . But good G-d, how could you wake up your child he should go to desecrate the Sabbath! . . .

He picked up the Mishna. He would immerse himself in it and drive away his troubles. But he found himself turning to the portion about the Sabbath. The clock on the wall chimed six. "I must awaken him. . . . But no, how is that possible? How can

I?" . . . A terrible thought ran through his head like lightning. "Run to the synagogue! Scream! Shake the world! G-d in heaven, a million Jews, may they all be well, in New York, and can't they do something so that a man should not have to work on the Sabbath."

He took another look at the wall clock. "It is already late. I have to wake him up!" With one hand he held the Mishna and with the other hand he approached to wake him up. He came over to the bed, his old heart beating, trembling, and he heard himself crying in an unrecognizable voice, "G-d in heaven you punish me too much. Do you want to see, oh G-d, if I will be able to withstand this test? Yes! I can! I will not wake my son to go and desecrate the Sabbath!" And he burst into deep, heavy sobs.

There were many religious Jews in America. But they knew that their way of life would probably end with them and that the children would feel no remorse in seeing their parents' way of life disappear from their family.

In the *Jewish Light* of April 6, 1923, the following article appeared.

> Judaism in America is without heirs. The synagogues are filled with old people and there are almost none of that group which is called "youth." Our young men and young women are not seen in the synagogues. They have no interest in our Holy days. They are interested neither in the national ideal of the Holiday of Freedom nor in the religious ceremonies of eating Matzah on Passover. . . .
>
> The Jewish father is a relic of the past. The father is bound to the old foundation and the children are floating somewhere and don't care that they are hurting the parents so deeply.
>
> In a house where there is a religious father, it is most likely that he is the last link in the golden chain of Judaism in his family. He has no heirs. The American children have no concept of their great ancestry and no respect for it. They are not interested in their parents' old books. And they let their father know quite openly that with him ends the old-country Judaism and then starts something new and something different.

Millions of Jews came to America, a vast number of them religious, devoted to Torah, many of them great rabbis and scholars. They brought with them the light of Torah. But as succeeding generations were growing up, their children were leaving them.

In the United States in 1939 the sunshine of Torah came from the many dedicated Torah-observant immigrants and from several thousand children in the Yeshivot. But whatever was shining seemed to be heading for decline.

In 1939, America was not aspiring to become the Torah center to take the place of Eastern Europe. The sun did not seem to be rising in the United States.

12

JEWS IN PALESTINE

After the destruction of the Second Temple, the people of Israel were exiled to the four corners of the world. The land of Israel lay desolate for centuries. It was not completely deserted, for in all the generations there were some few hardy souls who sacrificed all earthly feelings to breathe of the sanctity of the Holy Land. But their number was very limited. The forbidding conditions made it extremely difficult to exist on the land.

Some attempts were made by groups of Jews to settle in Palestine. For many centuries these efforts were small and temporary. But in the sixteenth century came an effort that had a lasting effect on the rebirth of the "yishuv," as the settlement was known.

After the exile from Spain, a group of Spanish Jews including Rav Yosef Caro, the author of the Shulchan Aruch, settled in Safad. They established a center for Torah learning, and the settlement struck roots. The Sefardim made a place for themselves and their customs in Palestine.

The first aliyah of the Ashkenazi Jews took place in 1700 when a group of several hundred Jewish families from Poland, led by Rabbi Yehudah Hachasid, came to Palestine. But this move did not strike roots. Rabbi Yehudah died soon after his arrival in Palestine and many of his followers returned to Poland.

The first successful attempt by the Ashkenazi Jews came in 1747 when the talmidim of the Baal Shem Tov went up to Palestine. In 1758 a second group of his followers arrived in Palestine and in 1778 a group of 300 men arrived.

In the year 1808 the talmidim of the Gaon of Vilna began to come up to Palestine, and their aliyah continued for over fifty years. With great sacrifice and determination they established themselves in Palestine, first in Safad, then in Jerusalem.

As a result of the activity of these hundred years, Palestine turned from a land unnoticed by all the nations of the world to a land that became a focus of attention for many nations. Countries opened consulates in various cities in Palestine. One of those countries was Great Britain, which opened its consulate in Jerusalem in 1838.

The yishuv expanded. The Jews were centered in four major cities—Tiberius, Safad, Jerusalem, and Hebron—and in some places farm settlements were established.

Until this period in the history of the Jewish settlement of Palestine there was one uniform attitude and therefore one educational system. The Jews were in Palestine to live in its holiness and to be ready and waiting when the redemption came.

The educational system was entirely one of Torah content. There was no other learning taught in the cheder. No subjects dealing with adjustment to the land were part of the educational content of the schools. Though it was deemed valuable to teach the child a trade, that was not undertaken by the school; it was the personal obligation of the parents.

However, during this period there were Torah scholars who formulated new attitudes. They believed that the Jews in Palestine should not confine their work in the Holy Land to Torah and prayer—rather, they should work to improve the living conditions of the land to prepare it for its settlement by the Jewish people. They believed that it was the will of the Almighty to make the land ready for His redemption. They believed that the active settlement of the land, and energetic diplomatic efforts among the nations of the world, would bring the redemption closer. This was the theme of the works of Rabbi Kalisher and Rabbi Alkalai. These new beliefs gave birth to the movement called Chibas Zion, or Love of Zion.

Chibas Zion

In the years 1840 through 1880 this new attitude was building among the Jews inside and outside of Palestine. The believers in the new ideas attempted to introduce their thoughts into the schools. They felt that the school curriculum should be expanded and, besides intensive Torah learning, subjects should be added in mathematics, Hebrew, and foreign languages.

But though the leaders of the movement were acknowledged Torah scholars and pious Jews, their attempts at establishing schools with this program were heatedly opposed. The leaders of the yishuv were very much aware of the Reform movement in Europe and the changes it had wrought in Torah loyalty. They were fearful that any mixture of secular learning into the Torah learning of the cheder would be the forerunner of the creeping secularization of the school.

Many of the Torah leaders of the new movement withdrew. But others persevered and succeeded in several attempts at establishing schools with the new curriclum.

In *The Jewish Yishuv in Palestine 1840–1881*, Dr. Ben Zion Gat tells the story of the establishment of the Lemel School.

> In 1855 the Lady Hertz, from the aristocratic Lemel family, informed the leaders of the Jewish community in Austria that it was her will to establish a school in Palestine in memory of her father. In this school the children would learn from their youth, to walk in the ways of the Almighty, to observe His commandments, and to love an occupation.

One of the people of that generation, Yehoshua Yellin by name, tells in his memoirs the story of the founding of the Lemel School.

> I was then twelve years old. One day after davening, people gathered together and began to scream and many of them were crying, "Oy, woe to us! Help us! There is a fire in the city! A heretic has come to our city and wants to establish a school! He wants to teach our children heresy and burn their souls!" And after all the screaming they announced a sentence of excommunication on the school and on Mr. Frankel, its head.

But despite the storm that raged among the Ashkenazi Jews, the school was received warmly by the Sefardim. For the first term twenty children were registered.

Thus the Lemel School came into being in Palestine. This was one of several schools established during this period. In the same way, facing the same kind of reception, the new movement established the school Doresh Letzion and later Kol Yisrael Chaverim and several smaller schools.

Notwithstanding the great controversy that was aroused, this movement presented no threat to the Torah commitment of the yishuv. All involved in the controversy agreed to the principle of the supremacy of the Torah. Torah was unchallenged as the primary learning in the educational system of the yishuv.

The growth of the Palestine settlement captured the attention of the Haskala thinkers, who viewed Palestine as the land the Jews needed to be a nation. They recognized Palestine as the center for the Jewish people and saw it as the seat of its culture and the place for the rebirth of its language. Nationalism and secularism were the ideals of the maskilim and they saw their fulfillment in Palestine. They were inspired with the ideal of Zionism.

Both ideals, the ideal of Torah building of Palestine and the ideals of secular Zionism, converged in the Chibas Zion movement.

The First Aliyah, which took place in 1880, was led by the Chibas Zion movement. It brought 25,000 people to Palestine during the years 1880 to 1890. The overwhelming number of "olim" were Torah-observant Jews. But, for the first time, along with them came maskilim and assimilationists. They were joined by a group of fourteen young university students who called themselves "Bilu." These young people were inspired with the ideal of working the soil of Palestine and realizing their dream of secular Zionism.

In 1882 Rabbi Mohliver, a leader of Chibas Zion, visited Baron Rothschild, a Torah-observant Jew, and enlisted his support for the settlement of Palestine. Baron Rothschild dedicated himself to that cause. In forty years of unselfish support of the yishuv, he spent millions of francs. He helped maintain the Torah schools. He supported the establishment and maintenance of forty settlements, and he acquired for the settlers 400,000 dunam of land.

By 1890, Palestine had increased its Jewish population to 47,000. The people were for the most part devoted to Torah. The educational institutions founded by the leaders of Chibas Zion were Torah schools and, in line with their dream of the settlement of the land, they added work-oriented learning.

But the Zionist movement, which had begun to stir in the

middle of the nineteenth century, was building and soon was changing the direction of life in Palestine in fundamental ways.

New Winds

In 1895 the Dreyfus affair shook France and sent shudders through the Jewish world. One of those present at the trial was Theodor Herzl, a Viennese journalist for the *Neue Freie Presse*, one of Europe's leading newspapers. The intense anti-Semitism displayed there made an indelible impression upon him. He became convinced that there was no solution to the problem of the Jewish people in exile—they had to be a nation in their own home.

Herzl began his efforts to found a Jewish state by trying to establish connections in diplomatic circles. He was determined to lay his plan before the mighty of the world. He sought audiences with the sultan of the Ottoman Empire, of which Palestine was a part, and with the German kaiser.

In his first visit to Constantinople, he met with leading officials, including the grand vizier, the secretary-general of the Foreign Ministry, and a great many other officials. He did not succeed in meeting the sultan.

The news about his mission spread. Upon his return from Constantinople, at the Sofia railroad station he was greeted by masses of Jews, kissed on the hand, and hailed in speeches as the leader, the Heart of Israel. Soon visitors and letters began to arrive from all parts of the world.

Herzl convened a small committee in Vienna. There it was decided to convene a Zionist Congress in Basle, Switzerland. On August 29, 1897, the First Zionist Congress was opened with 197 delegates. The congress resolved that "Zionism seeks to secure for the Jewish people a publicly recognized, legally secured home in Palestine." It was recognized that a powerful organization was needed to lead this movement. It was decided that the Zionist Congress should become the supreme organ of the movement.

Jewish and non-Jewish newspapers from all over the world reported the congress. Herzl had succeeded in fashioning a dynamic movement to support his diplomatic efforts.

Zionism grew rapidly. The Second Zionist Congress, held one year later, reflected the growth of the movement. The number of

Zionist groups grew from 117 to 913. The number of delegates grew to 400.

As the Zionist movement grew, doors opened wider for Herzl. In November 1898 he met with Kaiser Wilhelm and appealed to the kaiser to intercede with the sultan in support of the aspirations of the Jewish people for Palestine. His request was deferred by the kaiser, who replied that further investigation was necessary.

In May 1901 he succeeded in gaining an audience with the sultan on three different occasions. He was received with great honor, and he spoke to the sultan longer than most ambassadors. But, when the conferences were over, he had made no progress.

Herzl met with the British leaders, hoping to establish a Jewish state in a British colony. In October 1902 he met with Lord Chamberlain, the Colonial Secretary of England.

In 1903 he visited Russia and met with Plehve, the Minister of the Interior, and with Witte, the Minister of Finance. He hoped that Russia would intercede with the sultan. His appointments resulted in no tangible successes but their effect on the Jewish masses was electric—the image of a representative of the Jewish people meeting with kings had magical effects upon the people.

In his Russian visit, he stopped in Vilna. There, he was welcomed tumultuously. Tens of thousands shouted, "Hedad, Hail" as he passed. Never before, in modern days, had a Jewish leader been greeted with such wild acclaim.

In the end Herzl's efforts did not achieve any practical success. When he died in 1903, there was no concrete result to which he could point, but his diplomatic efforts had made a great impact on the Jewish people. Zionism seemed no longer to be an impossible dream. To hundreds of thousands of Jews the dream of a Jewish national home began to take on real substance in the form of the land of Palestine.

Organizations of young Zionists proliferated. Many young people were inspired with the thought of aliyah. And, when the Kishinev pogrom and the pogroms of the "Black Hundreds" struck in 1903, thousands of young people became chalutzim and left for Palestine in the Second Aliyah.

The Second Aliyah began in 1904 and was almost entirely an aliyah of the youth. The chalutzim were inspired with the dream of a new life in a reborn Jewish state. They envisioned a new language, new customs, and a new social order. Some idealized labor and dreamed of the "Conquest of Labor" in the land of Palestine. Some dreamed of socialism and communal life. But, invariably, their dream was of a break from the past, and from the Torah that was a symbol of that past.

During this aliyah, in 1905, the first kibbutz or agricultural collective settlement was founded in Degania. The life-style was communal and totally free of all Torah values.

The Second Aliyah lasted from 1904 to 1914. It brought between 35,000 and 40,000 dedicated young chalutzim to Palestine.

Conflict

Herzl's efforts as head of the World Zionist Congress were largely concentrated on political Zionism. Herzl believed that diplomatic activity was the most important method of achieving the Jewish state. He believed that formulation of the cultural program was not yet vital and too divisive.

But he could not restrain the speakers and thinkers at the World Zionist Congress. Entire sessions of the congress were dominated by cultural discussions. Most of the spokesmen of the congress were intense believers in secular Zionism. They called for a new beginning, a spiritual renaissance. They rejected the Torah as having no relevance to the new, modern Jewish state.

Despite the overwhelmingly secular climate of the World Zionist Congress, the rabbis and religious Jews of the Mizrachi persisted and joined in the activity of the World Zionist Congress. They believed that the unity of the Zionist movement was paramount but tried to gain whatever concessions they could on behalf of their Torah values.

But the greater number of rabbis and religious Jews were repelled by the hostility of the leaders of the World Zionist Congress, which was thus left almost completely in the hands of the secular Zionists.

The religious Jews moved to establish their own organization. The organization was initiated by Yaakov Rosenheim, the secretary of the United Religious Jews. In 1908 in a letter to the membership he wrote, "We are far from being the minority of the Jewish people. But we do become the minority if we close ourselves within our four cubits, if we shut off the millions of our brethren from any attachment to the new era."

The leaders of religious Jewry met in 1909 and resolved to establish an international body to represent religious Jewry.

The final push for the establishment of this body came when the tenth World Zionist Congress in 1911 resolved to include culture and education in their program, and to establish schools in Palestine and in the diaspora in the spirit of secular Zionism. Many religious Jews who were participating in the World Zionist Congress left and joined in the establishment of the Agudas Israel.

In 1912 three hundred delegates from all over Europe met in Katowicz on the border between Germany and Russia. Among the speakers at the founding meeting was Rabbi Breuer. He declared:

> Are we to gaze from a distance and leave in the hands of our brothers, who possess ambitions contrary to ours, the title "Saviors of Israel"? No, no! We must be independent and take into our own hands the leadership of those interests which are to us most precious and sacred.

But, at this time, the most influential organization of political Zionism was the World Zionist Congress, and that was in the hands of the secular Zionists.

The Balfour Declaration

In 1914 the First World War broke out. Dr. Chaim Weizmann, a prominent British scientist and one of the leaders of the World Zionist Congress, was convinced of an Allied victory. He believed that Palestine would then pass under Allied influence. He saw Great Britain as the key to the realization of the Jewish national home. He began a series of diplomatic efforts to persuade the British leadership to adopt Palestine as a British protectorate.

Weizmann met first with Herbert Samuel, a minister in the cabinet of Lord Asquith. He discovered that Herbert Samuel was strongly committed to Zionism and that he was working diligently to persuade his colleagues to support Zionist aims.

In January 1915 he met with Lloyd George, the Chancellor of

the Exchequer. Lloyd George assured Dr. Weizmann of his support. He told Weizmann that Zionism, represented, for him, a tradition for which he had enormous respect.

Samuel and Lloyd George were, however, the only members of the cabinet who supported the idea of making Palestine a British protectorate. The prime minister, Lord Asquith, evinced no interest in the plan. He considered it an invitation to Great Britain to accept an unnecessary and unwanted burden on her imperial responsibilities.

Weizmann met with Lord Balfour in 1915 and 1916 when he was first lord of the admiralty. Balfour promised unequivocal support. He told Weizmann that he believed that the world owed the Jews an immeasurable debt for their contributions to mankind and their years of suffering.

Weizmann found some important support in the British government, though not enough to make the protectorate plan a reality. However, in December 1916 events developed that changed British policy. A cabinet crisis struck the British government; Lord Asquith resigned. Lloyd George was named prime minister and Lord Balfour, foreign secretary.

On July 18, 1917, with the help of Lord Rothschild, a draft of a resolution was submitted to the Foreign Office proposing British support for a Jewish national homeland.

The memorandum was discussed at several cabinet meetings. Finally, at the cabinet meeting of October 31, 1917, Lord Balfour was authorized to send the following letter to Lord Rothschild with a request that he bring it to the attention of the Zionist Federation. "His Majesty's government views with favor the establishment in Palestine of a national home for the Jewish people, and will use their best endeavors to facilitate the establishment of this object."

The news was published on November 8, 1917, in the British press. The Jewish people greeted the news with jubilation. It touched off a new wave of optimism and created the momentum for the Third Aliyah that began in 1919.

The Third Aliyah took place in the years 1919 to 1923 and brought 37,000 immigrants to Palestine. As in the Second Aliyah most of the "olim" were young "chalutzim." They came from the cities and shtetlach of Russia and Poland consumed with the ideal of building the land. Their zeal and determination to rescue the land of Palestine from the desert and the swamps knew no bounds.

In the book *Toldot Hahityashvout Hatzionut*, Alex Bein quotes the letter of a young girl, Chana, writing to her friend in Russia in January 1921.

> The land is beautiful. There isn't, I believe, another land like it among all the nations. I worked in Shuni, a settlement of sixty-five people. We dug ditches, we dried swamps. The first month passed like a wonderful dream. On the week-days we worked, and on the Sabbath we had discussions and took walks. And you know, there are no walks like in Israel. Every place, every corner is a world by itself, each one is so different from the other. And Shuni is so beautiful. You go up to the mountains, you walk for ten minutes and the sea unfolds before you. On the other side is a dry land unplowed and sown with rocks. And here and there the land is spotted with islands of orchards, pomegranates and figs. Behind Shuni is a mountain with palm trees rising up. And overhead hangs the sky, the skies of Italy are like nothing compared to them. In Shuni the evenings are wonderful. After our work we sat in the fields, we sang and played and rejoiced in our hard work. We rejoiced in everything.
>
> But then came the disease. One after the other they began to get sick. To get fully well was impossible because there was no medicine and no medical help. From day to day the number of sick grew. Day and night we took turns to watch the sick. Just imagine, at one time only seven people went to work, though there were no lazy people amongst us. The wages of the few workers was not enough for medical expenses.
>
> We began to conserve food. More than once we went to work without breakfast. Despite all the hardships our spirit did not fall. But in the end, everyone had to leave Shuni because of health reasons.
>
> It is good, at least, that we finished the work in the swamps. Now the group that replaced us received equipment and everything they needed and they are not sick like us. At least we have the recognition that we were a pioneer group which prepared the way for the group that came after us.
>
> Four of the members of our group had to leave the country

because of their poor health. After the malaria they developed heart trouble and the doctors forbade them to do physical work. They did not want to remain in the country and be a burden to the working community, and to be of no use either to others or to themselves. They decided to leave. Do not think that their spirits fell. No, they were very hurt that they had to leave the land. They will complete their studies and return. How they will pine for their beloved land.

I forgot the most important thing. Do not send to Israel people who have no skill. Today there are many Chalutzim in Jaffa without work. And every week more boats arrive filled with Chalutzim.

In the years 1920 to 1923 the Jewish population grew from 57,000 to about 95,000. In 1920, 8,223 came; in 1921, 8,294; in 1922, 8,685; and in 1923, 8,175. More than 35,000 Jews came to Palestine during this period of immigration.

The young men and women who came to Palestine from the towns of Eastern Europe were not raised as farmers and stone cutters, but they believed that the land of Israel needed labor.

They came to Palestine and challenged the desert, scorched by the sun and scourged by disease. They worked endlessly to bring life to a land that had known no life for centuries.

In the book *Pioneer Youth in Palestine*, Bardin describes the chalutzim and their dreams.

> They were filled with national devotion and fitted for hard struggle. They were united in the denunciation of life in the Diaspora, having come in almost all cases under the influence of the Russian revolutionary climate of opinion. They were united by the idea that a Jewish National Home implies a profound reconstruction of Jewish life.

When the Second and Third Aliyot came to an end in 1923, the composition of the population of Palestine had changed greatly. No longer was Palestine typified by the religious inhabitants of the old yishuv. The majority of the population was new, having come to Palestine in the twentieth century. These immigrants had different values than the members of the old yishuv. They believed in socialism and they did not follow the Torah.

In April 1920 Great Britain was given the mandate to administer Palestine. Article Four of the Mandate stated that "an appropriate Jewish agency should be recognized as the public body for the purpose of advising and cooperating with the Administration of Palestine in such economic, social, and other matters as may affect the establishment of the Jewish National Home and the interests of the people in Palestine."

The Jewish Agency was constituted on August 11, 1929 with Dr. Chaim Weizmann at its head. The Jewish Agency was recognized by the British government as the official body representing the interests of the Jewish people. All authority and finances were placed in its hands. The Jewish Agency became the quasi-government of Jewish Palestine and came into control of all aspects of public service.

The Palestine Yishuv, which had begun to change with the growing influence of the immigrants of the Second and Third Aliyot, was now firmly in the hands of the secular Zionists.

Education

For many years the only education that existed in Palestine was in the cheder, the Talmud Torah, and the yeshiva. The curriculum was purely Torah and the language of instruction was Yiddish. All attempts to introduce any other kind of learning were successfully resisted by the Torah leaders of Palestine.

But in the twentieth century, changes began to be felt, and with the coming of the Second Aliyah the changes could no longer be controlled. In 1914 the Teachers Union and the Zionist leaders founded the Vaad Hachinuch; the board of education. The goal of the board was to advance nationalism and Hebrew language teaching in the schools. The budgets of the affiliated schools were subsidized by the Zionist organizations. Twelve schools placed themselves under their supervision.

The Vaad Hachinuch gained immediate acceptance as the supervisory agency of Palestine and grew rapidly. In 1918 forty schools were under its supervision. In 1920, 110 schools with a student population of 12,830 children were supervised by the Vaad Hachinuch and subsidized by the Zionist Organization.

In 1918 the British military government recognized the World Zionist Congress as the official representative of the Jewish people. All authority and finances were placed in its hands and philanthropic contributions were funnelled through it.

With growing authority and capabilities, the Zionist Congress embarked on an effort to accomplish an aim that was very dear. It decided to establish a uniform and united system of schools for Palestine and succeeded in gaining the acceptance of most political parties and schools in Palestine.

In 1918 the Zionist Commission, headed by Dr. Chaim Weizmann, came to Palestine and met with the Torah leaders. It offered to subsidize their educational institutions if they would place their schools under the supervision of the Vaad Hachinuch.

Rabbi Sonnenfeld, speaking for the Torah leaders replied,

> The Yeshivas and the Talmud Torahs are ours. We will conduct them as we deem proper. We will not permit anyone who does not share our beliefs to have any say in their direction, neither in their curriculum nor in their organization.

The education system of the Zionists was divided into two departments, the general and the Mizrachi, or religious system. The program of the general school was non-religious. Torah had very little place in the curriculum. It was left to the parent to provide religious training for his child.

The Mizrachi schools were religious schools and the teachers were Torah-observant. The curriculum was evenly divided between Torah and general subjects. The Mizrachi schools provided Torah learning, but much less than the Torah-centered education of the cheder and the Talmud Torah.

In 1918 the Zionist school system was made up of fifty-six general schools with 6,200 students and twenty-three Mizrachi schools with 2,100 students.

During this period the Labor Zionist party was growing. It conducted its own separate network of schools. In 1925, in addition to the ninety-seven general schools with 11,000 pupils and the forty-five Mizrachi schools with 4,500 pupils, there were twenty-seven Labor schools with 700 pupils.

In 1926 the British government recognized the Zionist school system as the official public school system of Palestine. It was given a percentage of the education budget of the British Mandatory government.

The Labor Zionists requested that they be admitted to the Zionist school system as a separate department. In 1929 their request was granted. The Zionist public school system thus consisted of three departments, general, Mizrachi, and Labor.

More than two-thirds of the children of Palestine were enrolled in the Zionist public school system. Seventy to 80 percent were in the general and Labor branches. About 20 to 25 percent of the Zionist public school children received a Torah education.

The Fourth Aliyah took place during the years 1924 to 1929. This aliyah was composed mainly of middle-class Jews from Poland, fleeing from the discriminatory tax decrees of Minister Grabsky, and brought 84,000 Jews to Palestine. The Zionist public school system increased, but the pattern of enrollment remained generally the same.

In 1932 there were more than 23,000 students in the Zionist school system. Some 14,000 of them were in the general schools, 6,000 in the Mizrachi schools, and 2,800 in the Labor schools. The private schools consisted of about 13,000 students. The number of students in the schools of the Agudas Israel and the cheder, or Talmud Torah as it was often called, was about 4,000.

The Fifth Aliyah took place from 1932 to 1936. Over 150,000 Jews arrived in Palestine, many German Jews fleeing from the growing persecution in Germany. The majority were from Poland, fleeing from what they anticipated would be frightening times in Poland.

The number of students in the Zionist school system increased greatly. In 1939 there were 55,000 students in the Zionist public school system: the general schools had about 32,000 students, the Mizrachi schools about 13,500, and the Labor schools about 10,500. Private schools enrolled 25,000 students. The Agudas Israel schools had about 3,000 students, and the Talmud Torah schools also about 3,000.

In 1939, of the approximately 100,000 children in the public and private schools of Palestine, less than a quarter were receiving a religious education. And of those, only a small minority were receiving a Torah-centered education.

The educational scene reflected the great changes that were taking place in Palestine. In 1939 the social climate was predominantly secular.

The Mandate

The flow of immigration was dependent upon the policies of Great Britain, which held the mandate over Palestine. The number of immigrants was fixed by the Mandatory Power and the consideration of Great Britain in determining the number depended upon her political interests. The Balfour Declaration, as administered by Great Britain, was not a single open-door policy for all Jews who wished to enter. Every passport was a diplomatic decision.

The policy of Great Britain was affected not only by the situation of the Jews, but also by the attitude of the Arabs. As long as peace reigned between Jew and Arab, Great Britain was content to have the Jewish immigration continue without controls. But in 1929 the growing Arab discontent with the rising Jewish population resulted in riots throughout the land. In Hebron the Arabs killed 59 men, women, and children. In Safad 41 Jews were killed or wounded. The attacks spread into the outlying districts of Jerusalem and lasted for a week. By the end of the week 108 Jews were killed, 87 were wounded, and the financial loss ran into hundreds of thousands of pounds.

Lord Passfield, the secretary of state for the colonies, appointed a commission of inquiry headed by Sir Walter Shaw. In its report the commission declared that the outbreak was an attack by the Arabs on Jews. However, they attributed the cause of the disturbance to "the disappointment of their political and national aspiration and fear for their economic future." They recommended that an equal balance be struck between the interests of the Jews and the Arabs.

The commission also stated that in order to prevent future disturbances the immigration of Jews should be limited to the agricultural capabilities of the land. The commission's report was followed by the Simpson Report that declared that "at the present time with the present methods of Arab cultivation there is no margin of land for agricultural settlement by new immigrants with the exception of undeveloped lands as the various Jewish agencies hold in reserve."

Based on these findings the British government issued a statement policy in 1930 known as the Passfield White Paper. It declared that "any hasty decision in regard to more unrestricted

Jewish immigration is to be strongly deprecated." It emphasized the need to control Jewish immigration to ensure that such immigration did not cause Arab unemployment.

The White Paper brought great outcries from the Jewish people. The repercussions caused Prime Minister MacDonald to write a letter to Dr. Weizmann informing him that the Mandatory Power did not intend to stop Jewish immigration to Palestine. But the unwillingness of Prime Minister MacDonald to issue a new White Paper was an indication that Great Britain was turning away from the unrestricted immigration envisioned by the Balfour Declaration.

At the same time that Europe saw the rise of the Nazis to power in Germany, anti-Semitism was rising in Poland. Immigration rose sharply. In the year 1933 over 30,000 Jews entered Palestine; in 1934, over 42,000; in 1935, over 61,000.

The rising immigration of Jews increased the hostility of the Arabs. The British, deeply concerned with the attitude of the Arabs, became increasingly strict in their policy of Jewish immigration. In 1936 disorders erupted in Jaffa and were followed by a general strike of the Arabs. As a result the number of certificates of immigration issued by the British was drastically curtailed. Immigration into Palestine was held to less than 15,000 a year.

Disorder and unrest mounted. The British exerted strong efforts to bring the Jews and the Arabs together, in 1938 convening a conference between Jewish and Arab leaders. The Arabs were firm in their insistence on their rights to Palestine and the Jews insisted on their rights as formulated in the Balfour Declaration. The conference ended in failure.

When the conferees failed to reach agreement, the British government imposed its own plan on the Jews and Arabs. In May 1939 the British issued the White Paper that sent shock waves through the Jewish world. The White Paper declared that "it was the objective of the British government to establish a Palestine State within ten years."

In order to implement the new policy the white paper declared that for the next five years Jewish immigration would be permitted at the rate of 75,000 per year. That would bring the Jewish population up to one-third of the population of the country. After that the British government "will have no further obligation to assist in the establishment of the Jewish National Home."

The British government, confronted with the conflict of Jewish and Arab interests, sided with the Arabs. The door to Palestine was to be shut to the Jews fleeing from persecution in Europe. The chapter of Jewish immigration into Palestine and its further development as a center of Jewish life was closed by the great and mighty power of Great Britain.

The future of the Jewish people in Palestine was grim. The chalutzim, who had toiled with such fervor and sacrifice to reclaim the desert and to drain the swamps for the settlement of the Jewish National Home, had succeeded in reclaiming the desert and draining the swamps but not for the Jewish National Home. It seemed that their incredible self-sacrifice was all for the sake of what was declared to become an independent Arab state.

And as a home for the Torah the situation too held very little promise.

Before the First World War there were approximately 4,000 Jewish students in the schools of Palestine. Most of them were in seventeen Yeshivot, twenty-two Talmud Torahs, and many small Talmud Torahs. Twenty-five years and over a half million immigrants later the number of students in these Torah-centered schools had gone up to only about six thousand. About 13,500 students were learning Torah in the Torah-Work schools of Palestine. During this same period the secular schools had grown from hardly any students to over 75,000 in the public and private schools of Palestine.

In *Divrei Ymei Yisrael* the historian Rabbi Rabinowitz writes:

> For many years the secularists were the main olim to Palestine, the main speakers for its rebuilding and the main workers for the preparation of its foundation. At the head of the olim were the secular youth who dreamed of a secular life and saw no hope for their kind of life in Europe. Before they left they worked at Hachsharah preparing for a hard life of working the land. The religious Zionist youth also took part in Hachsharah but they were few. Because of this the Yishuv took on a mostly secular personality, although there were some happy evidences of Torah living in the general society.

The happy evidences Rabinowitz mentions were the thousands of children learning Torah. Though they were but a small minority of the total, they nevertheless were a source of Torah. There were also great and famous yeshivot in Palestine. The Torah Jews could point proudly to the yeshivot of Jerusalem, Bnei Brak, and Tel Aviv.

But in the total view of Palestine at the time that the doors were closed to the Jews by Great Britain, the sun of Torah in Palestine was overcast by a thick cloud of secular Zionism. And the dream of Zionism that the secularists had put in the place of Torah was proclaimed by the British to have come to an end. Not only had the sunshine of Torah grown dim in Palestine, the very existence of the settlement was shrouded in uncertainty.

In 1939 the sun of Torah did not seem to be rising in Palestine.

13

WHAT OF THE PROPHECY?

In 1939 what had never happened in all the thousands of years of Jewish history seemed to be coming.

King Solomon prophesied, "The sun rises and the sun sets," and the Talmud explains that there is always a sun of Torah rising somewhere before the sun of Torah sets. This had been true in all generations of Jewish history. But in 1939 the sun of Torah seemed to be declining everywhere.

It was declining in its center, Eastern Europe. It had set in Russia. And in the United States and in Palestine where Torah had been planted, there too it seemed to be on the decline. The Jewish people seemed to be on a road leading to self-extinction.

What of the promise of Hashem as prophesied by King Solomon that "the sun rises and then the sun sets"?

PART III

"WITH FURY POURED OUT"

Ezekiel 20

14

"LOOK DOWN FROM THE HEAVENS"

For generations the people of Israel have recited the following prayer in their morning services:

> Look down from the heavens and see that we have fallen to shame and ridicule among the nations. We have been considered as sheep led to slaughter, to kill, to destroy, to beat, and to shame. But in spite of all this, Your Name we have not forgotten, please do not forget us.

Through exile after exile, as they wandered from one place to another, the lot of the Jewish people was the same. They made their home in the country that accepted them, suffering abuse and beatings and death from the inhabitants, all the while accepting with meek gratitude the hospitality of the nation. They stayed until they were no longer welcome, and then they made their way to another country where they faced the same fate. The liturgy describes, with pathos, the pathetic heroism of the long-suffering Jew, the incredible measure of toleration the Jewish people possessed. The factor that made possible their toleration was their faith that Hashem would not forget them as they did not forget Hashem.

For generations their faith remained firm, their loyalty to the Torah unswerving. And in 1939 this generation, as earlier generations, was steady and undoubting.

But human beings have their limits and the Jewish people had reached theirs. The Jews of succeeding generations could no longer bear to be the shame and ridicule of nations, as a sheep led to slaughter. They would forget the Name of Hashem.

The prophet Ezekiel had said,

> And that which ascends upon your spirit shall not be, that which you say let us be like the nations, like the families of the lands, to serve wood and stone.

In the twentieth century there was descending upon the Jewish people the desire to be like all other nations. The younger generation of the scattered remnants of the Jewish people was seeking other values. The young chalutzim of Eastern Europe were seeking European socialism and secular Zionism. The children of the immigrants in America were seeking the materialism of the "Golden Land."

But it was the will of Hashem that the Jewish people, the bearers of the Torah, would not forsake the Torah. The present generation of righteous would not be the last. The ambition of the coming generation to be like all the nations of the world would not be.

Hashem knew that the oppression of the Jewish people had to end or the sun of Torah would set. The Jewish people had to be redeemed and returned to the land of Israel. Only in the land of Israel would they find freedom from the suffering that was inevitably their lot in the lands of their exile.

When they would be returned to their land and the burden of oppression lifted from their backs, the heaviness would be removed from their hearts. When their hearts and minds would be free, they would seek and find themselves. The "pintele yid," the spark of Judaism that is in the heart of every Jew, would be awakened. The sunshine of Torah would rise.

This was therefore the moment in the divine history of the Jewish people that Hashem judged to be the time for redemption from oppression.

The Talmud describes the process of redemption. In the tractate Megilah the Talmud explains the order of the blessings of the Shmone Esray. Rashi tells us that there are four blessings dealing with the four stages of redemption. They are: redemption from oppression, ingathering of the exiles, the return of Jerusalem, and the crowning of the Kingdom of David, which is the Kingdom of Hashem.

The prophet Ezekiel had said,

> As I live says the Lord that only with a strong hand and an outstretched arm, and with fury poured out will I be King over thee.

The road to the Kingdom of Hashem, beginning with redemption from oppression, would be preceded by "fury." Not just fury, but a fury of unprecedented magnitude—a "fury poured out."

The beginning of redemption was to be ushered in with all of its prophetic accompaniments. It meant the coming of the fury. It meant a holocaust.

The Talmud says that when Rav Nachman read the prophecy of Ezekiel, he said, "May Hashem let forth an anger such as this upon us and may He but redeem us."

Rav Nachman knew that the fury of the Holocaust would be spent on the righteous. He knew that that supreme moment called for martyrdom and only the righteous could bring sanctity to the Name of Hashem out of the tragedy.

Rav Nachman, speaking for the righteous of all generations, accepted the horrors of the Holocaust.

Martyrdom

In the liturgy of Yom Kippur the poet tells the story of the Ten Martyrs, the great classic epic of martyrdom that took place during the days of the Roman Empire about two thousand years ago. And thus says the poet,

> These will I remember, and my soul will I pour out. Evil men have swallowed us and eagerly consumed us. In the days of the tyrant there was no reprieve for the ten who were put to death by the Roman government. . . .
>
> Give us three days, they said, so that we may ascertain whether this has been decreed from heaven. If we are condemned to die, we will accept the decree of The One who is all Merciful.

Trembling and shuddering, they turned their eyes to Rabbi Ishmael the High Priest, and they asked him to pronounce the name of G-d and ascend to the heavens and learn whether the decree was issued from G-d.

Rabbi Ishmael purified himself and pronounced the name of G-d in awe. He ascended to the heavens, and inquired of the angel robed in linens, who said to him, "Accept the judgment upon yourselves, you beloved and pure, for I have heard from behind the curtain that this is your fate."

Rabbi Ishmael descended and related to his friends the word of G-d. Then, the evil man commanded to slay them with force. And two of them were taken first for they were the leaders of Israel, Rabbi Ishmael the High Priest, and Rabbi Shimon Ben Gamliel, the president of Israel. . . .

The angels of heaven screamed in anguish, "Is this the Torah and this its reward. Behold the enemy blasphemes Your great and revered Name, and scorns and curses Your Torah."

A voice replied from heaven, "If I hear another sound I shall turn the world to water, I will devastate heaven and earth. This is My decree, accept it, you who love the Torah."

Thus were slain men of spotless conduct. They led forth Rabbi Akiva, who explained all the letters of the Torah, and they raked his skin with iron combs. . . .

Thus the poet mournfully describes the passing of the ten great leaders of Israel, including Rabbi Chanania ben Tradion, Rabbi Hutzpith the Interpreter, Rabbi Chanania ben Chochinai, Rabbi Yeshavav the Scribe, Rabbi Judah ben Dama, and Judah ben Bava.

The poet concludes,

Thus has befallen us, and we have narrated it with grief. And we have poured out our sad and humble hearts. From the heavens hear our prayers, thou great G-d of Mercy and Compassion.

The Talmud, Brachot 61, tells us that when Rabbi Akiva was being taken to his death it was the time for reciting the "Shma," the prayer accepting the Kingdom of G-d. As they scourged his flesh with combs of iron, he was concentrating on his prayer with great love. His students said to him, "Even now you can say it with love?" And he said to them, "All my days I have been disturbed that I am not fulfilling the verse which commands you to love G-d with all your soul, which means, even if He takes your soul. Now that I have that opportunity, should I not be glad to fulfill that command?" He said the words of the Shma with feeling and his soul left him as he completed saying, "G-d is One."

These righteous men defined the way of the martyr. Martyrdom can achieve its divine purpose only when it is fulfilled with pure faith. When the martyr dies proclaiming his trust in His Truth, those who witness the death of the martyr are inspired to follow his example. They dedicate themselves to the service of Hashem with faith and love as did the martyr. Then when Hashem chooses to fulfill His promise, their dedicated service makes the will of Hashem come to pass. Their deeds are endowed with His blessing.

But if the victim dies without love of Hashem and without faith in His promise, the survivors derive no faith and hope from the martyr's death. They are not inspired to serve Him. They despair of salvation and reject His will. They do not follow Hashem, and their deeds are not blessed. The divine purpose cannot be realized with their death. Only when the voice of the martyr rings out with pure faith does the sacrifice of the martyr achieve its purpose.

Hashem knew that this was the last generation of the exile that lived in the spirit of Rav Nachman, that had the sanctity to sing "Ani Maamin" with their last breath. Hashem chose this generation for Martyrdom. Their Martyrdom would bring the blessing of Hashem upon the work of those they left behind. And with their deeds the Jewish people would be redeemed from the oppression of their exile and the sunshine of Torah would rise again.

Hashem hid His face and He did not protect His people from the evil that was in the hearts of His enemies.

15

THE SIX MILLION

The Second World War broke out in September 1939. Poland quickly fell before the Nazi blitzkrieg. Soon thereafter the Germans conquered Denmark, Norway, Belgium, Holland, and France. Austria and Czechoslovakia had already been occupied by the Germans before the war began. In June 1941 the German army invaded Russia and quickly moved deep into Russia. By the end of 1941 most of the Jews of all of Europe were in the lands occupied by the Nazis. In March 1944 the Germans occupied Hungary and the Jews of Hungary were added to the number already under the heel of the Nazi conqueror.

The Germans immediately undertook a campaign to rid Europe of its Jews. The first step was to concentrate the Jews into ghettoes that were to be established in the major cities. They were to be removed from the shtetlach and from most parts of the city and "resettled" into a narrow walled section of the city.

Food for the Jews of the ghetto was strictly rationed. The amount of food allocated by the authorites for the ghetto was pitifully inadequate. The Jews were always hungry and many starved to death. Children begged in the streets. It was a common sight to see children lying dead in the streets. The Jews of the ghetto existed in the shadow of death.

But all of this was only a prelude to the "final solution." The fate the Nazis had in store for the Jews was total extermination. The Jews in the ghetto were awaiting their turn to be shipped to the crematoria.

Though the Jews in the ghettoes and in the extermination

camps were caught in a web of horror unmatched in the history of "civilized" man, never did they waver in their faith that the Jewish people would survive. Who would live and who would die? This question they could not answer. But they did not doubt that the Jewish people would outlive their enemies.

They knew that it was only a matter of time when the enemy would fall and the Jewish people would raise their heads again. They knew that many would die. But they knew that there would be a "saved remnant" to keep the Jewish people alive.

The following account is related by M. Prager in *Tnuat Hachasidut Bitkufat Hashoah.*

> When the murderer Globotchnik came to Lublin at the end of 1939 he commanded that all the Jews be gathered together in an empty field at the edge of the city. When all the Jews assembled, trembling with fear, he suddenly announced that everyone should start singing a happy Chassidic song. Someone in the frightened crowd began to sing the sweet Chassidic song "Lomer Zich Iberbeten Avinu Shebashamayim" (Let Us Make Up, Our Father in Heaven). But the song did not catch on. At once Globotchnik commanded his troopers to beat the Jews who were not following his orders. The Nazis swooped down upon the Jews and began to beat them mercilessly. Suddenly a loud clear voice rose up in song, "Mir Vellen Zei Iberlebben Avinu Shebashamayim" (We will Outlive Them, Our Father in Heaven), singing to the same Chassidic melody. In a second, the song caught on. Everyone began singing and then they all joined together dancing a stormy, whirling dance before the eyes of the murderers. The Jews were so intoxicated with feelings of hope and faith that Globotchnik stood there bewildered and confused and began to scream with a shrill voice, "Stop! Stop at once!"

This unshakable faith in the survival of the Jewish people is reflected in the writings of the Holocaust diarists. Many of the Jews of the ghetto took pen in hand and wrote diaries, setting down their experiences and thoughts, recording them for the posterity they knew belonged to the Jewish people.

Chaim Aaron Kaplan in *The Scrolls of Agony* writes in his entry of February 9, 1940:

The Jews refuse "krepieren" (to die like animals). It appears to me that the Fuehrer is as mistaken as were Pharaoh, Nebuchadnezar, and Haman.

On August 1, 1941, he writes:

A nation that can live in such terrible circumstances as these without losing its mind, without committing suicide, and which can still laugh, is sure of survival. Which will disappear first, Nazism or Judaism? I am willing to bet! Nazism will go first!

As they waited for their salvation, they went on with their lives as Jews, finding courage, hope, and even joy in their Jewish heritage. They studied Torah and observed Jewish practices. Neither suffering, nor pain, nor the fear of death discouraged them.

The following account was related by Zalman Kleinman at the Eichmann trial and published in *Ani Maamin* by Mordecai Eliav.

One day as I was lying on my bunk in the children's ward in Auschwitz, I saw a guard carrying a big rubber hose, going to whip someone. I jumped from my bunk to see whom they were going to whip. The guard went over to one of the bunks. The boy that was lying there already knew what was coming and he was waiting. The guard said, "Get down." He came down and bent over. The guard began to whip him.

I and the boys who gathered around, watched and counted. The boy did not cry, did not shout, did not even sigh. We were astonished, we did not understand . . . and the whipping went on. He had already passed twenty-five lashes; as a rule we were given twenty-five lashes. He passed thirty. When he passed forty, he turned the boy over and began to whip him on his head and on his legs. The boy did not groan, did not cry, nothing . . . a boy of fourteen and he did not cry.

The guard angrily finished fifty and left. I can still see this great red blotch that streaked the boy's forehead from one of the blows of that rubber hose.

We asked the boy why he was whipped. He answered, "I

brought some prayer books to my friends. It was worth it." He did not add a word. He got up, went to his bunk and sat down.

On the holidays the Jews gathered together for services. Their synagogues were closed down but they managed to find ways to pray together.
In *The Scrolls of Agony* Kaplan writes about Rosh Hashanah in the Warsaw Ghetto.

> There are secret Minyanim by the hundreds. In every part of Warsaw, congregations are conducting services and they don't leave out any words of the services. There are even sermonizers for the services. Everything is just like in the earlier days.

The following is told by Rabbi Z. H. Maizlish in his book *Mkadshei Hashem.*

> On the day of Rosh Hashanah I went from block to block with the Shofar in my hand though I knew that this involved great peril, and Thank G-d, I was able to blow the hundred blasts of the Shofar about twenty times. This greatly lifted up the spirits of the unfortunate and calmed their consciences a bit. They were thrilled that they were able to fulfil the command of hearing the Shofar on Rosh Hashanah even in Auschwitz. Now, fourteen hundred boys who were locked in a block and condemned to the gas chambers found out that I had a Shofar. They begged and implored that I go to them and blow the hundred blasts of the Shofar so that they could fulfil this precious commandment in their last moments.
> I did not know what to do, because this was an extremely dangerous thing, and if the Nazis would come in at the time that I was there with them, there is no doubt that they would take me with them to the gas chambers.
> However, the pleas of the boys did not let me rest, they aroused great compassion in my heart, and I resolved that I would not refuse them.
> After much pleading and for a large sum of money which was collected, the Kaypos agreed to let me in, but they warned me that if I heard the sound of the bell at the gate, which is a signal that the S. S. is coming, at that moment my fate would be

sealed along with the boys, for they would not let me out under any conditions.

I accepted it all and I joined the boys. Where is the pen and where is the writer who can put on paper the feelings of my heart as I came into that locked block. . . . After the blowing of the Shofar when I wanted to leave, one young man arose and said, "Dear friends, the Rabbi has given us words of strength. He had told us the words of the Talmud that even if a sharp sword is placed at the neck of a man he must not despair of G-d's mercy. I say to you we can hope for the best but we must be ready for the worst. For the sake of G-d let us not forget at our last moment to say Shma Yisrael." And they all recited with intense feeling the sentence Shma Yisrael. Another boy arose and said, "We will not say thanks to the Rabbi for granting us the privilege of fulfilling the commandment of hearing the Shofar. However, we all join in blessing him that the Almighty help the Rabbi to leave this place healthy and unharmed." And all of the boys shouted Amen in a great voice.

Leib Garfunkel tells about Yom Kippur in the Kovne Ghetto in *Kovne Hayihudit Behurban.*

A short time after the decree, the Jews took courage and reopened the closed-down synagogues and conducted services and studied Torah without concern for the dangers involved.

Minyanim were organized to hold services on Yom Kippur, and one of the Minyanim was held in the hospital. On Yom Kippur in the middle of the Musaf Services, as the entire Congregation was pouring out its heart in fervent prayer, the news spread that two officers of the Statkomissariat had entered the ghetto and were walking in the direction of the hospital. Like lightning, every sign of the "great sin" was removed. They disguised the Ark, put out the candles, concealed all the prayer books, and the worshippers hid in an inside room. The two Germans circled around in the hospital for a short time and found nothing suspicious. When they left, everything was returned to place and they continued the Services.

Yaakov Kurtz in *Sefer Ha'aidut* tells of the time during the holiday of Succos when he saw an old Jew sitting in a succah and singing zmirot in a loud voice. He entered the succah and asked the old man if he realized the great danger of what he was doing. The old man shook his head this way and that and continued to sing. After a while he turned to him and said, "What can they do to me? They can take my body but not my soul. Over the soul they have no authority. Their power is only in this world. Here they are powerful. But in the Other World they are powerless!"

Kaplan in *The Scrolls of Agony* tells of the Simchat Torah celebration in the Warsaw Ghetto.

> We have not shamed our eternal Torah. This was not a raucous celebration but an inner one, a heartfelt joy, and for that reason it was all the more warm and emotional. Everywhere holiday celebrations were organized and every prayer group said the wine blessing. The Chassidim were even dancing as was their pious custom. Someone told me that on the night of the holiday he met a large group of zealous Chassidim, on Mila Street, and they sang holiday songs in chorus out in public, followed by a large crowd of curious people and sightseers. Joy and revelry in poverty-stricken Mila Street! When they sang they reached such a state of ecstasy that they wouldn't stop until some heretic approached them shouting, "Jews! Safeguarding your life is a positive Biblical Commandment, it is a time of danger for us. Stop this!" Only then did they become quiet. Some of them replied in their ecstasy, "We are not afraid of the murderer! The devil with him!"

In the most bitter conditions of slavery and oppression the Jews studied Torah and gained strength from their studies.

The following account published in the *Jewish Morning Journal* of September 24, 1945, was taken from the memoirs of Dr. Leo Baeck.

> It took place in the concentration camp of Treisenstadt. Every day, every hour, each one of us was prepared to take his last walk. None of us knew when the murderers would decide to kill us. And what did the Jews do? Did they sit and cry? No! They displayed superhuman, supernatural powers. They gathered in the attics in the dark of night to study the Torah, to discuss Judaism and to listen to lectures on matters of eternity.
>
> These gatherings in the attic in the night were dangerous not

only because of the possibility of discovery by the Nazis. But there was also an added peril. The men worked in the daytime doing back-breaking work. After their work they needed rest. And here, instead of resting they gathered for the nightly study sessions. It would seem that this would have weakened them even more. However, strange as it may seem, the truth was that these "spiritual injections," these lectures, in the attic did not weaken them. On the contrary, they were strengthened, they gained new power to withstand their sufferings.

I will never forget these gatherings. We used to gather in the darkness because lighting a candle, even a match was fraught with danger. But in the midst of the darkness I felt a light. A kind of divine light shone from the faces of the Jews who gathered in the attic of Treisenstadt as we spoke about G-d, about the Jews and world, about the eternity of Israel.

And if on the next day I would ask one of them if they felt weakened by the late hours of the night before, they would answer me, "You are mistaken if you think that these lectures weaken us. They give us strength not only spiritually but even physically. They help us overcome our weakness."

The following account is related in *Eilah Ezcrah*, Volume IV.

Great institutions of Torah were closed. Yeshivos and Batei Medrash in which the voice of Torah was heard for hundreds of years were destroyed. But, Rabbi Avraham Weinberg did not change his daily schedule at all. He dedicated all his days and nights to Torah and service to G-d. The "Group" of Rabbi Avraham continued and the learning did not cease even for one day. Every day a large group of young men gathered in his house and listened to his Torah lectures.

The group of Rabbi Avraham grew daily. Behind the Ghetto walls were crowded more than half a million Jews. Many young people attached themselves to their Rabbi with all their heart and soul.

The situation in the Warsaw Ghetto was worsening. The murderers began to kill hundreds of thousands of the inhabitants of the Ghetto. Many were being sent to the death camps. Many others were "lucky" and were taken into work groups. The students of Rabbi Avraham resolved not to leave their Torah learning and not to try to join the work groups. They went every day to the house of the Rabbi to hear his lecture.

The destruction was drawing nearer. The murderers were surrounding sections of the Ghetto, taking out the Jews and sending them to Treblinka. Rabbi Avraham did not move, did not go to the factories and did not interest himself in being saved. He continued to say his lectures, continued to teach Torah, and his faithful students stayed with him. Thus he sat, until one day the murderers came, took out the Rabbi and many of his students, and led them to Treblinka. They did not give them a chance to close their books of Talmud and they remained open to page nineteen in the tractate Bchorot.

There were others among the Jewish people who chose a different path for Kiddush Hashem, the sanctification of His name. They believed that the glory of G-d and Israel would be better served by resistance. They knew that G-d would bring His vengeance upon the murderers of His people. "A G-d of vengeance is the Lord" said the prophet in Psalms. They believed that the Jewish people would sanctify the name of G-d by fulfilling the divine quality of vengeance.

Rabbi Menachem Zembe, quoted in the *Hatzofeh* of Tishrei 17, 5706, declared:

I speak to you with calmness and I say to you: This is the way! Rise up! Fight! Whoever is able, teach the children of Judah to fight!

I have studied the subject of vengeance in the Torah. I have always been troubled by this subject. Vengeance is forbidden in the Torah. But yet, in a just war, there is the commandment in the Torah to avenge. The explanation is simple. If the avenger is thinking about himself and finds in his vengeance, vulgar gratification, that is a sin. However, in a just war, vengeance is not for the individual, it is for the group and that is a proper fulfillment of the positive commandment. When we remove from our hearts personal consideration, we raise up our voices in prayer and say, Our Father Our King, avenge the Blood of your Servants.

Therefore, I am convinced that resistance with all the weapons of war is a positive commandment, for, in the vengeance of the "blood of your servants" there is no possible personal gain. What personal gain can there be in vengeance when one knows that he will himself die. However, it is a sanctification of the name of G-d. This is a just war, and in a war such as this it is a positive commandment to avenge, with sacred knowledge and will.

They believed that the world would misunderstand the martyrdom of the millions of Jews who when faced with death turned away from the murderers and faithfully accepted the will of G-d. They feared that the world would not recognize their silence as martyrdom but rather would look upon it as hopelessness and helplessness.

They believed that the name of G-d and Israel would be most glorified by resistance. They were convinced that the world would recognize only resistance as bravery.

In a little jar that once contained gasoline, in the rubble of the ruins of the Warsaw Ghetto, was found this letter written by a Jew who identifies himself as Yossel Rockover. The letter was written in the last hours of his life, as the Warsaw Ghetto was going up in flames.

In this situation I don't, of course, expect miracles and I don't ask of my G-d that He should have pity upon me. I will not try to save myself and I will not try to escape. I will make it easier for the fire to do its work by soaking my clothing in gasoline. Three bottles of gasoline are still in my possession, after I emptied many tens of them on the heads of the murderers. . . .

A tank suddenly burst into our street. From all the fortified houses bottles of burning gasoline rained down upon it, but they missed the mark. I and my friends waited until the tank passed right before us, then we threw it at them through the half closed lattice. The tank went up in flames and six Nazis ran out of it with the fire licking at them. They burned like the Jews who were burnt by them. However, they screamed more than the Jews. Jews don't scream. They accept death as their redeemer. The Warsaw Ghetto crumbled through war, through shooting, through fighting, through fire, but not through screaming. . . .

Death can no longer wait and I must complete my writing. From the steps above me I hear the shots becoming weaker and weaker. Now the last of the defenders of our fortress are falling, and now the great Warsaw, the beautiful, G-d fearing, Jewish Warsaw, is falling and dying. The sun is setting and I thank G-d that I will not see it anymore. The red of flames bursts through the lattice and the piece of sky that I see is red and stormy like a torrent of blood. In an hour at most I will be with my wife and children and with millions of my people who died, in that better world, where G-d rules alone. . . .

May He be praised forever, the G-d of the dead, the G-d of vengeance, the G-d of truth and justice, who will again light His Countenance on the world. Hear O Israel, the Lord our G-d, the Lord is one. In Your hand I place my soul.

Many Jews chose to die resisting and avenging. They died in the flames of the crumbling ghettoes, but before they died they destroyed large numbers of the enemy and showed the world the bravery and courage of the people of Hashem.

The six million took different paths to martyrdom. Silent, praying, and fighting, they gave their lives in sanctification of His Name. When the moment arrived that the martyrs recognized as their last, they faced death without fear. They did not grovel, they did not scream or plead for mercy. They believed that it was the judgment of G-d to take their souls. They surrendered their souls to Him with undiminished love for Him and with the affirmation of trust in His judgment.

In the book *The Crooked Shall be Made Straight*, Dr. Jacob Robinson quotes the statement of a non-Jew who witnessed life in the Cracow Ghetto.

Except for only a few cases which I happened to notice, I did not see people crying. People calmly looked death in the eye, resigned but also proud. The Germans did not succeed in seeing these people show sorrow or ask for mercy, and this aroused their brutality still more.

They did not turn against their murderers, they were oblivious of them. The following account was published in the *Jewish Forward* of March 3, 1946.

It happened during Succos of 1941. The Rabbi of Dombrow, Rabbi Chaim Yechiel Rubin, and about twenty followers were brought to the cemetery on Friday. The Nazis held him the whole day. . . . When evening came the Rabbi said the Shabbos services with feeling. At a distance stood the murderers armed and ready for the order to kill the Jews. In the afternoon they had forced the Jews to dig their graves with their own hands. The Jews had done so, and inside this grave they were saying the Sabbath services.

After the services the Rabbi began to sing the Sabbath songs and to preach words of Torah. In the midst of his words of Torah, he became filled with great feeling and he began to sing and dance. His spirit took hold of the Jews that were there with him and they all burst into song and began to dance in the grave, purifying their souls along with the Rabbi. The Nazi Commander gave the order to shoot, and in the midst of their dancing their souls departed them.

As they prepared to surrender their souls to G-d they thought only of the purity of their souls. The following event described by Rabbi Alter Mayer was published in the *Haboker* on the tenth of Tevet, 5711.

It happened in Treblinka. The time for extermination arrived. They were transported like cattle to the slaughter. Silently they accepted their judgment. The people going to their death did not let even a sigh escape from their lips. They did everything the evil Nazis commanded. They rode, they walked, they washed and prepared themselves for their departure. Before they were sent into the gas ovens Rabbi Yerucham Hanushtate arose and said, "This is our final journey in life. We are all being led to destruction, fathers, mothers, and children together. No one will live. So, I say to you, let us ourselves say the kaddish that in normal times our children and relatives would say after us. Let us declare our acceptance of G-d's judgment and sanctify the Name of G-d whose deeds are righteous and holy."

The great kaddish was proclaimed. They all recited the kaddish with holiness and purity and with the serenity of people who were privileged to sanctify the Name of G-d in the world.

When the leaders of Israel saw the holy people who were the victims of the Holocaust they knew that this was not a punishment from the Almighty. They knew that this was the fury that precedes redemption. They therefore cried out to their people to purify their souls in affirmation of their faith, to bring the redemption that they were being called upon to bring about with their souls.

The following event, related by Rabbi Oschry in *Churban Lita*, took place in the Kovne Ghetto.

On the eleventh day of Tamuz 5701 a group of great Rabbis were gathered in the ghetto of Kovne and were studying Torah. Suddenly the gates were burst open and a group of Lithuanian fascists sprang into the room. They were all deeply engrossed in their study and ignored the intruders. When the murderers saw that no one was paying attention to them they began to fire their revolvers, and the Rabbis trembled and arose. . . .

The order was given. "Line up! Come with us!"

The Rabbis understood what the order meant. They stood in line. While they were getting ready to march Rabbi Elchanan Wasserman turned to the prisoners and said, "It seems that in the Heavens they have seen amongst us great righteous men, for they want us, with our lives to bring forgiveness upon the people of Israel. We must therefore repent now immediately, on this spot, for time is short. We must remember that we will surely sanctify His Name. Let us go with heads held high and let no imperfect thought enter it lest it blemish our sacrifice. We are now fulfilling the greatest commandment, to sanctify His Name. The fire which will consume our bones is the fire that will give birth again to the Jewish nation."

Thus they marched, the march of the holy, with pride and honor they went to bring forgiveness to the people of Israel, thirteen of the elders of Israel, and at their head the great holy Rabbi Elchanan Wasserman, were killed that day.

In the book, *Toldot Hadorot Haacharonim*, Friedner tells of an account related by a Jew who was saved from the gas chambers of Treblinka and who told the following to Chief Rabbi Herzog.

At the time that they led the Rebbe from Grodzhisk, along with thousands of other Jews, men, women, and children, to the gas ovens in one of the German death camps, the Rebbe asked for permission to say several words to the masses of Jews. The Rebbe began his remarks and said, "Brothers and sisters! One of our sages in the days of the Talmud said in his time, 'May he come but may we not see him.' Meaning may the Messiah come but may we not see him. That sage did not want to see with his own eyes the terrible suffering that the people of Israel would suffer before the Redeemer comes. However only he could permit himself to make such a request because he knew that the Redemption was still very distant. However, now, we are standing on the threshold of the Redemption. Now when we are washing and purifying the road before the Redeemer with our blood, at the time that we are purifying the people of Israel with our ashes so that they should be worthy to welcome the Righteous Messiah, now it is forbidden for us to make such a request. On the contrary, we have to view ourselves as fortunate that it has fallen to us to pave the road before the Redeemer who is on his way and to accept with love our binding for the sanctification of His Name, may He be blessed. Let us come, therefore, fellow Jews, and call out with joy, 'Hear O Israel'. Let us sing Ani Maamin, I Believe." And so it was. With an intense holiness they sang Ani Maamin. And with a song on their lips they went to the gas chambers.

The Jewish people fulfilled their part for the realization of the prophecy. They accepted with love the judgment of Hashem. And as the great rabbis foresaw, Hashem began to fulfill His share of the prophecy and extend His rule over the people of Israel.

PART IV

THE SUN RISES

16

"AND WITH THE CONSENT OF THE KINGS OF NATIONS"

In the thirteenth century the Ramban wrote in his commentary on "The Song of Songs" by King Solomon:

> And with the consent of the kings of the nations and with their help the Jewish people will go to Israel as it says in Isaiah Chapter 66, "And they will bring all your brothers etc." And the kingdom will continue and not cease forever.

In the grand design of Hashem for the Jewish people the time had come for the fulfillment of this prophecy. The Jews were to be redeemed from persecution with the consent of the nations of the world. The White Paper of 1939 was not to be—it would be a victim of the survivors of the Holocaust.

Events began to unfold that climaxed in the recreation of the Jewish national home.

Displaced Persons

On May 6, 1945, the Nazis were defeated. The victorious Allied armies liberated the concentration camps and the remnant of European Jewry were saved from destruction. The Holocaust was over. But with survival their problems did not end. They were now confronted with the question, where were they to go?

The Jews had lived in Eastern Europe for hundreds of years. They had lived through all manner of anti-Semitism and countless pogroms. Never were they shaken from the feeling that Europe was their home in exile. They prayed fervently for the Messiah, but in the meantime they were grateful to the Almighty that they had found a country that did not drive them out. They accepted the pogrom as the price they had to pay to be permitted to stay. They bowed their heads and hunched their backs and waited prayerfully for the storm to pass. And when the storm did pass, they gratefully thanked Hashem for His mercy and the countries of Europe for their kindness in permitting them to live in their land. They regarded the pogrom as the inevitable suffering of the exile.

But the Holocaust was not just another pogrom. The shattering experience of the Holocaust, which brought with it the almost complete annihilation of European Jewry, totally destroyed their feeling that Europe was their home, however temporary. How could they tread foot in lands that were the graveyards for their families? They could not go back to their former European countries. Where could they go?

They dreamed first of Palestine. And with the end of the war in Europe, Jews all over the world expected that the doors of Palestine would be opened to the survivors of the concentration camps. But that was not to be. The White Paper restrictions were not to be relaxed. They could not go to Palestine.

Even if they wanted to, most of them could not go to Great Britain or to the United States. Those countries had their own quotas restricting immigration. Most of the survivors neither wished to nor could go to America or Great Britain.

Where could they go?

Many of them chose to stay in the displaced persons camps that the Allies had set up in their zones. They hoped that somehow they would yet get to Palestine.

Many others did return to their former European homes. They hoped that they would see a new beginning, free from anti-Semitism. But they looked upon the prospect of peace with great uncertainty and viewed the future with hope mingled with fear. Their incredible fortitude in the face of the pogroms was gone.

With trepidation, the Jews began to come back to their former homes. But, as they feared, they were received with unconcealed hostility. Anti-Semitism was no less prevalent than it was before the Holocaust.

On February 1, 1946, the *Manchester Guardian* published a full report of the situation of the Jews still in Poland. The four headlines of the report read:

"Jews Still in Flight from Poland"
"Driven Abroad by Fear"
"Political Gangs out to Terrorize Them"
"Campaign of Murder and Robbery"

The newspaper reported that since the beginning of 1945 some 353 Jews had been murdered by Polish thugs. "Unfortunately," it added, "anti-Semitism is still prevalent in spite of the government efforts to counteract it. . . . Since the end of the war, ritual murder accusations have been made against Jews in Cracow and Rzeszow."

This hostility was directed not only at the Jews of Poland. It was repeated in Slovakia, in Germany, in Austria, and in most of the countries of Central and Eastern Europe. The mutterings "they should all have burnt" were heard in many countries.

Many Jews found the hostility unbearable and they left. They sought shelter in the displaced persons camps until they could somehow get to Palestine, the only place in the world they could see as home.

In the displaced persons camps to which the refugees turned, conditions were very difficult. In 1945, Earl O. Harrison was sent by President Truman to study the situation in the camps and report to him. In his report of July 1945, Harrison stated, "As matters now stand we appear to be treating the Jews as the Nazis treated them, except that we do not exterminate them." President Truman was alarmed by the report. He referred it to General Eisenhower, the Supreme Commander of the military forces in Europe, with instructions to act immediately to improve conditions in the camps.

President Truman also asked Prime Minister Attlee to allow 100,000 Jewish displaced persons to enter Palestine. Attlee replied by suggesting the appointment of a committee to study the entire Jewish problem. On November 13, 1945, an agreement was made between the United States and Great Britain to jointly investigate conditions in Eastern Europe and Palestine and to make recommendations on their findings to the British Mandatory Power.

The inquiry of the Anglo-American Committee began in December 1945 and ended in April 1946. In the book *Behind the Silken Curtain*, Bartley Crum, one of the members of the Anglo-American Committee, reports on his observations during the months of the study. In his visit to the DP camps in Frankfort, Germany he spoke to the Jews and he spoke to the military administration. He tells of a conversation he had with a spokesman of the Jewish displaced persons.

> I asked him, was there still anti-Semitism in Stuttgart? He smiled wryly, "I can only tell you that I myself heard Germans pass by our Jewish Community Center and say aloud, 'It is a shame that they did not burn all the Jews.'"

Another statement during the conversation was,

> "We receive ration cards like the Germans and stand in the same queues," he said. "Often when we reach our turn the merchant has no more rationed items to sell, but when we pass on we see that he has managed to find those items for the non-Jew behind us."

What the Jews used to look upon as expected and accepted discrimination they were no longer able to live with. The spectre of the tragedies of the Holocaust haunted them and they could not be soothed into believing that they need not fear any more.

Crum also states:

> Time and again witnesses told us, one way or another, "Yes, of course Hitler and the Nazis sought to exterminate us. Hitler made the plans, but it was the people of Europe, regardless of nationality, who were our executioners."

Most of the Jews saw no hope anywhere else but Palestine. He reports, "In one poll I was told the DPs were asked to put down a second choice if Palestine was unavailable and hundreds wrote 'crematorium'."

One of the visitors observed that it was disturbing to think that

Jews wished to leave Europe so completely and to build so separatist an existence. The displaced person answered,

> When we will have a nation in Palestine of two, three, or four million Jews, then the Jews in America and in the other countries will also have peace, because then the world will know that there is a Jewish State somewhere in the world.

The author concludes his visit to Europe with these words:

> It was evident to anyone who wanted to hear, to anyone who wanted to see, that no Jew facing the bitter realities of his position would dream of remaining in Central and Eastern Europe.

The committee published its report on May 1, 1946. Among its recommendations was the immediate grant of 100,000 immigration certificates to the Jewish survivors. The recommendation was not accepted by the British.

During 1945 and 1946 several thousand Jews a month left their European countries. On July 4, 1946, a pogrom in the city of Kielce in Poland shook the Jewish people. In a vicious outbreak, mobs attacked the Jews of Kielce; forty-two Jews were killed and many more were injured. A flood of refugees were released. The face of Europe was covered with thousands of wandering Jews trying to get to Palestine.

President Truman had established a policy in December 1945 in which the American Zone of Occupation was declared to be a "temporary haven for displaced Jews." It was estimated that the number of refugees would be 200,000 and the displaced persons camps in the American Zone were prepared to accept them.

Most of the refugees headed for the American Zone. It was to them a station along the way to Palestine. Others headed for the ports, hoping to become one of the "illegal" immigrants that the Haganah was bringing to Palestine.

Escape

In the face of the British refusal to relax restrictions on Jewish immigration, the yishuv in Palestine was filled with anger and resentment. They viewed the British policy as a betrayal of the Mandatory commitment. They refused to accept Britain's right to declare Jewish immigration illegal and determined to bring the immigrants to Palestine regardless of the will of the British.

Hundreds of thousands were in the DP camps and many thousands more were wandering through Europe, dreaming that they would somehow get to Palestine. The Jewish people of the yishuv were determined to help them realize their dream. To guide the refugees to Palestine they sent Bricha, or escape, workers whose mission was to help the refugees cross countries and climb mountains while avoiding the watchful eyes of the British.

Many of the refugees travelled through Czechoslovakia, which was a gathering point and a major crossing point for the refugees, especially for those fleeing from Poland. The trip was fraught with peril, but the refugees remained undaunted. Men, women, and children asked that they be placed in the first group to cross the mountains.

In the book *Sefer Hamaapilim*, edited by Moshe Basuk, the story is told of a mother who was to be left behind with her child, as her group prepared to climb up the Alps. She pleaded,

> Please do not delay my trip. All my children were killed by the Nazis except for my little five year old daughter Rachel. She is my whole world. I must go with her to Palestine. Believe me, I can climb mountains carrying her. With my finger nails I will hold on to the rocks and carry her.

The Bricha workers selected the routes of escape and also chose the people they would take on each trip. The guides feared that the whole group would be endangered if one would weaken and slow them down. Only after the group was inspected and declared fit did they start on the journey. But the desire to go was so strong that pregnant women often hid that fact and joined transports that had to climb mountains and go very long distances on foot to cross borders.

A Bricha worker tells of an incident that took place in the mountains between Poland and Czechoslovakia.

> In the beginning of June 1946 a group of thirty was climbing the mountains along the borders of Poland and Czechoslovakia.

The crossing of the mountains was very good in regard to avoiding the Polish border guards. But physically it was very difficult. We had to climb very steep mountains and travel great distances on foot.

This time, as always, the leaders of the group had gone through the regular procedure and they were certain that everyone in the group was healthy and able to withstand the rigors of the trip. But we soon found out that it was not so.

The group was on the steepest point of the mountain, where it was necessary for each member to extend his hand to his friend to help him scramble over the rocks and boulders. This was about 20 miles from Poland but still in the no-man's land between the borders of Poland and Czechoslovakia. Suddenly the screams of a woman were heard, a woman giving birth. In a few moments a boy was born and his cries reverberated through the fields. There was no time for questions to find out why she had lied about her pregnancy. There was only one thing to do, to run to the nearest Czech village to get a sled for the mother and the infant and to bring them to the home of a peasant in the village.

The leader of the group wondered how she could have hidden her condition from him. There had been inspection of the entire group the night they were getting ready to leave.

When the leader came to visit her in the house of the peasant he told her that he wasn't angry with her, only curious about how she managed to get away with the deception. She said, "It was very simple. I sent my younger sister for line-up and inspection. And in the hours after midnight when we were getting ready to leave I took her place and nobody noticed."

The escape through Czechoslovakia was not legal. But not only did the Czechs not interfere, they assisted the refugees to make their way safely through Czechoslovakia to their next destination.

A report by the Ministry of Social Welfare in Czechoslovakia describes its activities concerning the Jewish refugees for the year 1946.

> Jewish refugees are coming into Czechoslovakia from Poland, Hungary, and Romania. Their direction is towards Germany and Austria by way of Czechoslovakia, but their real goal is

Palestine or the countries across the oceans. Altogether in the year 1946, in the points of Nahoud Dianska to Novourus, 71,046 people were transported with special trains. Since the beginning of the works 209,697 were transported through Czechoslovakia. The expenses amounted to 52,406,750 crown.

Their next destination was Vienna, the city that played the greatest part in the escape. More people passed through this city than any other.

The stream to Vienna came from the Rumanian and Hungarian borders bringing the Jews of these nations, and from the Czech border bringing the Jews of Poland. There the workers of the Joint and of the Bricha received them and provided temporary shelter, gave them food, and sent them on their way. From 1945 to 1949 more than 200,000 Jews escaped through Vienna.

Most of the refugees who passed through Vienna went on to Salzburg, the capital city of the American Occupation Zone of Austria. Salzburg was the crossroads. There the refugee had three choices. He could remain in one of the camps of the American Zone of Austria and wait; he could travel to one of the camps around Munich in the American Zone of Germany and wait; or he could try to get to Italy and hope that he would not have to wait too long to board a ship to Palestine.

The way to Italy led from Salfelden in the American Zone of Austria over the Alps directly into Italy, or from there to Innsbruck in the French Zone of Austria over the Alps into Italy.

The journey to Italy was full of great hazards. Everywhere the British patrols were active and alert. The refugees had to go on foot from the borders of Austria and Germany through the snowy, treacherous Alps, and they had to use the most hazardous routes to avoid the patrols of the British or of some other Allied unit.

In the book *Sefer Hamaapilim* a Bricha worker tells of the efforts of the Bricha to find routes across the mountains undetected by the patrols.

Because of the pressure of the British upon the Italian authorities the Bricha had to open new points to cross the borders of Italy. The passages through the Alps were few and known to the British. We were compelled to find unknown paths through the Alps.

After much inspection of maps and many scouting trips on the mountains, we chose a certain village near the Austrian border, where we would set up a "trial" station. The choice was not ideal. Most of the months of the year the mountain paths were closed by the snow. The few paths we found were blocked by strong water-falls. We had no choice but to erect temporary "bridges" over the falls. Even after we decided to lead the refugees through the mountains, our hearts were full of doubts. Are we allowed to imperil the lives of old men, women, and children by leading them across these steep mountains, deep valleys, and high snow? Our doubts were deepened by the fact that the traveling usually took place at night.

The most difficult problem was, where were we to get a house to shelter all the refugees who would be coming to us. As we scouted the place we found that an Italian police unit was stationed there. All around there were uniformed men of all descriptions, Italian police, border guards, customs guards. We decided to add a group wearing another uniform, "American uniforms." At midnight we all arrived at the selected location wearing American uniforms. We were stopped many times by guards who immediately saluted when they saw our uniforms. And after distributing American cigarettes we were given information about the condition of the roads. We rented two rooms in an inn in the mountains. The officer in charge of security in the area appeared sleepy-eyed and asked us the purpose of our stay. We informed him that our purpose was to establish a convalescent home for the people attached to the American camps in the area.

Thus we established our station in the Alps, 2,500 feet up. The transports of Jews were brought to the "Convalescent Home" in the mountains as "Convalescing American Officers." We became very friendly with the officers and the heads of the Carbineri. At night when we had to move the transports we held parties. We even engaged musicians to entertain our friends among the soldiers and the peasants of the village. Some of our group took part in the party while the other members of our group took care of the refugees.

With incredible determination many Jews escaped into Italy. But the pressures of the British were relentless and many did not get through.

A British newspaperman tells of such an incident that took place in the middle of 1947.

> Two hundred and sixteen Jews crossed the borders from Austria into the beautiful little town of Merano at the foot of the Austrian Alps. They were going to Palestine. They had drifted here in small parties, never more than six. Sixteen women were with them and nine children. Some had crossed the Alps at almost inaccessible spots, climbing over ice-covered rocks 8,000 feet up. At Merano, Italian police rounded them up—the first time Italy had stopped a march of Jews. And tonight, 215 of the Jews have gone back to Austria in lorries and under guard. The 216th, Abraham Schutzman of Vienna, is in a Merano Hospital. He said, "Another Jew and I started out on an 80 mile walk from Innsbruck. Five days and nights we spent on the Alps seeking to get into Italy and avoid the frontier guards. I hoped to reach Genoa last Friday. I was told that friends would get me aboard a ship there for Palestine. If I am sent back to Austria I will try again."

The British were determined to prevent the refugees from settling in Palestine. They hounded the immigrants every step of the way, trying to turn them back. They tracked them through Europe, scouted their boats, stopped them before they could dock. They boarded the boats and took off the passengers, peacefully or forcefully. And many of the boats were turned back to Europe.

In the book *Illegal Immigrants Cross the Seas*, one of the immigrants who made it from Italy to Palestine describes the feelings of the refugees who participated in the escape.

> We escaped through Czechoslovakia, through the plains of Hungary, through the snow-covered mountains of the Alps, and through the sun-drenched land of Italy. We crossed borders and wire fences. The darkness of the night covered us, we disguised ourselves in various ways, we used every means to get to the sea ports from where we could go to the Promised Land.
>
> We know that many long days of waiting are ahead of us. Days of wandering in strange ports will be our lot before we reach the

miraculous day when we take our first step towards Aliyah. We surely will sail in a small boat, one of those boats which sail the seas with assumed names and strange flags. Many days we will sit crowded below the decks, and the stink of the rats and the salt water will choke our throats. The British birds of prey will follow us threateningly. But the hour will come, and through the dark clouds we will see the harbors of Palestine. And our eyes, red from sleepless nights, will be fixed upon the shores of the Promised Land and our hearts will beat.

Across the Sea

Most of the boats that they boarded failed to elude the British. However, a number succeeded in bringing their passengers into Palestine.

In the six months from the end of the war to the end of 1945 about a dozen schooners, none over 250 tons, brought about 4,400 illegal immigrants to Palestine.

One of the little boats crowded with immigrants was the Greek fishing vessel *Demetrius*, renamed the *Berl Katzenelson*.

The following is the account of its arrival in Palestine, as described in the book *Sefer Hamaapilim*.

> From the waters of Herzliah a boat was seen approaching in the darkness. Row boats, which were waiting in the port, went towards the boat which bore the name *Berl Katzenelson* (formerly *Demetrius*) and took aboard about 200 illegal immigrants who had come from various European countries. As soon as they came on shore they were transferred to vehicles in which they were taken to various places. The newly arrived were welcomed joyfully.
>
> Before all of the passengers were landed on shore, a British destroyer was seen approaching the ship which was anchored a short distance from the dock. It is reported that naval airplanes had discovered the boat with their radar and had informed the warship of the landing of the immigrants. Arab fishing boats were drifting near the docks. Police boats from Jaffa port arrived and held two of the boats with twelve men. It found that these men were citizens of Palestine and that they had fishing permits. The fishermen were brought to Jaffa for interrogation

and were then taken to Latrun. They are charged with aiding illegal immigrants.

In December 1945 the *Hannah Senesh* discharged its load of passengers in the port of Nahariah. The following is a description of its arrival.

> The sea had no mercy on the little boat. A powerful storm shook it, raised it up to the tops of the high waves, and threw her down. The ship held fast, even though the storm was unusually fierce. The passengers were not used to the rolling waves, and all of them without exception became seasick. However, they were all used to storms, perils, and wanderings, and their spirit held fast. The boat came close to the port, tossing in the storming waves. As the boat drew closer a current grabbed it, raised it high, and hurled it tens of meters forward. The boat landed on a reef. The roaring motors tried to move it. The boat shook, and dug deeper into the sand.
> A row boat which was lowered from the ship immediately turned over, one of the passengers was almost drowned, and the man who saved her almost drowned. One of the sailors almost lost his life. A second boat also filled with water. The rope between the dock and the boat broke. For a few moments and maybe for about a quarter of an hour, it seemed as though all hope was lost.
> And then a way was found, a rope was wound in another rope, and the boat was tied to the dock. Boys and girls stood in the icy waters in the darkness in the stormy sea, and directed the immigrants to the shore. Some came to the shore hanging with both hands from the rope as though they always went from place to place this way. Some hung and held the ropes with their hands and feet, and some didn't have the strength and jumped into the water. But, quick hands, the hands of brothers, pulled them out and passed them on to the second, to the third, until they reached the shore.
> More than one salty hot tear fell into the salty cold waters of the sea. Tears of happiness, the happiness of the one who had the greatest privilege in the world, to extend a helping hand to save a brother.

In this way some immigrants were able to come to Palestine. And as time went on, a growing number of immigrants managed to get past the British. These were the totals released by the British for the six-month period starting December 1945: In December 1945, 252 immigrants came; in January 1946, 911; in February, 15; in March, 973; in April, 90; in May, 1,662; in June, 1,745; and in July, 3,800.

With the swelling number of immigrants, Britain took added steps to discourage the immigration. On August 12, Britain announced this new policy: "Immigrants arriving illegally will henceforward be conveyed to Cyprus or elsewhere and housed in camps there until a decision can be taken as to their future."

On August 12, 1946, the vessel *Yagur* with 758 illegal immigrants aboard, and the *Henrietta Szold* with 540 immigrants, including 200 children, were caught and brought into Haifa harbor.

There, anchored in Haifa harbor and waiting for the boats to dock, were two large British ships, the *Empire Rival* and the *Empire Haywood.* Strung along the decks of the two ships were wire fences.

One of the immigrants aboard the *Yagur* describes what took place upon the arrival of the boats to the waters of Palestine.

> Thirteen days our illegal boat the *Yagur* sailed over great oceans, and it was as though nobody noticed us. But on the 13th day of our voyage an airplane suddenly appeared and we were discovered. The plane circled over us and not only did we not go down from the deck, we jumped up higher and higher. Our Hebrew flag was raised up, and the song Hatikvah burst from the lips of all of us standing crowded on the deck. And the plane circled overhead. . . .
>
> Our boat was coming closer to the shore when suddenly we noticed that we had escorts, two destroyers were following us.
>
> Suddenly the destroyers came close and called to our boat to stop. In a second, British sailors jumped on our deck. They tied the boat, surrounded the captain and his crew, pulled the boat close to the port, threw down the anchor, placed a guard of Arab police over us, and left. Night passed and then morning and around us all was quiet.

Towards noon a destroyer appeared, pulling another immigrant boat. It drew near to our boat and we saw on its deck hundreds of people and many, many children. This was the children's boat *Henrietta Szold*.

We all went over to one end of the deck so that we could get closer to the children in our sister ship. At that moment we forgot our suffering and our hunger, and without any instructions, the men began to give everything they had to the people of the *Henrietta Szold*. Every drop of water, chocolate bars, boxes of food were passed over there. The faces of the children showed the suffering they had gone through in their voyage across the sea. When the feeling spread that we would be chased from the land, we could not believe that they too, the children, would be sent away.

Soon from the ship there came a voice over a loudspeaker saying in Hebrew, "You are requested to go to the ship in order. It is a good ship, not crowded, good sanitary conditions. You will be given food and water and medical care. You can go according to families." There was not a word about us being chased away or what would be done with us. But the lines of wire which rose from the ship told wordlessly of the deceit. We all cried out, "We already heard words like this in Auschwitz. We don't believe you. We won't go!"

Again the voice called asking us to cross over to the ship. And again the voice was answered with cries of scorn. Everyone began to sing Hatikvah, and then sang songs of the ghetto and songs of the Partisans, powerful and deep singing burst from the hearts of all of us. I can not remember ever hearing singing like that. The soldiers stood quietly, listened to the singing and did not try to board our boat. But when they saw that time was passing and no one was moving, they jumped up on deck. At first they acted gently. But when we refused to come they began to get rough. Pregnant women were lying on boards on the deck. They grabbed the women by the hair and began to drag them. When this did not help, four at a time grabbed a woman, one by a hand and another by a leg, and they dragged her across the deck. We ran down below deck. We searched for things to throw at them but we could hardly find any thing. The soldiers bent down, grabbed someone by the hair and pulled up, while we grabbed the person and pulled him down. We were almost tearing the person apart. We succeeded in pulling many of our friends away from the soldiers.

When they saw that this would not work, they brought hoses of water and turned them upon us. This also did not work. Then they took the boards out and came after us. Their strength was greater than ours. We were weak and tired from the long trip. We did not go quietly. We fought. We did not surrender easily.

Action and Reaction

The war of Great Britain against the Holocaust survivors created shock waves in and out of Palestine. In Great Britain opposition mounted against what was seen as a hopeless and costly British policy. In the United States there were vociferous protests against Great Britain's policy restricting immigration. World opinion was aghast at the repressive measures the British were taking against the refugees.

In Palestine sporadic incidents of terror and reprisal had been taking place since 1945. On December 27, 1945, British police headquarters in Jaffa was destroyed by a bomb. In Tel Aviv a British corporal was slain in an attack on an arms depot by fifty men. The British responded by arresting between 1,500 and 2,000 persons and deporting fifty-two men to Eritrea.

But as the measures against immigration increased, violence escalated. On June 10, 1946, three trains were derailed and blown up between Jaffa and Jerusalem. On June 16, eleven bridges were blown up. On June 17, railway workshops near Haifa were blown up and set afire. On June 18, five British officers were kidnapped in Tel Aviv.

One of the most costly of these acts of violence took place on July 22, 1946, when terrorists' explosives damaged the King David Hotel. The seven-floor building was the seat of British Military Headquarters in Palestine and contained the Mandatory Government Secretariat. According to the official announcement, the victims totalled ninety-one dead and forty-five injured.

On October 4, 1946, President Truman cabled Prime Minister Attlee, again urging that substantial immigration of Jewish displaced persons in Europe begin at once. The cable read,

In the light of the terrible ordeal which the Jewish people of Europe endured in the recent war and the crisis now existing, I cannot believe that a program of immediate action along the lines suggested above could not be worked out with the cooperation of all concerned.

Terrorism and reprisal continued in Palestine with no one able to stop the bloodshed. The Jewish Agency tried over and over again to halt the terrorism, but with no success. On December 4, 1946, the agency called for "the immediate end of these activities." They called the attention of the entire yishuv to the "grave dangers and disasters that threaten it if the terror and outrages of these isolated groups do not immediately cease."

But extremist terrorism continued unabated. On January 26, 1947, terrorists kidnapped Major Collins, a banker and retired British military officer. On January 27, the terrorists kidnapped Ralph Windheim, chief judge of the Tel Aviv District Court.

On January 31, 1947, in a debate in the British House of Commons, Labor members joined in the opposition against British policy. Labor member Richard Crossman said, "We should appreciate the position of the Moderate Jew in Palestine. He is between the devil and the deep sea. . . . Ruthless measures of repression without a policy will produce war in Palestine. The Mandate is unworkable."

Barnett Janner, another Laborite, agreed that the government had tried everything possible to combat terrorism and to keep order. But he expressed doubt that this goal could be achieved merely by military action. If immigration into Palestine were available to more displaced persons from Europe, terrorism would fail as a policy and cease almost at once, he asserted.

Winston Churchill, leader of the opposition, summed up the Conservative opinion:

> We have not fulfilled our promises, made at the election, and having found ourselves unable to carry out our policy, we have no right to stay there for motives of policy. It is said we must stay because, if we go, there will be civil war. I think it very likely. But is that a reason why we should stay? The responsibility for stopping civil war in Palestine ought to be borne by the United Nations and not by this overburdened country. . . . We

really cannot go about in all directions taking on burdens which drain the strength of Britain.

In the face of the mounting opposition in Great Britain and in the United States to the British policy, and in the face of the mounting bloodshed in Palestine, the hopelessness of their policy was becoming increasingly evident to the British.
On February 18, 1947, the British government asked United Nations Secretary General Trygve Lie to summon as soon as possible a special session of the General Assembly "for the purpose of constituting and instructing a special committee to prepare for the consideration of the problem of Palestine."
On May 13, 1947, the United Nations Political and Security Committee voted 13–11 to set up the United Nations Special Committee on Palestine. An eleven-member committee was immediately created and began its study of the entire Jewish situation.

UNSCOP

Jorge Garcia Granados was one of the members appointed to the United Nations Special Committee on Palestine. In his book, *The Birth of Israel*, he relates the things he and the committee discovered during the months of study.

Their first stop was Palestine. On the day that the committee began its first official duties in Palestine, they found tensions in the yishuv at a feverish pitch. That day three members of the Jewish underground who had participated in the Acre Prison break were to be sentenced to death. In this incident 100–150 armed men breached the walls of the prison and the prisoners escaped. Three Jewish attackers were killed and one British constable was injured.

Granados describes the emotional scenes at the trial and writes, "The news that the three were to be hanged for a deed which elsewhere in the world would have meant a prison sentence was certain to have serious repercussions."

The committee learned very quickly about the cycle of terror and reprisal that gripped Palestine.

They learned of the repressive measures the British had instituted against the yishuv. In an interview with the attorney for the young men they learned that under British regulation a person could be detained by any soldier or constable and held for years without trial. The prisoners arrested were tried before military courts, without the right of appeal.

Granados declared, "Palestine was a Police State in the most tragic sense of the word."

Before the committee left Palestine, they came face-to-face with the issue at the root of the confrontation, the issue of Jewish immigration to Palestine. The committee was there when the *Exodus* arrived from the displaced persons camps of Europe with 4,500 Jewish refugees.

Granados writes,

> An event occurred which brought the temper of the Jewish population to its highest pitch in many months and left the most neutral observer convinced of the brutality and illegality of the course Britain had adopted toward Jewish immigration.
>
> One morning word came that the *Exodus* had been intercepted off the shore of Palestine, boarded by British sailors, and after a violent battle brought under arms into Haifa.

The members of the Committee were appalled by the accounts they heard of the violence the British had used against the immigrants, who fought the blazing guns of the British with potatoes, canned goods, and their bare hands.

He continues,

> The story of the *Exodus* was to grow more tragic in the days that followed; for the refugees were not sent to Cyprus, but by a British decision which must go down as one of the most heartless and stubborn ever made by a civilized government, were returned to Germany, the country of Jewish death and horror.

The next stop of the committee was the displaced persons camps of Europe. It did not take long for them to be convinced that the Jews could not live in Europe.

In an interview with Rabbi Philip Bernstein, advisor on Jewish affairs to the United States Army, they were told, "Gentlemen, if the United States Army were to withdraw tomorrow, there would be pogroms the following day."

The committee visited Vienna, the stopping point for thousands of Jews wandering through Europe. There they visited the Rothschild Hospital, which was once a famous hospital and had become the main center for the housing of the refugees in Vienna.

Dr. Garcia Granados describes the Rothschild Hospital at the time of his visit in 1947:

> Little by little as we began slowly to explore this incredible building, it dawned upon me that I was in the presence of one of the great shames of modern times. We began with what had once been a hospital ward. Beds placed head to feet almost completely filled the room and where there were no beds there were cots and mattresses. There was no place for people to stand and so all of them either sat or lay on their beds.
>
> We moved through other rooms in which every possible inch of space was similarly taken by cots and mattresses occupied by men, women, and children. Some lay on the floor.
>
> Hundreds of people swarmed in the corridors. I could scarcely push my way through. In the courtyards hundreds more men and women were camping. There was no room for them inside. Wherever I looked men, women, and children were sitting or trying to sleep curled up on the earth. I descended to the basement of the hospital. It had been divided into large windowless rooms. After our eyes became accustomed to the gloom, we realized there were scores of people lying there. Huge pipes, part of the water system, crisscrossed the ceiling, and from them clothes were spread to dry.
>
> The heavy odor seemed to permeate my being. I felt I was going to be sick .... By a tremendous effort I pushed my way through the people to the door. There I found the Iranian alternate Dr. Ali Ardelan. His face was haggard. He said in a trembling voice, "This is a crime against humanity. I never thought I would witness anything like this." I crossed the doorway and ran to a window opening on the courtyard. I remained there for two or three full minutes breathing deeply, and sick at heart for all mankind.

After months of study the committee arrived at its decision, recommending that Palestine be partitioned into an independent Jewish state and an independent Arab state.

On November 29, the recommendation of the committee was voted on by the General Assembly. In an unusual demonstration of agreement between the United States and the Soviet Union, the General Assembly passed the resolution with the required two-thirds vote. The vote was 32 for, 13 against, with 11 abstentions. With the consent of the kings of nations, the Jewish people were given permission to return to their land.

The state was to come into being when the British handed over the Mandate to the United Nations. The British informed the United Nations that they would terminate the Mandate on May 15, 1948, and the Jewish people would then be free to take over.

But the enemies of the Jewish people did not give up so easily. War broke out between the Arabs and the Jews in Palestine. The British and members of the United States delegation in the United Nations cited the disorders in Palestine as proof that the vote of the General Assembly should be repealed. They began to push for a United Nations Trusteeship in Palestine.

The debates in the United Nations continued while the days passed, coming closer and closer to May 15. On May 14, in New York, in the middle of the debate on a United Nations Trusteeship for Palestine, the news spread through the chambers of the United Nations: the government of Palestine had proclaimed its independence, and the United States had recognized the Provisional Government as the de facto authority of the new State of Israel.

Other nations followed soon after.

On May 15, the British handed over the authority to the government of the State of Israel. All restrictions on immigration ended. The Jewish people were free to return to the land of Israel.

17

FREEDOM FROM OPPRESSION

The United Nations vote for the establishment of a Jewish state in part of Palestine was received with great emotion by both Jew and Arab. The Jews all over the world danced and sang in the streets. But the Arabs angrily rejected partition and vowed that they would never permit a Jewish state to exist in Palestine, no matter how small.

And they did not wait to carry out their threats.

The day after the United Nations vote, a bus carrying Jewish passengers was attacked by rifle fire on the road from Netanya to Jerusalem and five passengers were killed. A number of Jews were killed in Haifa, snipers harassed passers-by in Tel Aviv, stores were looted and shopkeepers slain in Jerusalem. A three-day general strike was called by the Arabs. The Undeclared War had begun.

And for all of this, there was no help for the Jews from any source. Great Britain, which held the Mandate, stated that it would remain neutral. Riots took place, with the British police standing by and making no move to intervene. The only step the British took was to disarm the Jews. They blocked all arms shipments to the Jewish defenders.

The British refused to permit any other power into Palestine as long as they held the Mandate. Therefore, the United Nations did not attempt to place any force between the Arabs and the Jews. The United States was unable to help. No power felt able to control the riots. The Jewish people were left to their own resources.

But the Jewish people who for centuries had suffered persecution with passive acceptance no longer accepted the role of helpless victim. They fought with courage and fury.

The 650,000 Jews of Palestine found an Arab enemy inside and outside Palestine that far outnumbered them in men and equipment. The Arab population inside Palestine numbered 1,200,000. They were augmented by Arab "irregulars" mobilized by the neighboring Arab nations. These armies were made up of "volunteers" who moved freely across the borders to join in the attacks against Jewish settlements.

The Arab attacks consisted of three parts—terror attacks in the cities, attacks on isolated settlements, and blocking of the vital roads.

The Arabs mounted attacks against the settlements of Kfar Etzion, Yechiam, and Tirat Tzvi. In all cases the defenders held their positions and the Arab forces were forced to withdraw.

Parallel to these attacks on the settlements, the Arabs intensified their terrorist attacks in the cities. They spread death and destruction in the main cities, especially in Jerusalem.

The main Arab effort was directed towards disrupting the Jewish lines of communication, and they succeeded in cutting a number of main axes throughout the country. By the end of March 1948 the Jewish settlements in the Negev and the Etzion bloc of settlements had been completely cut off, and the roads between Jerusalem and the coast were under heavy fire. For the first three months of this period the situation looked hopeless. The Arabs were attacking all over Palestine.

But slowly and dramatically the tide turned. In April the Arabs besieged the settlement of Mishmar Haemek in an attempt to cut off the communication between Tel Aviv and Haifa. If Mishmar Haemek fell, Haifa would be isolated. An Arab force of over a thousand men supported by artillery attacked the settlement. For days and nights the battle raged, but the Jewish fighters prevailed and the Arab attackers withdrew.

At the same time Arab forces attacked the settlement Ramat Yochanan. For two days the battle raged. Then the Arab lines broke and they withdrew—the Arab attempt to isolate Haifa had failed.

The Jewish forces went over to the attack. In mid-April they captured the city of Tiberius. On April 21 the Haganah mounted an attack to capture the Arab section of Haifa and succeeded in cutting Arab Haifa into three parts. The Arab commander of the city fled to Beirut, the Arabs of the city surrendered, and the Jewish forces occupied all of Haifa.

Safad was vital to maintain the Jewish position in the Galilee in the face of the imminent Arab invasion. On April 30 the Haganah launched an attack on Safad and on May 15 it fell into Jewish hands.

At the end of April the Haganah attacked Acre. On May 17 the city fell to the forces of Israel.

The city of Jaffa, which was adjacent to and a continuation of the city of Tel Aviv, was assigned to the Arabs in the United Nations Partition Resolution. The Jewish armies refrained from attacking the city. But the Arabs of Jaffa were constantly attacking and sniping at Tel Aviv. On April 25, the Irgun attacked Jaffa and, with limited Haganah support, cut Jaffa in half; the city surrendered.

An astonishing effect of this phase of the Arab-Israeli conflict was the mass evacuation by the Arabs from most of Israel. Many left because they were certain they would defeat the Jews. And many left because they feared being defeated by the Jews.

The Arab leadership sent an uninterrupted flood of propaganda to the Palestinian Arabs urging them to leave the country. An appeal was constantly rebroadcast over Radio Cairo from March 18 to 24, declaring:

> We shall drive the criminal Zionists into the sea. Not one Jew will be left in Palestine. In order that our victorious armies may accomplish their holy mission without the risk of harming our Arab brothers the latter must leave the country for a while so that our fighting forces will have complete freedom to carry out their mission of extermination.

The constant urging by the Arab leadership and the victories of the Jewish armies precipitated mass evacuations. It all began with the battle for Tiberius. The Haganah cut the city in two and isolated the Arab population—the Arabs chose to evacuate the city.

In the battle for Haifa, after the Jewish forces cut Arab Haifa into three parts, they demanded the surrender of the Arabs. At the same time they urged the Arabs to remain and continue to live peacefully in the city.

In the book *Arab Israeli Wars*, Chaim Herzog describes the Arab response.

> Major General Hugh Stockwell, commander of the British 6th Airborne Division, convened a meeting of the Arab and Jewish notables of the city. . . . The Arabs went into caucus and were subjected to the urging of the representatives of the Mufti and of Kaukji, who advised them that an Arab military invasion was imminent, that the Jews would be wiped out and that their property would be fair game for the Arab population. They could return after the Jews had been driven out. Following the Arab decision, the Jewish Mayor addressed them movingly, and promised them that they could continue to live side-by-side with their Jewish neighbors; but the Arab leaders persisted. General Stockwell and some of the leading Arab citizens also attempted to dissuade them, but again these efforts were unsuccessful. A five day truce was arranged and a mass evacuation began. Out of an Arab population of 100,000 only a few thousand Arabs opted to remain in Haifa.

When the city of Jaffa was defeated, the bulk of the Arab population fled. Only a few thousand remained of its former 70,000 inhabitants. The same took place after the Arab defeat at Safad, where there was a mass Arab evacuation from the city. The same pattern was repeated in most cities. When the Arabs faced defeat they decided to take advantage of the presence of the British forces and left under their protection. These evacuations reduced the Arab population in the Jewish section of partitioned Palestine from 700,000 to about 150,000.

In spite of these successes the situation of the Jewish people was still deeply troubled. In May the Etzion bloc of settlements fell into the hands of the Arabs after holding out heroically for several months. Jerusalem was under siege by the Arab Legion—the city was being pounded with artillery, and food and supplies were very low. The siege of Jerusalem was a cause of deep concern.

The nations of the world viewed the situation in Palestine with alarm. They feared that the new Jewish state would not be able to withstand the onslaught of the Arab armies poised to invade as soon as the British left. But on May 14, 1948, the Jewish state bravely proclaimed its independence. And on May 15 the armies of five Arab countries invaded the new State of Israel.

Independence and Invasion

The day of the invasion was a day of celebration in the surrounding Arab countries. The armies were sent off with wild cheers and clapping from the crowds. The troops themselves were jubilant because they expected to return victorious in two weeks.

The armies came from Lebanon, Syria, Transjordan, Iraq, and Egypt. In addition the Arabs fielded two armies of irregulars, the Arab Liberation Army and the Moslem Brotherhood.

The Arab armies had many more resources than the Jewish defenders of Israel. Not only did they outnumber the Jewish army, their equipment was vastly superior—they had tanks, planes, and artillery. The Jewish armies faced them with a limited number of light weapons, a few ancient pieces of artillery, and several small planes.

The Syrians invaded from the north. Their first goal was to control the entire Galilee by linking up with the Arab city of Nazareth. From that vantage point, they would have a firm jumping-off ground to move to Haifa. Only several settlements with small numbers of defenders stood in the way.

They massed tanks, armored cars, and artillery and moved against the settlements of Degania A and B. But the settlements repulsed attack after attack. Several days later the Syrians withdrew and made no further attempt to drive south.

The Degania victory had an electrifying effect on the whole of the Jewish population of Israel. The morale of the Israeli defenders was lifted enormously.

The Syrian army turned its attention to the north, making a major effort to capture the settlement of Ein Gev. Here a small number of about 100 ill-equipped defenders held off the Syrian Army with its armor and artillery.

Meanwhile the Arab Liberation Army, also operating from the northern front, made an all-out effort to capture the village of Sejera. After bitter fighting the Arabs broke and withdrew. In all their campaigns until the first truce the Arab Liberation Army scored no victories.

The Lebanese army played only a limited role in the invasion. They attacked and captured the lightly held village of Malkiya. But when they attempted to continue their march and attack the settlement of Ramat Naftali, they were beaten back. They were content with their capture of Malkiya and gave up active military participation.

Simultaneously with the Syrian invasion in the north, the Iraqi army crossed the Jordan farther south. After bitter fighting for the town of Jenin, which the Iraqi army took, and after unsuccessful attacks on the settlements around it, the Iraqis gave up their plans for offensive action until the end of the war.

The Egyptians invaded from the south. They were supplemented by the irregular army known as the Moslem Brotherhood.

The Egyptian army envisaged a quick march to the approaches of Tel Aviv and Jerusalem. Along the route they found that the settlement of Kfar Darom posed a threat to their communications and they attacked the isolated Jewish village. But an assault by tanks and artillery was beaten back by the thirty defenders, with heavy Egyptian losses. The Egyptians did not continue their attack.

The Egyptians also mounted an attack on the village of Nirim. Here a group of forty-five defenders succeeded in beating back an Egyptian assault, causing heavy losses. The Egyptians did not continue this assault.

The Egyptians decided to push along the highway to the center of the country and bypass the settlements. But they could not ignore the settlement of Yad Mordecai, situated on the Gaza-Ashkelon highway, which blocked the Egyptian advance northwards.

For five days the settlers held off the main Egyptian forces. Fierce battles raged for days until the Egyptian army finally overcame the heroic resisters. But very valuable time was gained by the Israeli army, which was now prepared for the invaders and stopped the Egyptian advance before Tel Aviv.

The Arab Legion of Transjordan, trained and led by British officers, had as its mission the capture of Jerusalem and the area surrounding the Holy City.

At the time of the invasion the town of Latrun, blocking the road to Jerusalem, was held by the Arab Liberation Army. Latrun was turned over to the Arab Legion.

The Legion directed a major thrust against the Jewish Quarter of the Old City. Most of the Old City was inhabited by the Arabs. The Jews, isolated in the Jewish Quarter, were besieged by the Arab Legion; the Haganah fought gallantly to lift the siege. At one point they succeeded in breaking into the city but they could not maintain their position in the face of savage counterattacks and so were forced to withdraw. The Jewish Quarter was once again besieged. The defenders fought valiantly. After desperate hand-to-hand fighting in the narrow alleys, the Arab Legion captured the Old City of Jerusalem.

The Arab Legion then tried to bring about the fall of the New City of Jerusalem by tightening its hold on the Jerusalem road, especially around Latrun. But the Haganah succeeded in building a road through a mountainous, seemingly impassable area. This road, which was known as the "Burma Road," became the lifeline for the Jews in Jerusalem. The siege of Jerusalem was lifted. The next day the United Nations cease-fire came into effect.

The first twenty-eight days of fighting leading up to the first truce were marked by Arab offensives. In spite of the Arab initiative, they had captured very little. None of the invading armies had accomplished their major objective.

When the first phase of the fighting ended the Israeli defenders had succeeded in blocking the Arab invasion on all fronts. They had blocked the Arab invasion by way of the Galilee. The Egyptian army was unable to take Tel Aviv. And though the Arab Legion held the Old City of Jerusalem, the New City of Jerusalem held out against the Legion. When the truce ended ten days later, the Jewish army, aided by arms purchased abroad, was ready to take over the offensive.

The second phase of fighting lasted ten days, until the United Nations established a second truce. During these ten days the Israeli Army mounted an offensive against the Arab Legion aimed at taking the cities of Lod and Ramle to relieve Jerusalem and remove the threat to Tel Aviv. The offensive succeeded and the Israeli forces captured Lod and Ramle. When the ten days of fighting ended the situation of the Israeli forces was considerably improved. The second truce saw the tide of battle swinging to the Jews.

Several months later, the fighting resumed. In a battle for Tarshisha the Israeli Army defeated the Arab Liberation Army decisively and the remnants were either taken as prisoners or driven out of the Galilee.

The Arab Liberation Army ceased to exist as a force. The Israeli Army retook Malkiya from the Lebanese Army and the forces of Lebanon ceased to threaten Israel. For all practical purposes the war in the north had ended.

In the south, fierce fighting continued between the Israelis and the Egyptians. Haleqat, which was a key to the Negev, was the scene of a very crucial battle. In the fight for Haleqat the Israeli Army defeated the Egyptians and opened the road to the Negev. They then moved against Beersheba and took the city. The fortress of Iraq Suedan, which had resisted many attacks, was taken by the Israelis. After the Israeli Army defeated the Egyptians at El-Auja, the entire Beersheba-Auja road was in Israel's hands. The Egyptian government then entered into negotiations for an armistice agreement.

The armistice agreement with Egypt was signed on the island of Rhodes on February 24, 1949. An armistice with Lebanon followed on March 23, 1949.

The Israelis knew that the positions held at the time of the armistice negotiations would determine the final boundaries of Israel. They decided to consolidate and expand their positions in the Negev before the armistice agreement with Jordan, which had some military control of the Negev. In March, before the armistice with Jordan, they succeeded in taking Eilat. On April 3 the armistice agreement was signed with Jordan and the shooting war was over.

On April 11 the new State of Israel was accepted into the United Nations.

The armistice with Syria was signed on July 20.

After twenty months, from the time of the United Nations vote for partition to the cease-fire, the Jewish people emerged with a new image in the eyes of the world and in their own eyes.

The Jewish people did not live any longer in the sad realities of the liturgy, which described them as "the ridicule and derision of the nations, viewed as a lamb led to slaughter." No longer were they a homeless people—the whole world had consented to return them to their land. No longer were they thrust upon the mercy of the world—they had fought for their survival alone, against all odds, and prevailed. No longer were they ridiculed—they were viewed with respect, even admiration. No longer were they oppressed—in their own home no one would belittle them.

Their image in the eyes of the world was of a brave and resourceful people. Their image in their own eyes was of a proud and vibrant people. This pride and self-respect was as real to the Jews outside Israel as to the Jews in Israel.

Now all that remained was for them to discover their true identity and the sun of Torah would rise once again to shine brightly wherever Jews dwelt.

18

SUN RISING IN THE WEST

In 1938 the situation of Torah in America was very sad. Millions of Jews had come to America from Europe in the twentieth century, most of them Torah-observant. But they were not holding on to their children, who were leaving the old Jewish Torah culture behind for the melting pot of America.

But despite all this, America was not a desert, arid of Judaism. The generation of Torah-observant Jews that came to America was still large and strong. They had established Yeshivot and many synagogues. Kosher food, mikvaot (ritual baths), religious books, and religious articles were available. Societies to aid the poor and the immigrant were founded.

In the late 1930s, when the situation in Europe became perilous and the Jews attempted to flee, there was a place of refuge waiting to accept them. The Jews of the United States were ready.

As the flood of Jews came to America from Europe, they joined with the Jews who welcomed them to build Torah institutions in the United States. And the Torah forces who had known only frustration in America and foreboding in Europe suddenly met with great success on all levels of Torah learning. At first gradually, then with ever-increasing rapidity, America witnessed the blossoming of day schools, yeshivot, and kollelim—Torah institutions for students of all ages.

The Day School

Traditionally, the child's intensive Torah education started when he began his education. In 1938, when the after-school Hebrew school was the major institution for Jewish learning, most American Jewish children were not given an intensive Jewish education, nor did their Jewish education begin when they began their secular education.

Only a handful of elementary school yeshivot, or Hebrew day schools, existed then in America. But the decade of the forties saw the remarkable growth of day schools and students, and the dawn of the day school movement.

In 1945 the number of day schools grew to 69 with a total enrollment of 10,000. By 1955 the number had grown to 110 with an enrollment of approximately 35,000 students.

The growth of the day school was steady and rapid, with no down periods, not even a plateau. Each year new day schools were founded and enrollment increased. The student body was made up of children from Torah-observant homes and from homes that were not Torah-observant. The students came from every social status in the Jewish community.

It was not because the parents were dissatisfied with the public schools. As a general rule the parent of the Hebrew day school student had a high regard for the public school.

In the *Congress Weekly* of May 1952, Trude Weiss-Rosmarin writes, "The Jewish Day Schools are not a protest against public education but the affirmation of the desirability, even the need, to impart Jewish knowledge to our children."

In *The Parent and the Jewish Day School*, Dr. Louis Nulman studied the parent body of the Hillel Academy of Pittsburgh, Pennsylvania, for the school year 1954-1955. He found that of approximately one hundred families only thirty-five could be considered observant. He found also that most parents themselves did not have a Torah education of any consequence.

Every parent knew that the child was being taught Torah values that might be in conflict with the conduct of the home. Also, the parents were not all wealthy, and the cost of tuition was often a strain on the family budget. In spite of this, the parents sent their child to the Hebrew day school.

This phenomenon, which was observed repeatedly in the day schools, prompted Dr. Joseph Kaminetsky, Director of Torah Umesorah, to write in the *Jewish Life* of March-April 1952,

> The boys and girls attending the ever-increasing number of Day Schools in the cities and towns of America are not only

growing Jewishly themselves, but are genuinely revolutionizing the religious feeling, and in many instances, the religious conduct of the homes.

In 1965 the number of day schools was up to 323, with 63,500 students. The incredible growth of the day schools elated the leaders of the movement.

Noting the steady growth of the day schools and their proliferation in the cities and towns of the United States, Mr. Feuerstein, president of Torah Umesorah, wrote in the Annual Report of 1963, "In the hundreds of communities today, an earlier pessimism concerning the hope for the survival of Torah has been replaced by a pulsating and vibrant optimism."

The Day Schools were not limited to certain sections of the United States. They were springing up across the length and breadth of the country, wherever Jews settled.

In 1970, Torah Umesorah, a leader in the Day School movement reported that "with the establishment of the school in New Orleans, Louisiana, every city with a Jewish population of 10,000 or better has a Day School." In 1971 it announced,

> In the fall of this year a new Hebrew Day School opened in Indianapolis. This marks a milestone in the development of the Day School movement on this continent. The Indianapolis Jewish community was the last community with a Jewish population of 7,500 or over which did not have a Hebrew Day School. This now represents a heroic climax to a significant chapter in the development of the movement.

In 1975 there were 427 day schools with over 82,000 students.

In 1976, Dr. Kaminetsky wrote in the Annual Report of Torah Umesorah,

> We have written finis to wasteland, devastation, and plague, with the 446 Day Schools in the United States. It is this success story replicated in hundreds of communities and thousands of homes which makes each year another year of achievement.

In 1982 there were 497 Hebrew day schools in the United States with a total enrollment of 86,000 students. Dr. Bernard Goldenberg, Director of Torah Umesorah, wrote, "These years have been filled with moments of triumph; replete with a host of accomplishments."

With the growth of the day school, Torah education was starting at a very young age. The great increase of elementary school yeshiva students created a solid base for the expansion of the advanced yeshivot of America.

Yeshivot

The advanced yeshivot, in which young men beyond the age of cheder devoted themselves to Torah learning, were the pillars of the Torah in Europe. But in America in 1938 there were only seven yeshivot with a total enrollment of under a thousand students.

From 1939, during the war years, five more yeshivot were established, headed by great scholars who had established their name and fame in Europe. The yeshivot, were further bolstered by the arrival in the postwar years, between 1947 and 1951, of approximately 120,000 immigrants from Europe, most of them coming from the displaced persons camps. Among them were great scholars and leaders of European Jewry who were immediately invited to join the Torah leadership of America. New yeshivot were founded and the enrollment of the established yeshivot increased.

In *The World of the Yeshiva* William Helmreich states,

> The outbreak of World War II had a lasting impact on the development of Jewish education in America. With it, a thousand-year-old culture that had existed in Europe came to an abrupt and tragic end for the Jewish communities. Millions of Jews were slaughtered, especially in Eastern Europe, the home of the advanced Yeshivas, and only those fortunate enough to have left in time, or lucky enough to have survived the Holocaust remained. Among this group were leaders of numerous European Yeshivas who came to the United States and found institutions of higher learning modelled after their European predecessors. These leaders, or Rosh Yeshivas, as they are commonly known, were successful beyond their wildest dreams.

The new yeshiva students were not just the immigrants. American-born children, from religious and non-religious homes, attended the yeshiva in ever-increasing numbers. The yeshivot and their student bodies grew steadily and rapidly and before long had increased many times over.

In 1964 there were approximately 4,000 students in advanced yeshivot in the United States. By 1978 there were about 100 advanced yeshivot with over 9,000 students and by 1982 over 10,000 students in the yeshivot of the United States.

The yeshiva was led by the European rosh yeshiva, and the program of the yeshiva was similar to its traditional European counterpart—the American yeshiva was not adjusted to meet the expectations of the American student.

The American yeshiva student spends all day and much of the night in the yeshiva. He begins his formal learning day with morning services at approximately seven thirty and does not complete it until approximately ten at night. This is the usual formal program. However, many students are to be found in the bais medrash for hours beyond the time established by the yeshiva.

The centrality of Torah in the American yeshiva is as total and all-embracing as it was in the intensive European yeshiva. The American yeshiva student learns and accepts, just as did his European counterpart, that all learning is to be found in the Torah and that all codes of social and ethical conduct are directed by the Torah. His social and intellectual life is lived almost exclusively in the yeshiva world.

The students of the advanced yeshivot of America were inspired with a fervent desire for Torah learning and saw the conclusion of their yeshiva learning as a sign of their growth and their readiness for higher learning. Thus another institution of Torah learning, the kollel, was added to the pyramid of Torah schools.

The Kollel

The kollel is a more recent development on the Torah scene in America. The kollel student is a young man who has completed his yeshiva learning and is married. He continues to learn full time and is supported by the kollel. In most instances, the sponsor of the kollel in which the student is enrolled is the yeshiva in which he had been studying and that added a kollel program to its functions. Often the kollel may be an independent institution that has only a kollel program.

There the young man studies for an unspecified number of years, depending upon his own judgement and sometimes on the program. The number of years varies from school to school and from student to student. The length of stay is usually around five years.

The same steady upward growth experienced by the yeshivot and the day schools has also been the history of the kollel in the United States since its beginning in the 1940s. In 1982 there were approximately a thousand kollel students in America.

Today most advanced yeshivot have a kollel as part of their programs. Independent kollels have been founded in most major cities of the United States. It is no longer only the outstanding student with great powers of concentration who is the kollel student; it has become almost standard behavior for the yeshiva student to continue his Torah learning in the kollel for at least several years.

In *The World of the Yeshiva*, Helmreich quotes a student at a kollel who describes this trend. "Today Kollel is not for the elite . . . it's part of your membership in the Torah club."

Many cities sponsor a kollel with a program that integrates learning with community service. Rather than engage in full-time personal study, the kollel student undertakes to spend part of the day serving and strengthening Torah in the community. The student learns Torah within the kollel all day, but the evening is usually reserved for community service. He studies Torah with individuals in the community or teaches classes in the local synagogue.

The community kollel aims to mobilize the latent Torah aspirations of the local Jewish population. It has succeeded in drawing people of all ages to share in Torah activity and often inspires other young men to engage in serious Torah learning.

The *Jewish Observer* of March 1983 tells of one such incident. The writer Abby Mendelsohn tells of his introduction to and his involvement in the Kollel.

> It was Shavuos, the first Shavuos that I had been in a synagogue since my confirmation on Long Island and Ben

Zimmer, a talented young psychiatrist, asked me if I would be going to Kollel Bais Yitzchok later that night. . . .

Shavuos night at Kollel Bais Yitzchok convinced me. . . . I began to attend classes and lectures at Kollel Bais Yitzchok more often. . . . Pittsburgh and I have grown Jewishly and we would not have done so without Kollel Bais Yitzchok. The "Yiddishe Neshama" has reverted back to form—it has cried out for more Torah, more learning, and institutions such as Kollel Bais Yitzchok have steadfastly answered that need. . . . Torah has seeped gradually into my life, touching all its parts. What's more, it has become something I want to externalize as well, to share with fellow Jews. Two years ago, I created a "shiur" in downtown Pittsburgh in the office where I was then working and a number of us learned every Wednesday at noon. Now Rabbi Miller and I are organizing a "shiur" in my house.

People at Kollel Bais Yitzchok are very kind, they call me Dr. Mendelsohn. . . . But one time the question arose—what kind of doctor? Ph.D. in English, I said, University of Pittsburgh 1976. The question followed as to my dissertation topic. I shifted uneasily as I explained: I applied French anthropologist Claude Levi-Strauss' structural studies of Myth to English Renaissance poet Edmund Spenser's epic *The Faerie Queen.* It was a singularly arcane dissertation, the last senseless hoop through which I had to jump to get out of graduate school.

Then the thought occurred to me that I was not alone. In all likelihood I am akin to hundreds—perhaps thousands—of bright, young Jews brought up with a love of books and reading, but without any real Yiddishkeit. Looking for an outlet for my talents and profound intellectual desire I fell like others, into the shady and stultifying grave of American academia.

Outside the Yeshiva

The American yeshiva student appreciates that the knowledge of Torah is a life-long pursuit. Therefore, the kollel is by no means the end of Torah learning—it goes far beyond that point.

In a study of the graduates of the yeshiva, Helmreich found that slightly less than two-thirds of the alumni study Talmud almost every day and an additional 19 percent study Talmud once or twice a week. He writes, "There are today thousands of persons in the United States who study Talmud for one, two, even three or four hours daily while holding down full-time jobs."

The ever-growing popularity of the daf yomi program is evidence of continued learning by men of all ages.

The daf yomi, or daily page, study program was introduced in Europe about sixty years ago. In this program, all Jews in all parts of the world unite in the daily learning of the same daf, the two sides of a page of the Talmud. Every day a daf is completed and the Talmud, which comprises 2711 dafim, is completed in approximately seven and a half years.

Although the daf yomi achieved great popularity in Europe, in 1939 it was hardly studied in America at all. But after World War II groups began to form. In 1967, when the cycle of the daf yomi was completed and the participants had completed studying the entire Talmud, a daf yomi celebration was held in the Bais Yaakov school in Brooklyn. A capacity audience of about a thousand people crowded into the auditorium.

The daf yomi was catching on in the Torah community. Many daf yomi groups were formed. At the next siyum in 1975, some 5,000 people converged on Manhattan Center to attend what was then called the largest siyum in history.

On November 14, 1982, the next cycle of Talmud was completed and another siyum was celebrated. The tremendous increase in participants during this seven-year period gave rise to a celebration of immense proportions. Ten thousand people crowded into and outside of the Felt Forum of Madison Square Garden. This is how the event was described in the *Jewish Observer* of December 1982:

> There was a special tingle of anticipation as, on highways all over the New York Metropolitan area, cars crowded with hatted or beyarmulked passengers, recognized fellow pilgrims bound for a common destination—part of the stream of thousands of celebrants, joining thousands more that were surging forth from subway exits, converging on the Eighth Avenue entrance to Madison Square Garden's Felt Forum. . . . Thousands more followed, facing closed doors, yet staying on hoping for a chance that another seat might be found within; some latecomers settling begrudgingly for a place by one of the loudspeakers stationed outside. . . . One well-known Rav later remarked,

"When the curtains opened, the view from the dais of the vast crowd, stretching from wall-to-wall, from the foot of the stage all the way up to the eaves, gathered for the sole purpose of giving honor to limud HaTorah—it was absolutely breathtaking!"

The Agudas Israel of America, which sponsors a great many Torah activities, noted its accomplishments with a tone of pride and exhilaration. The book of the Agudas Israel movement called *The Struggle and the Splendor,* published in 1983, points to the great advances in every facet of Torah activity.

The daf yomi celebration, which the Agudas Israel sponsored, grew to tremendous proportions. Its summer camps attract some 1,000 children every summer. The Agudas Israel sponsors youth groups, led by 1,500 volunteers to serve 20,000 boys and girls each year. The Jewish Education Program, an outreach program for non-yeshiva youth, attracts about 1,500 children every year to its Shabbaton, or group Shabbos, program.

The book concludes by saying, "The past is bright, the future is brighter. . . . Never have its aspirations been higher, its challenge greater, its promise brighter."

The material signs of Torah observance have grown dramatically since 1939. In the book *Dimensions of Orthodoxy,* published in 1983, Reuven P. Bulka describes the Jewish scene in America.

> The once-treife land, the same place which some famed Jewish religious leaders advised against living in, as it would endanger Jewish commitment, now boasts of an institutionalized Kashruth which is mind-boggling when it is viewed in the historical context. Major national and local producers pay for the privilege of having their products endorsed as kosher if they comply with the strict regulations usually demanded.

The author goes on to list an imposing array of material evidence of Torah observance such as the availability of religious articles, Torah books published in English, a great number of mikvaot or ritual baths, and eruv structures that make it possible to carry within a designated area on Shabbos.

Torah study and observance had grown visibly in America.

Old New Winds

At the start of the twentieth century the youth of Eastern Europe were Torah-centered, but as the century progressed they were drawn away from the Torah-centered life to other pursuits. As the twentieth century continued, the youth of America drew away from the other interests they had been pursuing and renewed a Torah-centered life.

The youth of the yeshiva were not attracted by secular learning. They had no desire to become "enlightened" by secular knowledge—Torah was the paramount wisdom they sought. Thousands of yeshiva boys spent their maturing years in the halls of the yeshiva totally immersed in the study of Torah.

And not only did the yeshiva student find no attraction in being "enlightened" by secular knowledge, many Jews who were already firmly established in various fields of secular knowledge drew towards the Torah as the source of true knowledge. They held the Torah to be supreme, their secular fields of knowledge limited. Their search for intellectual gratification brought them to Torah.

The youth were not leaving the bais medrash of the yeshiva, the main area of interest and center of activity for the yeshiva student. There the student spent all of the day and most of his waking night. His friendships and his social interests were initiated by the bais medrash.

The youth of the yeshiva were not joining political parties and other organizations. The only organizations they joined were those that advanced Torah causes. The convention of Agudas Israel featuring Torah luminaries was the attraction that drew the greatest number of Torah youth.

The Shabbos, which had been losing its grip on the youth in the early part of the century, was being observed with a growing consistency in the latter half of the twentieth century.

The children were not leaving their parents. Parents were sending their children to the yeshiva and the children were happily remaining under its influence, sharing a love of Torah with their parents.

In May 1984, at a Parent Teacher Association meeting in Long Island, a group of parents were asked whether they expect their children to be Torah-observant. Almost all of them answered that they do expect all of their children to be Torah-observant.

Rabbi Elkana Schwartz, rabbi of Congregation Kol Israel in New York, summarized this developing trend when he said in June 1984,

> It used to be that when a parent was asked if he expected his child to be Torah observant, the non-Torah observant parent would be sure. He would say with confidence, "No." And the Torah observant parent would answer with doubt, "I don't know." Today it is just the opposite. The Torah observant parent answers with confidence, "Yes," and the non-Torah observant parent answers, "I don't know."

The great Torah leaders described, in glowing terms, the condition of Torah in America. Rabbi Dr. J. B. Soleveitchik, rosh yeshiva of Yeshiva University, speaking on November 11, 1968, at a Torah Umesorah dinner said, "The last twenty-five years witnessed the reclamation of a continent that was spiritually wasteland."

On January 31, 1982, speaking at a Torah Assembly, Rabbi Henach Liebowitz, rosh yeshiva of Yeshiva Chofetz Chaim, said,

> The miracle of the Jewish peoples' survival, over centuries of wandering, rivals that of the Exodus from Egypt. So said Rabbi Yaakov Emden two hundred years ago. Were he here now he would have found the flourishing of our Torah community equally miraculous.

On May 14, 1973, Rabbi Shneur Kotler told a Torah Umesorah convention,

> North America represents the very last diaspora stop in the long history of the Torah wandering, since its first exile some two thousand five hundred years ago. The last Torah diaspora cannot exit through a whisper but rather through an enthusiastic, triumphant Torah blast.

Rabbi Shneur Kotler was the rosh yeshiva of the Bais Medrash Gavoha of Lakewood. The yeshiva was founded by his father, the rosh yeshiva of the famed Yeshiva of Kletzk in Poland, who had managed to flee from the Holocaust. He began the yeshiva in

Lakewood in 1943 with a handful of advanced students. In 1973, when Rabbi Shneur Kotler delivered his address at the Torah Umesorah convention, it had grown to become one of the outstanding yeshivot in the world, with an enrollment of about a thousand Torah scholars.

When Rabbi Kotler called America the last Torah diaspora, he was referring to the incredibly prophetic statement of Rabbi Chaim Volozhin, who said in 1780, "America will be the last station for the wandering of the Torah in the Exile."

This remarkable statement of Rabbi Chaim was made at the dawn of American history, before there was a hint of Judaism in America. Rabbi Shneur Kotler, rosh yeshiva of Lakewood, speaking to the leadership of the day schools of America, declared that the prediction of Rabbi Chaim had come to pass.

The sunshine of Torah was rising in the United States.

19

DELAYING THE EASTERN SUNRISE

The Jews who escaped to Palestine from the fires of the Holocaust and who came from the displaced persons camps of Europe were mostly observant Jews. Among them were leading roshei yeshiva. They joined with the Torah-committed Jews and made a great impact on Torah life in Palestine. New yeshivot were established, old yeshivot were expanded. The Torah elementary schools also gained new strength from the influx of these immigrants.

As the Jewish population of Palestine increased so did the number of children studying Torah. In 1940 there were 13,000 students in the 77 schools of the Mizrachi, about 2,800 in the religious schools of the Agudas Israel, and about 3,000 in the Talmud Torahs. By 1945 the number reached close to 19,000 in the Mizrachi schools, over 4,000 in the Agudah, and about the same number in the Talmud Torahs. In 1948 Palestine had 26,500 in the Mizrachi schools, over 7,000 in the Agudah schools, and about 5,000 in the Talmud Torahs. As the population grew, the voice of Torah gained strength.

The flow of immigrants from religious backgrounds brought with it a clash between the Torah Jews and the secular Jews. The Torah Jews of Palestine wanted to provide the new arrivals to the Holy Land with the environment for a Torah life. They wanted to offer the children of Torah-observant Jews the opportunities for a Torah upbringing.

But the secular Zionists felt strongly that the new Israel of which they dreamed should be a modern, forward-looking society, not held back by the Torah that they viewed as a "throwback to the Middle Ages." They therefore were determined that the children arriving in Israel be imbued with the new spirit of secular Zionism.

In the conflict between these divergent aspirations, the situation of the secular Zionists was far more powerful. The position of dominance in what was then Palestine, and which later became the new State of Israel, had passed from the Torah forces to the secular forces. The kibbutzim and the moshavim of the secularists far outnumbered their religious counterparts. The majority of the population in the cities was not Torah-observant. Even in Jerusalem the inhabitants of the new yishuv far outnumbered the Torah-committed inhabitants of the old yishuv. And the administrative leadership of the nation was in the hands of people who were strongly committed to other values.

The secular Zionists were strategically situated to bring their message to the new immigrants. The new arrivals, coming from the displaced persons camps and from their wanderings across the face of Europe, were received by the Jewish Agency's Department of Youth Aliyah. And they used every means in their power to win the new immigrants over to their way of life.

The first episode in the struggle for the hearts and minds of the new olim came with the arrival to the gates of Palestine of the "Children of Teheran."

The Children of Teheran

A number of Jews managed to escape the flames of the Holocaust, as they spread through Eastern Europe, by fleeing across the Russian border. Among them were families with children and children without families. They wandered through Russia and Siberia, always pointing to the land of Israel. Many people died along the way, and many times only a young child remained. He buried his parents in the snows of Siberia and continued on his way. Many of these children reached Teheran, the capital of Iran.

In Iran there was an office of the Polish government-in-exile. It established camps for the children and turned to the Jewish Agency to provide the guardianship for them. The Jewish Agency accepted the offer and the Polish government placed 733 Jewish children under its care. The Jewish Agency immediately established a camp in Teheran and began to prepare for the aliyah to Israel of "the children of Teheran."

The Jewish Agency believed that it had a duty not only to arrange for the permanent settlement of the children in Israel but also to educate them for their integration into the social fabric of the nation. And since the leadership of the Jewish Agency believed strongly in secular Zionism, their program for the integration of the children was that of secular Zionism.

In the foreword of the handbook distributed to the madrichim, the leaders, from the Hashomer Hatzair, was written,

> Our goal must be to bring the children to understand that their belief in G-d has no logic or rational basis, and that religion is the product of reactionary government and has no right to exist in a land where the people are endeavoring to establish a forward-looking, modern nation.

These goals guided the madrichim, who did everything they could to influence the children. This was not easy, for as it was soon realized, 80 to 90 percent of the children were from Torah families and had been students of the cheder and the Bais Yaakov in Poland. But the madrichim worked ceaselessly to achieve their goals. They started in Teheran and did not stop until the children were directed to their permanent place of settlement.

Yehudah Levenberg, a member of the Hashomer Hatzair, was appointed to head the camp in Teheran. Mr. Levenberg selected sixty-five madrichim, most of them from the Hashomer Hatzair. Almost all of them were not Torah-observant; many of them, especially those from the Hashomer Hatzair, were zealously anti-Torah.

The camp was established as the holiday of Rosh Hashanah approached. On the eve of Rosh Hashanah the children gathered for the maariv services. They prayed with heartfelt prayers and tears. In the midst of the services Mr. Levenberg entered and ordered the services halted and instructed everyone to prepare for a festive celebration that was planned for the children.

On the morning of Rosh Hashanah the children asked that High Holiday services be arranged. They were refused.

The meals served to the children were not kosher. Children who insisted on kosher food were admonished.

Children who said kaddish for their parents were punished.

At first the children were given a room to conduct daily services, but permission was suddenly withdrawn. When they held services in their bedrooms they were ordered to cease.

Rabbi Halberstam, a member of the Agudas Israel who was at the camp, sent a message to the central office of Agudas Israel in Israel, stating, "This week Dr. Hirschberg of Tshenstechov was engaged to teach the children Hebrew subjects. They told him that he could teach the children any subject he chooses except "religion."

In the *Hatzofeh* of March 7, 1943, Yonah Cohen reports on an interview he held with the children in the camp of Teheran.

> The main object of the leaders who guided the group was to guide the children for a "new life" in Palestine. The goals of this life were hard work and the achievements of man's efforts. "Dear children," they would say, "we are going to the land of Israel. You don't need your caps on your heads anymore."

It was not long before word of the conduct at the camp came back to Israel. When the religious leaders heard these reports they reeled from the shock. Protests began to pour in from all over the world. The religious organizations in Israel appealed to the Jewish Agency to halt their efforts to influence the children. But the approaches of the madrichim to the children remained unchanged for all the time they stayed in Teheran.

The next stop for the children was Atlit in Israel.

Atlit, the site of a government camp, was a temporary stop. The children were to be there only until they could be registered and distributed to more suitable quarters. The Sabbath of their stay in Atlit was just another day of hustle and bustle.

From Atlit they were to go to the transit camps. They would stay in the transit camps only until the determination and arrangements would be made for their permanent settlement.

The religious leaders asked that their permanent settlement be in an environment similar to the wishes of their parents and a continuation of the upbringing they had received at the hands of their parents. But the Jewish Agency judged otherwise. It decided that all children over fourteen would themselves choose their permanent settlement. They agreed, however, that children under fourteen were to be settled in places that were in line with their previous upbringing. In a case where their background could not be exactly determined, they would be settled in a place where they would be given a religious education.

The various organizations were asked to submit a list of proposed sites for the transit camps. All the organizations submitted lists of sites that met the conditions laid down by the Jewish Agency. Eleven transit camps were selected; from the eleven sites chosen, eight were from the non-Torah organizations, three from the Mizrachi, none from the Agudas Israel.

The organizations were asked to propose names of madrichim. The madrichim selected were: fifty from the non-religious organizations, twenty-eight from the Mizrachi, and five from the Agudas Israel.

When the children arrived at the transit camps, the madrichim intensified their campaign of persuasion. Incidents such as the following were legion.

In the camp Chavat Limud a girl was told to sew on the Sabbath. When she refused a madrich said to her, "You'll get used to forgetting such nonsense."

In Beit Chalutzot some of the children asked to attend the youth club of the Agudas Israel but were not granted permission to go. The madrichim arranged a party for them in the Gordonia Club, where they explained to the children that the best place to go was to the kibbutzim.

Yisrael Edelman reported that when the children arrived at Beit Chalutzot in Jerusalem, their tzitzis were taken from them "to be laundered" and never returned from the "laundry."

Rabbi Kalman Kahana reported that in the camp at Beit Olim the Agudah madrich, Mrs. Feldman, was forbidden to recite the Shma with all the children together. She was only allowed to do so individually with those children who requested it. Similarly the Mizrachi madrich was warned not to recite the blessing word for word for all the children "lest the children who do not know the blessing, learn it."

A madrich ordered the boys to remove their hats during their first supper in Bait Chalutzot. One of the boys stood up and said, "We are not in Teheran, we are now in the Holy Land. We will not remove our hats."

At a Shabbat party in Mikveh Yisrael some members of the Noar

Haoved, the working youth, induced some of the children to step into the gym where they arranged their own Shabbat party with cigarettes and instrumental music. A madrich explained that that was the way to prepare for "real life" in Israel.

The madrichim jealously guarded the children from any influence but their own. One day the Chief Rabbi of Israel, Rabbi Herzog, visited a transit camp and during his visit began to address the children. A leader objected angrily. In the middle of his remarks she called out, "Who gave you permission to come in here and speak!"

In an article in *Haderech*, an Agudah madrich in Bait Chalutzot reported on the effects of the constant pressure on the children. "Victims fell daily . . . . They began to forget to recite afternoon and evening prayers. Then they made light of their morning prayers. They 'did G-d a favor when they put on their Tefilin.' "

All these efforts at persuasion reached their climax in the last week before the poll to determine where the children would be placed permanently. Then instructions were sent out to all transit camps to arrange trips to the kibbutzim and settlements in the Jezreel Valley.

In the *Hatzofeh* of May 5, 1943, madrich Yehoshua Bachrach of the Mizrachi writes,

> Were the famous excursions, where children were taken on three day trips after they had been in the country only six weeks, weary from their wandering, coming down with fever every other day . . . were they a legitimate educational tool? They may give answers . . . but whoever had kept up with all the situations and all the talk that accompanied and hovered around the children can testify that an unforgivable, wholesale crime was committed here.

In *Yediot Achronot* appeared an article entitled "The Teheran Heroes."

> You can't depend completely on the madrichim to confuse the children. So you put the children on buses and take them to the Jezreel Valley. After the children return from their investigative trip as experts on agriculture, social systems, the Middle East,

afforestation, irrigation, religious and social problems—then the madrichim approach them one by one and ask, "Nu, nu—."

Mrs. Henrietta Szold, the head of the Youth Aliyah, declared quite plainly the purpose of the trips. In her report to the Jewish Agency, quoted in *Davar*, May 19, 1943, she wrote,

> Children's visits to different parts of the land were made in order to acquaint them with the land and the development of Jewish settlement. These excursions had great educational value in their Zionist influence and in directing children toward agricultural work. All the children, when it came time to choose their future, expressed a desire for agricultural training in the villages.

The efforts of the madrichim, from Teheran to the transit camps, had the effect they sought. When it came time for the final selection of their permanent settlement many children had been swayed.

The madrichim did not rest up to the very last moment. The day when the result of all their efforts was to be tested, they were ready.

In an article in *Haboker*, April 14, 1943, the process by which the children were assigned to their permanent settlement is described.

> During the day that the committee visits, the camps turn into real fairs. The Agency committee sits in a room and calls in every boy and girl separately to declare where they want to go, also to determine their religiosity. Outside, stand the madrichim and they try to "counsel" each child before he enters the committee room. The means of persuasion include promises of good treatment in the child's new home, primarily the promise of good food. Many children, when they step into the room, immediately announce the name of the settlement they wish to go to. For the most part they are settlements they have visited.

The voting was supposed to have been limited to children over fourteen years of age. The placement of children under fourteen, it had been agreed, was to be determined by the life-style of the parents and the previous education of the child. But in the end the children under fourteen were asked to choose. And even those who chose religious settlements were not all placed there. The Youth Aliyah found reasons to send many of them to non-religious settlements.

In the *Hatzofeh* of May 5, 1943, Yehoshua Bachrach, a Mizrachi madrich, writes, "Along with the older ones who had chosen non-religious settlement went their younger brothers and sisters, for how could anyone separate children of the same parents?" The final distribution of the children was published in the Hatzofeh of April 30, 1943. The list was given as follows: 334 children were assigned to non-religious settlements, 278 to Mizrachi settlements, 32 to Agudas Israel institutions, and the remainder to private homes and hospitals.

Thus ended the episode of the "Children of Teheran." They came to Teheran, by the most conservative estimate, 80 to 90 percent religious. But hundreds of them were turned away from religion, winding up in settlements that were not religious.

During the height of the conflict, a protocol was jointly issued to world Jewry by six of the religious leaders of Israel. They declared:

> These unfortunate children, almost all of them religious, many of them from the most prominent families in Galicia and Poland . . . children and grandchildren of rabbis and chassidic rebbes . . . as soon as they were given into the hands of their guardians, when they were yet in Iran, were immediately placed under madrichim and teachers who tried to persuade them to leave and forget their entire past and to get used to a new life without Torah and religion. And they used every method to make them forget the ways of their father and mother. . . . Let everyone know, this is not a question only of the nearly one thousand children who have already come. But let everyone be aware that preparations are being made to receive in Israel another thirty thousand children from Siberia and from other countries. It is therefore important that all Jews understand their responsibility at this time. . . .
>
> Signed with broken heart and bitter soul,
> Isar Zalman Meltzer   Avraham Mordecai Alter (Ger)
> Yitzchak Zev Soloveitchik
> Zalman Sorotzkin (Lutzk)   Akiva Sofer (Pressburg)
>   Yosef Kahaneman (Ponevez)

As the rabbis said, the episode of the children of Teheran was not only a question of close to one thousand children, it was a portent of the future for many thousands more. But as the rabbis did not know then, it was not only thirty thousand souls who were to be touched. It was many, many more. For in 1948 the State of Israel proclaimed its independence.

The news of the independence of the State of Israel was heralded with great joy all over the Jewish world. It let loose a great flood of aliyah, not only of the survivors of the Holocaust, but from the ancient Jewish civilizations of Asia and Africa. Hundreds of thousands of Jews came. The Jewish Agency and its department of Youth Aliyah were the agencies that received them, and the same problems, the same confrontations occurred over and over again. And those people, who were much more impressionable, were more easily molded. The effects of their exposure to these new forces went even deeper.

The people of the new State of Israel opened the doors wide to welcome all Jews who desired to come. They took the Jews out of the deportation camps in Cyprus. They welcomed the Jews who came from the displaced persons camps. During the first four months of the independence of Israel, 33,000 Jews came, 25,000 of them from the deportation camps of Cyprus. From September to December of 1948, 70,000 Jews came, most of them from the displaced persons camps of Germany, Austria, and Italy.

In the next four months, from January to April 1949, more than 100,000 Jews arrived. By the end of 1949 another 135,000 came. Thus from May 15, 1948 to December 31, 1949 over 340,000 immigrants came to Israel. In 1950 the great aliyah from the Eastern countries began with the aliyah of the Jews of Yemen.

Aliyah from Yemen

The news of the birth of the new State of Israel rang through the Jewish world and filtered into the most remote corners of the world. It penetrated into the isolated, ancient Jewish community of Yemen.

Some 45,000 Jews lived in Yemen in what was thought to be the oldest Jewish community in the world. They were deeply religious and steeped in the Bible. When the news of the creation of the

State of Israel came to them, they greeted the news as the announcement of the coming of the Messiah. They disposed of all their belongings and began a trek to Israel.

They travelled for months, on foot, along dangerous roads infested with robbers. They passed through territories ruled by sultans, whose collectors made them pay a head tax before they could continue on their way. They were robbed. They fell prey to disease. They starved and thirsted. But they went on.

The Jewish Agency became aware of the incredible wandering of the Yemenite Jews. It began intensive diplomatic activity with sultans to prevail upon them to let the Jews pass, and with the British who ruled the Protectorate of Aden to let the Jews pass through. The British agreed to set up a camp at Hashed outside the Port of Aden for the Yemenite Jews.

Thus began "Operation Magic Carpet," the name given to the operation that airlifted almost the entire Jewish population of Yemen and brought them to Israel.

The Jewish Agency welcomed the great aliyah of the Yemenite Jews with open arms. They set up transit camps for them to care for all their needs with warmth and concern. But there in the transit camps, the joy of the immigrant setting foot on the Promised Land was mixed with pain and confusion.

The Jewish Agency considered it a duty to absorb the immigrants into Israel and to integrate them into the economic and social life of their new land. It therefore included education in its program. As a strongly secular Zionist organization, it believed that religion was a hindrance to proper integration. The educational program they set up for the adults and children of the Yemenite families was for the most part, not religious. Very often the supervisors and madrichim carried out their mission of education with a zealousness that caused great pain to the immigrants.

Word of the treatment of the Yemenite Jews filtered out of the camps: non-religious madrichim, denial of religious education, discrimination in providing facilities for religious practice, religious visitors and teachers being denied entry to the camps, assignment of families to non-religious settlements, and cutting off of the traditional peos, or earlocks, of the Yemenite Jews. Cries of shock and protest poured in from every corner of the Jewish world.

An article in the *Jewish Morning Journal* of February 2, 1950, reports on a meeting of the religious organizations in America.

> Regarding the urgent problem of religious education in Israel . . . every Jew in America who holds Israel dear to his heart was deeply upset to read the daily telegrams arriving from responsible religious leaders in Israel. For months now these great personalities have been sounding the alarm about the terrible discrimination against religious education in and out of the immigrant camps. . . .
>
> Every Jew who possesses a spark of faith shuddered when reading the text of the telegram of January 23 from the Chief Rabbis Herzog and Uziel of Israel which we quote. "We pray that there will be a quick end to the shocking machinations; the removal of the children of religious Jews—believers, sons of believers, born of generations of G-d fearing Jews—to irreligious and even anti-religious education. The rabbis of Yemen attested, in our presence, in the religious courts, that in the camps the children are kept from education in Torah and G-d's commandments. . . ."

The hue and cry from inside and outside Israel could not be ignored. On January 17, 1950, Prime Minister Ben-Gurion appointed an Investigative Committee on Educational Matters in the Immigrant Camps. The committee questioned well over one hundred witnesses, and they heard stories such as these.

The minister of education remarked that,

> Of 170 teachers and counselors 77 are religious. . . . Regarding Beit Lid, of nine teachers only one is religious. Of thirty-eight men and women teachers in Ein Shemer, which has only Yemenite immigrants, only eight were religious. . . . Of twenty-five counselors in youth clubs only two were religious.

They heard a report from Rabbi Kahaneman of Zichron Meir who stated,

> I heard children, when they say Grace after the meals, say, "May He who is merciful revenge us. May He who is merciful punish Zipporah."

I thought this was a Yemenite custom because the children were of Yemenite immigrants. But it became clear that Zipporah was a madricha who cut off their peos.

In Ein Shemer, the director Aldama dismissed five of the Yemenite teachers and left nine. The nine who remained were harassed, and finally all the Yemenite teachers left. Rabbi Yosef David Madmon, also a Yemenite, testified that Aldama said, "There is no need to teach Torah."

Rabbi Fuchs and Rabbi Derner testified that they invited two religious teachers, Piltz and Schneersohn, after they and one hundred religious families decided to open a religious school in the camp. The teachers began to teach in the synagogue until the director ordered it closed.

In the immigrant home in Achuza, the parents persisted in their demand for religious education, and religious teachers were brought in. Rabbi Winkelstein relates that when the director ordered the learning stopped he told him he had fifty signatures requesting religious learning. Rabbi Winkelstein went on to say, "He asked for the list in order to examine it. That same evening he assembled the fifty parents who had signed and threatened them with suspension from the camp if the study of Torah were continued." The committee in its final report concluded, "The machinery was not adapted to the needs of a fundamentally religious element."

The aliyot continued. In March 1950 the Iraqi government enacted a law authorizing the departure of the Jews. A mass aliyah began, bringing to Israel 121,000 Jews out of a total Jewish population of 130,000.

The same problems that greeted the Yemenite Jews reared their heads again. The *Hamodia* of October 1952 reported about a meeting held on October 4 in the home of Chief Rabbi Herzog in Jerusalem. Those assembled issued the following statement:

> 1300 children just arrived from Iraq and have been placed in the care of Jewish Agency "educators" who are methodically weaning away the children from the faith of their fathers.
>
> These children who were reared and educated in religious homes by observant parents were brought to the anti-religious kibbutzim of the Histadrut and there the leaders who care for

the children spare no means to uproot every bit of religiosity from their young minds.

Children who have all their lives observed our traditional faith are being torn away from the belief and religion of their parents. Their leaders do not permit the children to pray. They compel them to desecrate the Shabbos, and deliver long lectures which aim to instil in their young minds disbelief about everything holy to G-d and His Torah. They do not hesitate to use any means toward that end.

The years of conflict and negotiations between the religious parties and the government continued. In 1953 the government made a decision. The children would be divided according to the "party key" or proportion of party membership. This meant that background, and the desire of the parent, would not be final. The families would be distributed according to the political affiliation of the general population of Israel. According to this formula the great majority of children would be settled in non-religous settlements. The Agudas Israel refused to accept this formula and left the government coalition.

The aliyot continued. In 1955, 37,400 Jews came from Morocco, in addition to 10,000 who came in 1950. They found the same problems of non-religious indoctrination. Charges of denial of religious education and placement in non-religious institutions resounded.

In an article in *Hatzofeh* of February 21, 1955, the writer states,

> From the moment the Great (North Africa) Aliyah began, the Jewish Agency has exhibited a prejudicial attitude toward the establishment of religious schools in new settlements. The buildings it has provided which were set up after long and wearisome campaigns, are very few and much too small for the number of pupils using them. The non-religious school system, however, is being provided generously with buildings, with no hardship or restrictions involved.

The publication of the P'Eylim gives this interview with a young immigrant from Morocco.

I, Mordecai son of Moshe Balalah, 17 years old, left Miknes in the summer of 1954. When we arrived in Israel they took us to Shaar HaAliyah and from there to Gadna (military training) at Ein Zeitim near Safad. At the conclusion of our training a man arrived from the Jewish Agency for the purposes of sending the boys to certain settlements.

We all pleaded with our commander that we were religious and wanted to be sent to religious places. His answer was that we must go where the Jewish Agency sends us. When we asked the representative of the Jewish Agency for religious placement he answered that the Jewish Agency does not provide religious places, and we must go to an irreligious place. Left without a choice, we went where they sent us.

Many aliyot came, from Asia, from Africa, from Russia. And the pattern continued with hardly a change. In the P'Eylim publication *Hachever Hatorati* of February 1960, the problem is summarized in the following manner:

A true understanding of the religious problems of Youth Aliyah cannot be reached without an awareness of the party "key" which dominates the religious immigration problem in general. In any arrangement for the distribution of immigrants to settlements it is this mathematical formula which is the point of reference. Conducted quite openly (though rarely publicized outside of Israel), the "key" directs about 80 percent to be placed in non-religious settlements. The arrangements set up to determine the immigrant distribution thus does not concern itself at all with the religious background of the immigrants themselves, but arbitrarily parcels them out on a quota basis determined by an entirely irrelevant factor, the configuration of the World Zionist Movement, from which the 80–20 ratio stems.

In Youth Aliyah, as in adult immigration, the "key" reigns supreme. The tragedy of Youth Aliyah lies in the fact that it is the political coloring of the Agency which generally determines where children in its care will be placed and not the highly religious background of the children themselves, nor the desires of their parents.

The absorption of the immigrants did not end the efforts to secularize them. The attempts continued during the process of integration into their settlements. Attempts to divert them from religious education came from the government authorities, national and local, and from the Histadrut, the national workers union.

Stories such as these were regularly appearing in various publications.

The *Jewish Opinion* of July 31, 1952, reported,

> In an address by Meyer Lowenstein, member of the Knesset and Agudah leader, he accused the heads of the villages of using terror tactics in order to compel its religious inhabitants who had recently arrived from Yemen to withdraw from the Torah-sponsored schools of the Agudah.

In the *Hatzofeh* of November 2, 1955, the following article appeared:

> In Beit Shemesh the non-religious school of 240 children was housed in a modern school building, while the 350 children receiving Government-Religious education studied in an inadequate, little building. Though the authorities promised the parents a new building by Chanukah, the promise did not materialize.

In the *Hatzofeh* of December 4, 1955, the writer reported,

> The parents here at Givat Dorot announced that they will not rest until a religious school is set up for them, nor will they send their children to the school prepared for them. . . .
> The parents of forty-one children submitted a written petition last June to the Minister of Education and to other officials, which was signed by the parents and contained all necessary information . . . and the request that religious schooling be arranged for the children. To this day they have not received an acknowledgment of the petition.

The *Yediot Achronot* of December 7, 1955, reported,

The officials went from parent to parent registering the children for the irreligious school without telling them what kind of school it was and that there were two systems, religious and non-religious. When the deception was discovered, the parents got in touch with Religious Education officials and sought their help in nullifying the registration. . . .

In the *P'Eylim Reporter* of February 1964, this statement appears:

I, Ouisi, Idel, arrived in upper Nazareth from upper Roumania with my wife and only son Baruch, aged nine. The boy is religious and G-d fearing. Three months ago I had an accident. I didn't fall during work, I can't receive compensation. My family and I live on the 61 pounds I receive from welfare. Since this tiny sum can't possibly support three people, I turned to the Histadrut Workers' Union and asked for aid. I spoke with Mr. M. Ariar, secretary of the Workers' Union, and he said that he would give me money to support my family on one condition; that I take my son out of the religious school. His words pierced my heart like a sword.

The *Hatzofeh* of November 23, 1955, sums up the painful situation in an editorial.

Government Religious education is fighting for its existence against the tactics of the Ministry of Education, officials of the Jewish Agency, and local authorities. Here they nullify a registration, there they force religious Jews to register their children in non-religious schools, and in other places they avoid their obligation to set up buildings for religious schools.

Despite their disappointment in these developments, the Torah forces were not disheartened. True, the great aliyot had not brought the increase of Torah education that they had expected. But they viewed these aliyot as a great blessing. They were thankful that hundreds of thousands of Jews had been rescued from oppression, and they knew that before long many thousands of them would come back to their tradition.

This feeling was expressed by the Belzer Rebbi in 1957 when he was asked for his assessment of the State of Israel. He said, "It is a great salvation from the Almighty that the Jewish people have a place to go."

The Torah forces dedicated themselves to the teaching of Torah in the elementary schools and yeshivot of Israel. Their efforts were successful beyond their greatest expectations.

20

SUN RISING IN THE EAST

As the 1930s drew to a close, the ominous signs of persecution in Europe touched off a great aliyah to Palestine. Hundreds of thousands of Jews fled to Palestine in those years. By 1948 the Jewish population had reached 650,000.

With the birth of the State of Israel many more aliyot came. Waves of immigrants came from Yemen, from Morocco, from Iraq. By 1952 the population had increased to over 1,300,000. In 1958, ten years after the birth of the State of Israel, the Jewish population had grown to over 1,700,000. Not only did Israel hold the central place in the hearts of the Jewish people, it had become a major population center of the Jewish people.

As the population increased, this question burned in the hearts of the Torah Jews, and equally but for opposite reasons in the hearts of the secular Jews: Would Israel become not only a population center but also a Torah center of the Jewish people?

Torah Elementary Schools

In 1948 when Israel became independent, the government established four "streams" of education. These "streams" were under the auspices of the different political parties. They included the general and the Labor systems, which were non-religious, and the Mizrachi and the Agudah systems, which were religious.

The Mizrachi and the Agudah schools differed in their curriculum and in the time and emphasis they gave to the Torah subjects. In the Mizrachi schools the day was divided into two equal programs, Torah and secular studies. The Torah curriculum was varied, not giving an unusual part of the day to the study of Talmud. In the Agudah schools, a greater emphasis was placed on continuing Torah learning. The greater portion of the day was devoted to Torah subjects, and Talmud, which was the main study of the advanced Yeshivot, was especially emphasized.

Another type of Torah elementary school was the cheder or Talmud Torah. In the cheder very little time was given to studies outside of Torah—only Hebrew grammar and mathematics were added to the curriculum. The Mizrachi and the Agudah schools were included in the government school system. The cheder was private.

In 1953 the government of Israel passed the National Education Act that consolidated the education system into two streams, the Mamlachti or general government school, and the Mamlachti-Dati or religious government school. The Mamlachti-Dati was patterned after the Mizrachi school. The Agudas Israel, whose school system differed from the planned program, refused to join. The Agudah Torah leaders determined to establish an independent school system; independent in curriculum and independent of the government in its supervision.

After intensive negotiations with the government they received a promise of partial support—60 percent of teachers' salaries for regular school hours. The Torah leaders recognized full well the burden of raising the additional funds. Besides the 40 percent they had to raise for regular teachers' salaries, they also had to provide salaries for the extra hours traditionally taught in Torah-centered schools. There were no funds for administration and maintenance, and there were no funds for classrooms.

But the Torah leaders in Israel and America were convinced of the indispensable nature of Torah-centered education. They founded Chinuch Atzmai.

Earlier in 1950, at the height of the dispute over the absorption of the children of Yemen, a meeting of the yeshiva students was called in America by the world-famous rosh yeshiva, Rabbi Aharon Kotler. The call was issued to the yeshiva students of America to join with the yeshiva students of Israel and to mobilize a drive to inform the new immigrants of their opportunities for a Torah education. An organization of the yeshiva students, named P'eylim, was established.

The P'eylim, immediately proved themselves to be a force on the educational scene in Israel. They embarked at once on a campaign to inform the new olim of their rights and opportunities. They visited the transit camps and the settlements where the new olim were housed. They spoke to the immigrants and guided them to register for Torah education. Between 1950 and 1952 the P'eylim helped to establish 150 Torah schools with a student body that averaged about 100 students in each school.

The efforts to keep Torah vibrant in Israel were thus concentrated mainly in the hands of the roshei yeshiva and the rabbinical leaders who headed Chinuch Atzmai, the yeshiva students of P'eylim, and the religious leaders of the Mizrachi who were in charge of the Mamlachti-Dati school system.

They were arrayed against the entrenched secular forces who headed the government both on the national and local level, and against "the street" where the voice of opposition to Torah was deafening.

In 1949 there were about 27,000 children in the Mamlachti-Dati schools and about 7,000 in the Agudah schools. By 1953, with the increase in population as a result of the aliyot from the Eastern countries, the Torah schools had increased to 53,000 in the Mamlachti-Dati and over 15,000 in Chinuch Atzmai.

The amount of increase was, however, painfully disappointing to the Torah leaders. The Eastern aliyah was predominantly religious, and the Torah leaders had expected that the children would be brought up in Torah schools. But the secular authorities had not turned the children over to Torah education and the religious schools' population had not increased at the hoped-for rate.

The disappointment of the Torah forces was evidenced by reports such as this which appeared in the *Shana B' Shana*, the official publication of the Chief Rabbinate of Israel.

> In 1948 the Mizrachi schools numbered 22.4% and the Agudas Israel 5%, a total of 27.4% of the total student population. But in 1953 both educational systems accounted for only 25% of the total, that is a decline of 2.4% and this despite a mass religious immigration.

Despite their disappointment at having lost many children from Torah, they took consolation from the fact that they were making strong gains in the total number of students enrolled in

Torah schools. In 1955 Mamlachti-Dati student enrollment went up to 55,000 and Chinuch Atzmai to 16,500. In 1956 the number of students in Mamlachti-Dati schools rose to over 61,500 and Chinuch Atzmai to over 18,500. In 1958 Mamlachti-Dati schools included over 81,000 students and Chinuch Atzmai about 20,000.

In 1958, a decade after the creation of the State of Israel, the Torah schools of Israel had recorded years of sustained growth. As a result of these reports confidence began to mix with the hitherto disappointed voices of the Torah leaders. The words of the Torah leaders began to resound with enthusiasm.

Gradually the realization began to dawn upon them that they had achieved a miracle. In spite of all the most intensive efforts of the secular Zionists the religious forces had remained staunch in their resistance. Israel was not being taken over by secularism. More than 100,000 children were being given a Torah education and all signs pointed to continued growth.

In an interview reported in the *Or Hamizrach* of January 1958 Rabbi Unterman, then Chief Rabbi of Tel Aviv, was asked, "Does the honorable Chief Rabbi believe that there is progress in the state of religion in the country?" The Rabbi replied,

> The answer to that question is clear. In every aspect of our life in Israel I see a movement of advancement. Religion is without doubt on the rise, though negative experiences are not uncommon. But the conflict in which religion is engaged arouses great hope.
>
> At first a false hope became embedded in the hearts of the secularists and free-thinkers that the spirit of religion in our people is expiring and soon secularism would replace religion in the land. And though they saw that in the Old Yishuv there still was strong religious belief, they thought that surely in the New Yishuv their rule would be boundless. Now they are filled with disappointment when they see, growing in the New Yishuv, young stalwarts who carry high the flag of Torah and the light of the Torah is a candle at their feet.

Ten years after the creation of the State of Israel Rabbi Unterman viewed the future of Torah in Israel with optimism.

Passing years continued to show spectacular growth in the

number of students in the religious schools, especially in the Mamlachti-Dati system. A sense of jubilation was becoming evident in the statements of the leaders of the Mizrachi as the reports of growth in the number of schools and students kept coming year after year.

In January 1959, the *Or Hamizrach* proudly reported, "The students of the Yeshivot and Day Schools in America number about 40,000 compared to 160,000 who receive Torah education in Israel with a population of less then two million."

The Mizrachi leaders were also enthused by the news that the students in the Mamlachti-Dati schools were staying for more years and more of them were going on to higher yeshivot. The *Shana B' Shana* reported in 1960, "Every fourth child who learned in Mamlachti-Dati went on to the higher Yeshivos. This is a new development in the field of religious education in Israel."

And in the *Shana B'Shana* of 1962 the following comment appeared.

> The shape of religious education was for many years a "pyramid," that is to say, the primary grades were full but the upper grades were sparse. In recent years, however, this pyramid has begun to straighten itself out and has slowly begun to take on the shape of a "box." In 1958 the first grade in Mamlachti-Dati had 12,388 children and the eighth grade 4,799, a ratio of 1:3. In 1961 the first grade had 12,500 children, the eighth grade 9160, a ratio of 3:4. In 1958 the first grade in Chinuch Atzmai had 2234 students and the eighth grade 1088, a ratio of 1:2. In 1961 the first grade had 3289 students, the eighth grade 2114, a ratio of 2:3.

In 1962 Mamlachti-Dati reached 100,000 students and Chinuch Atzmai 25,000. The *Shana B'Shana* published an interview with the Mizrachi leader, Minister of the Interior Chaim Moshe Shapiro.

> Since the enactment of the National Education Act, religious education finds itself in an upward graph. It has succeeded in establishing itself and in taking root along the length and breadth of the land, "from Metula to Eilat" and especially in the regions and centers which are absorbing the new immigrants,

where the percentage of students fluctuates between forty and fifty percent.

In 1973, after a quarter of a century of the State of Israel, the Mizrachi leaders were elated by the vitality of religious education in Israel. In the *Shana B'Shana* of 1974 the following report was given.

> In the twenty-five years of the State religious education has spread and branched out from kindergarten to religious colleges and universities including the network of Chabad schools and Chinuch Atzmai. In the beginning of the second quarter century the land of Israel has become the center of Torah and its crowning glory.

But while the Mizrachi leaders were elated, the Agudah leaders were restrained. True, the number of religious elementary schools and students had greatly increased. But they were not content with the aspirations of the Mamlachti-Dati school system.

They were not resigned to a Torah education in which Torah shared its goals equally with nationalism. And they were not contented by the knowledge that "every fourth child" went on to higher yeshiva learning. They looked to Chinuch Atzmai to spread the Torah-centered program of education. And they looked to Chinuch Atzmai to inspire the large majority of its graduates to continue on to higher yeshivot.

The Torah leaders noted the heartening advance of Chinuch Atzmai with cautious optimism. The optimism came from the success they were having in reaching the parents and children in the cities and the settlements in all parts of the country. With the help of the P'Eylim, successful rishum, or registration, campaigns were being initiated and they were thrilled by the results.

The *P'eylim Reporter* of September 1965 describes a rishum campaign.

> The crucial period is in May. It is then that the official Rishum-Registration period is in effect, when parents must choose and register children in the school of their preference. The vast organization and publicity superiority of the secular

forces in the country put religious systems at a great disadvantage. In helping fill the breach, P'eylim has played a vital role.

Teams of idealistic yeshiva students pack their bags and tramp strategic pivotal towns informing immigrant parents that they indeed do have a choice (a fact unknown to many) of a religious school, and shepherding them to the proper registration place. Often the task requires a great deal of persuasion and offers of help, for in many cases local authorities make it clear to parents that their jobs depend on sending their children to the secular government schools.

Last year's activities were successful to the tune of 1,000 new students in religious schools directly due to the effort of P'eylim. The entire outlook of certain areas was altered. Tiberius for example, had 271 new religious students and Tzfas 183. Most of these are for Chinuch Atzmai—all are aimed at providing Jewish children with a religious education.

The steady growth of Chinuch Atzmai was cause for optimism. But caution came from the awareness of the great financial burden that was entailed in the management of a network of schools.

In December 1956 Rabbi Itzchak Meyer Levin, Agudah member of the Knesset, is quoted in *The Yiddishe Vort:*

> Chinuch Atzmai has two possible prospects. It can, G-d forbid, break down under the weight of its great expenses. It can however realize great possibilities. It can in time become the educational system for 50,000 children and even more.

The Chinuch Atzmai brochure of 1962 included a letter from Rabbi Zalman Sorotzkin, one of the Torah leaders of Israel.

> Chinuch Atzmai has grown. It has struck roots and produced glorious fruit. Its framework has broadened immeasurably.
>
> But its existence is in grave danger. Now as before wise analysts have arisen who claim that Chinuch Atzmai has expended the last of its energies. In their pessimism they downgrade the untapped resources of Torah true Jewry.
>
> But, and this I state with all the power at my command, we have not even reached the half-way mark to our goal.

As time went on Chinuch Atzmai was managing to carry its financial burden. The Torah Jews of America and Israel supported it; in addition, the government gradually increased its support of the Chinuch Atzmai system. In 1977 the government agreed to pay 100 percent of the regular teachers' salaries. Although all other expenses of the many aspects of managing Chinuch Atzmai remained, the gravity of the situation was lessened.

The educational results were extremely gratifying. Thousands of children of the new generation were studying in the old traditional Torah-centered schools of Chinuch Atzmai. The voices of pessimism about the future of Chinuch Atzmai grew still.

The *Digleinu* of May 1974 published an interview with Rabbi Grossbard, director general of Chinuch Atzmai in Israel.

> The successful registration in this period is noted by the leaders of Chinuch Atzmai with especial satisfaction and they have real reason to rejoice in their achievements. A great portion of the registering parents belong to the group which settled in Israel in the past twenty-six years. In the past, most parents who registered their children in Torah schools were themselves immigrants who, in the land of their origin, were closely bound with religion and Torah. Therefore, it was not unexpected that they would register their children in Torah schools. But today most of the children who were registered are the children of the second generation. The parents are young and a great portion of them grew up in the Chinuch Atzmai schools. Therefore our joy is doubled, for this generation also chooses Torah education for their children.

In 1979 twenty-five years of Chinuch Atzmai was celebrated with great pride and emotion. The following progress report by Rabbi Henach Cohen, director of Chinuch Atzmai in America, was published by *The Yiddishe Vort*.

> Take a look at the map of Israel how different it is today than it was twenty-five years ago. Then the map was of a great spiritual desert. A great number of the Jewish settlements existed at that time but they were practically empty of Torah, the voice of Torah of little children was almost not heard. Torah

centers existed only in the large cities. In the rest of the land there were very few Torah institutions.

Today after twenty-five years of Chinuch Atzmai, the situation is altogether different. The voice of Torah of Jewish children is heard all over the length and breadth of the land, from Kiryat Shmona in the North to Ber Sheba and Dimona in the South.

Thousands of children were studying in Torah-centered schools and imbibing the old Torah values. They were identifying with the Torah leaders and following their ideals.

In 1980 at the World Congress of the Agudah, thousands of children assembled for the convention. They made a deep impression upon the Torah leaders. The assembly evoked memories of the past and what used to be. Ch. Dror, a delegate at the convention, wrote the following report of his impressions in the *Digleinu* of March 1980.

> The assembly of thousands of Jewish children in the World Congress of the Torah leaders of Agudas Israel was very touching and uplifting.
>
> The assembly reminded me of the National Congress which was held in 1944 when I was fortunate to be one of the tens of children who were privileged to appear as representative of their branches from all the sections of the country. The moment of greatest emotion which will never be forgotten was the appearance of the great Rabbi, the Chazon Ish, of sainted memory. We gathered strength and courage from him which up to this day accompanies us and has given us strength to endure the thirty-five years that followed. Those years were very difficult for religious Jewry, when great challenges stood before us waiting to destroy us, when the flood of secularism was uprooting all that was precious and holy. The number of Yeshivos and students was very small. The challenge to "the Yeshiva Bochur" cannot be described.
>
> Today we have been privileged to be part of a generation of Torah scholars, where thousands of parents send their children to Yeshivos.
>
> This was not the situation in Israel thirty years ago. Confusion and doubt reigned all over. Sending a child to a Yeshiva

was a very upsetting decision. "What would the neighbors say?" the parents would nervously ask.

Chinuch Atzmai continued its consistent growth of approximately a thousand a year. By 1985 it had about 40,000 children in elementary schools and kindergartens.

At the Chinuch Atzmai dinner of April 1985, Rabbi Grossbard reported about the successful rishum campaign of the past year and proudly announced that 95 percent of the graduates of Chinuch Atzmai went on to study in the higher yeshivot.

At the same time the Talmud Torahs of Israel were quietly going on with their work. The children were studying Torah intensely in the old tradition, and all of them went on to higher yeshivot when they completed their learning in the cheder. And their number was growing. In 1965 the American Joint Distribution Committee reported there were 5,231 students in the Talmud Torahs. In 1973–74 the number had grown to 7,652 and in 1983–84, 10,334.

In 1985 there were about 150,000 children in the Torah elementary schools of Israel, a rich reservoir for the yeshivot. Year after year they were sending an evergrowing number of students to the higher yeshivot.

The light and sound of Torah from the children was assurance of a bright future for Torah in Israel.

The Yeshiva Movement

In the years between 1939 and 1945 many Torah-committed Jews came from Eastern Europe to Palestine. They had an immediate effect upon the yeshivot there.

The great roshei yeshiva who led world famous yeshivot in Europe replanted their yeshivot in the Holy Land. The children of the new immigrants joined the new and the existing yeshivot.

In the book *Toldot Hadorot Haachronim*, Friedner describes the era between 1939 and 1945 as one of the most important in the development of yeshivot in Israel. He lists the great European yeshivot that were established in Israel at that time, including Mir, Ponevez, Kaminetz, Chidushei Harim, Slobodka, Pressburg, Chachmei Lublin, and Slonim.

This period ushered in an epoch of unparalleled growth for the yeshivot of Israel. Many more were established and the student body of the individual yeshivot grew and multiplied to numbers not imagined even by the most optimistic.

In 1944 there were about 2,500 students in 30 yeshivot in Palestine. In 1948 the yeshiva student population was about 2,950. In those years the sentiment of the authorities of the new government of Israel and of the general population was strongly anti-Torah. The prospects of long-term success for the Yeshivot seemed remote. At best, only the immigrants from the former yeshiva-trained families of Eastern Europe and the children from the families of the old yishuv could be expected to be attracted to the yeshivot. Even they were expected to be lost to the yeshivot in a few years.

But the Yeshiva leaders were not dismayed and they persevered. Up to 1948 the Yeshivot were concentrated in several large cities, especially Jerusalem and Bnei Brak. Starting in 1948 they spread to other parts of Israel. Friedner lists the period between 1949 and 1958 as another of the most important in the development of yeshivot and he says, "In the years between 1948–1958 Yeshivos were started in new sections, in places in which the voice of Torah was not heard since the destruction of the Holy Temple."

In 1958 there were 150 yeshivot across the country with about 7,500 students; in 1960, there were 165 with about 8,000 students; and in 1962, there were 200 with about 10,000 students.

The yeshivot were making great strides—the Torah leaders were awed by the magnitude of their own success. In 1958 the *Yiddishe Vort* quoted Rabbi Kahaneman, the rosh yeshiva of the Ponevez Yeshiva:

> The success of Torah learning in Israel is a miracle and a wonder. All the Yeshivos are succeeding to a degree which can only be described as "supernatural," and this in such a brief period of time. This is the great miracle of the post-Holocaust period, that Torah should not be forgotten by the Jewish people.

In 1960 the *Shana B'Shana* wrote,

> The history of the Yeshivos in Israel in recent years is rich and fascinating and is a reflection of the change that has taken

place in the Jewish community. About a thousand young people who knocked on the doors of the Yeshiva High Schools were not accepted because of lack of space. The thirst for Torah has increased and the Yeshivos are full of students who drink thirstily of it.

And in February 1962 Chief Rabbi Unterman told the *Or Hamizrach*,

> The number of students who are following the flag of Torah increased and there is a pressing need to add Yeshivos, for there are many who are knocking on the doors of the Torah institutions and there is no room to absorb them.

The Annual Report of the American Joint Distribution Committee for the year 1962–63 noted that

> "The Yeshivos in Israel continue to grow. Sympathizers of Yeshiva education are on the increase. Those who are not ready to identify themselves with this type of schooling, are nevertheless intrigued by its very existence."
>
> The newspaper *Al Hamishmar* of the extreme left Mapam party carried a story "The Yeshiva Bochurim in Israel" in the issue of December 26, 1962. The writer Jacob Ravi refers to Bialik's famous poem "Hamatmid" in the article:
>
> "The isolated cities of the diaspora were leveled by the wicked of the world. But our old candle was not extinguished. It shines, not in hiding, but in the main thoroughfare of the cities and on the lawns of villages, here in the State of Israel.
>
> "The matmid to whom Bialik dedicated a swan song about seventy years ago, persists with us today. He is part of the panorama of our life. Whether we like it or not his image accompanies us. The remnant of the old Beit Medrash is a very great remnant."
>
> These observations from the extreme political left testify to the fact that yeshivot are now rooted in the country.

Yeshivot continued to grow and spread into the communities of the olim from Yemen, Morocco, and the other Eastern countries.

The *P'eylim Reporter* of July 1966 carried the following account of the planned opening of the yeshiva in Rosh Ha'ayin.

Rosh Ha'ayin is a thriving town of 16,000 olim, all of them deeply religious. Rosh Ha'ayin is the Bnei Brak of Yemenite Jewry. Its Chinuch Atzmai school is one of the largest and best in Israel, and has been graduating over a hundred students every year. But for the Rosh Ha'ayin child, religious education ended with the eighth grade; there was no Mesivta.

The *Reporter* of September 1971 gives a follow-up report on the yeshiva in Rosh Ha'ayin.

Thousands danced in the streets of Rosh Ha'ayin last summer in celebration of the fulfilment of a dream, the dedication of P'eylim's new Mesivta which the local Yemenites called the "greatest Kiddush Hashem we have ever witnessed."

The *P'eylim Reporter* of September 1972 tells about the yeshiva in the new community of Ofakim.

Halfway between the thriving metropolis of Beer Sheba and the Gaza strip lies the Negev town of Ofakim. Twelve years ago the district was sparsely inhabited; today its inhabitants number over 10,000 resulting from an influx of immigrants from Morocco and North Africa.
The doors of the Yeshiva Ofakim opened in 1962. . . . At the inception, conditions for study were difficult. In 1965 the present quarters were erected . . . Yeshiva Ofakim is fast becoming a major Torah center in the Negev.

Thus yeshivot grew and flourished. They covered the length and breadth of the nation.

In 1973 there were 352 yeshivot in Israel with a population of approximately 22,000 students. In 1983 there were about 600 yeshivot with an enrollment of about 53,000.

The growth of the yeshiva movement is reflected in the number of students enrolled in 1983 in the yeshivot mentioned by Friedner that were founded in the period between 1939 and 1945.

In 1983 Mir had 972 students, Ponevez 1334, Kaminetz 133, Chidushei Harim 399, Slobodka 359, Pressburg 128, Chachmei Lublin 150, and Slonim 17.

Another important aspect of the growth of the yeshivot was the increasing number of years that the student stayed in the world of the yeshiva. A great many did not leave when they were married or when they reached the middle twenties, which was the average age for completion of yeshiva studies. They continued with their Torah learning in the kollel.

The kollel, or the yeshiva for married students, may sometimes have the same program as the yeshiva, that is, a program of all-day Torah study. Or, it may be a community service kollel. This type of kollel started in Israel in the late 1960s when the yeshivot sent groups of their students into towns and settlements to plant the seed of Torah in those communities.

The May 1969 issue of the *Moriah*, the publication of the kollel movement in Israel, describes the activity of the kollel in Migdal Haemek.

> On the Haifa-Nazareth highway stands the development city of Migdal Haemek with a population of about 10,000, most of them new immigrants, who are diligently building up their city to be one of the most beautiful cities in Northern Israel. . . .
>
> The head of the Kollel, Rabbi Asher Sofer, the noted Torah scholar who understands well the responsibilities of the hour to spread Torah and to bring the word of Hashem to the new immigrants, went out together with his dear friend Rabbi Grossman to Migdal Haemek. With the complete support and encouragement of the "Tenuah" (the Movement) he established a Kollel of young men, Torah scholars, who appreciate the importance of their mission. They came with their families, established a Torah center in Migdal Haemek, and immediately initiated a wide-ranging program of Torah activities among the adults and the youth.
>
> They arranged regular Torah classes in the synagogues. They are now conducting classes in twenty of the thirty synagogues in the city. Their warm, personal, contact with the inhabitants is very much appreciated by them and brings them great influence in the community.
>
> The young men of the Kollel established an afternoon Talmud

Torah for the public school students, and more than 150 children are studying there. Most of the classes are held in the homes of the young men of the Kollel.

The wives of the Kollel young men also share in the program of education in the community. They give classes for the women and for their daughters. These classes are also held in the homes of the Kollel students.

So that the young men would have sufficient time for their own studies, they get up at 4 o'clock in the morning and begin their studies when the community is still asleep.

The kollel movement, like all other phases of the yeshiva, spread and multiplied. In 1960 there were 712 kollel students; by 1975 the number had grown to 4,300 students. In 1984 the Ministry of Religion reported that over 14,000 young men were studying in the kollelim of Israel. The kollel became a vital part of the yeshiva movement in Israel.

Old New Winds

The yeshivot that had taken root in Israel were not "new," they were replanted in the Holy Land by the European roshei yeshiva or their followers. The yeshivot maintained the same customs and traditions, they taught the same curriculum, they followed the same schedule, and the students exhibited the same degree of commitment as in the famous European yeshivot.

In the *Yiddishe Vort* of July 1979 Moshe Prager writes,

> Some years ago I happened to be visiting with the Rabbi of Ponevez and sat talking to him till after midnight. Suddenly the Rabbi picked himself up from his seat and said, "Listen, my dear Moshe. Do you hear? In the Yeshiva hall they are still sitting and learning. Such diligent masmidim I have not seen in my life. . . . Come with me to a quiet corner and let us see what is happening."
>
> The Rabbi quietly drew close to a nearby window at the side of the great study hall, stood on tiptoe, peered over so that the students should not see him. I quietly followed him and I saw that the hall was full of students. "This is the greatest gift of

Hashem. Such diligence, such thirst for learning Torah was never before."

And in the same issue of the *Yiddishe Vort*, S. Gershuni describes the yeshiva bochur of the 1970s.

> Today there is no hint of the wild pursuit of "books" and "pamphlets" which poisoned the minds of some of our young people. Gone is the awe of every "writer." Today he knows to distinguish between a great Torah scholar whose vision embraces worlds, and between little people who ride high on high sounding prose which covers up the shallowness and emptiness of their writings.
> The modern Torah-loyal youth has freed himself of all these movements which drew him. Today he believes and feels that the crown of Torah is greater than all earthly achievements.

The yeshiva bochur of Israel recognized Torah as the source of all wisdom. He did not view Torah as "ancient" or as a "throwback to the Middle Ages." He saw Torah as the eternal chain binding all generations. The yeshiva bochur of the second half of the twentieth century in Israel saw the yeshiva bochur of yesteryear, of Eastern Europe and of generations before him, as the ideal to be emulated, and that is what he was like.

The yeshivot grew in all directions: in number of students, in number of yeshivot, in the breadth of the nation that they covered, in the length of years the student spent in the yeshiva, and in the dedication of the students to their Torah learning.

And just as Torah learning grew inside the walls of the Yeshivot, so did Torah learning grow outside the yeshiva. Jews who had never known Torah learning began to be touched by it in great numbers. This was the phenomenal rise of the teshuva movement, the movement of return, that spread through Israel.

The Teshuva Movement

In modern-day Israel, as in all periods of Jewish history, there were instances of "teshuva," Jews returned to Torah living. In the early days of modern Israel, the number of instances of teshuva was not perceived to be unusual. There was no general talk about a teshuva movement.

But in the aftermath of the Six-Day War in 1967 and the Yom Kippur War in 1973 the instances of teshuva began to mount.

Torah leaders began to take notice of the mass stirrings for teshuva. Special "baalei teshuva" yeshivot were established to respond to the special needs of the baalei teshuva. Yeshivot, which later became renowned for their successful inspiration of baalei teshuva, were established in those years.

Observers of Israeli society also began to be aware of the growing number of such instances. Very tentatively, very timidly, they pointed to signs of what they considered to be the emergence of a "movement."

In the *Bais Yaakov* of October-November 1974 the following article by the writer Nitzotzi appeared. It was entitled "Many Prominent Signs of the Strengthening of the Spirit of Judaism."

> What really changed? What is the result of all this yearning for Teshuva which multiplied especially since the Yom Kippur War?
>
> It is not easy to answer this question. Nevertheless, everyone will agree that something has changed in our land.

And in the *Bais Yaakov* of April 1975 Nitzotzi wrote,

> The number of secular kibbutzim in which magnificent synagogues are being built increases from year to year. And the building of synagogues is just one of the striking signs of a movement of greater closeness to Judaism. Another sign is the growing number of chaverim of the secular kibbutzim who are fasting on Yom Kippur.

In the *Bais Yaakov* of September 1976 the noted writer Moshe Prager wrote an article entitled "Are We on the Doorsteps of a Movement of Return to Judaism?"

> I will confess, and not be ashamed to admit, that for years I have been tempted to write about the revelation of Teshuva, before the waves flood the entire area. And I have given a name to this vision, "With the Current of Return"; a "current" because

that connotes something which breaks out from the depths, which one cannot hold back, and one cannot stand up against it.

Many laughed, many scoffed and shook their heads with an expression full of pity, "You are so naive. . . ."

Therefore I decided with all humility to research that subject; the Return to Judaism.

I innocently turn the pages of the Israeli newspapers, the day after Rosh Hashana, and I read an official report in the secular newspaper *Haaretz* under the heading, "The Number of Visitors to Resorts This Rosh Hashana Across the Entire Land Was Much Lower than Expected." In the recreation park Yaarot Menashe the number of automobiles yesterday was about 100, much less than usual. In the recreation park of Shacharia there were very few visitors. . . . In spite of the beautiful weather, the number of people going on outings was much smaller than in previous years. . . .

The synagogues and the places of worship which were set up especially for the holidays were filled in the entire city of Tel-Aviv for the two days of Rosh Hashana. In Ramat Gan the 150 synagogues of the city were all crowded. And in Ashkelon all the synagogues, 140, were full of worshippers.

What is happening here? We certainly cannot attribute all this to "pure coincidence." These reports did not come in from just one place. The reports come in from many, many places.

Let us keep a close watch on things as they develop, for we may be in for a lot of surprises.

As Moshe Prager predicted, the observers began to see the most surprising things. Signs of teshuva appeared all over and in the most unexpected places.

In the special Teshuva issue of the *Bais Yaakov* published in 1977 there appeared a review of the baal teshuva movement thirty years after the birth of Israel.

After thirty years of the establishment of the State of Israel, the movement of return to Judaism is strengthening and deepening and striking roots in Israel.

And we are not speaking of isolated incidents or individuals. The wondrous revelations of those who return to Judaism, are in all areas and all walks of life of the Israeli society. They are in the Bohemia, in the kibbutzim, and in the Israel Defense Forces.

In the weekly supplement of *Al Hamishmar* appeared this article written by one of the most militant anti-religious writers, "News began to arrive in bits and pieces from all directions. Once a young lady of the theatre was telling her friend about a young man who was known as a very wild person, who suddenly left Tel-Aviv, put a yarmulke on his head, and went to Jerusalem. There, she heard, he rented a little room and sits and learns Torah. A young man came over to join the conversation and he told about a certain photographer from a leading newspaper who reportedly tried everything and everywhere in the world and he too went back to religion."

The people about whom they were speaking were people of the first rank in the art set, the most popular stars, successful actors of the theatre, artists, and others like that.

In the secular newspaper *Haaretz* none other than the feature writer Montzer announced, "The kibbutz members are returning to religion."

The newspaper *Maariv* describes a kibbutznik of Ein Gev, about twenty-five years old, born in the kibbutz, educated in the kibbutz, and grown up in the kibbutz youth movement. He has a yarmulke on his head, wears tzitzis, and says a blessing before any food goes into his mouth.

The *Maariv* published an article entitled, "Officer of the Golani Batallion Leaves to Become a Yeshiva Student."

The young man was Offie Fein, known as one of the most promising young officers, who was in many operations, including the "Entebbe" operation. Here is what the writer Erez tells about his departure to the Yeshiva. "The top officers in the IDF including Field Marshall Eytan and the head of the paratroopers Uri Simchoni, received the news of his move, not only with understanding but even with a blessing. And he is not the only one. Many of the military have come to occupy regular benches in the Yeshiva."

In 1977 the writer Moshe Prager was convinced that the incidence of teshuva in Israel had established itself as a movement. Writing in the *Yiddish Vort* of September 1977 Prager declares:

What is now certainly clear and obvious is the mighty rise of a mass teshuva movement in Israel. I assume that not everyone of the readers will say, "Of course, we know that." And I must admit that I myself did not realize how far the teshuva movement had reached. I just recently happened to have an experience with a Baal-Teshuva that was so remarkable and so emotional that it gave me a lot to think about.

One day I heard in the streets of Jerusalem that the sensational performer, one of the most popular and beloved comedy artists in Israel whom everybody calls "Pupik" suddenly became a Baal Teshuva. He had gone off to study in a Yeshiva in Jerusalem and changed his name to Arnon. He was invited to lecture at the great student club on Mt. Scopus about "The Revolution in My Life." . . .

When I got there the hall was packed to overflowing. More than a thousand students, boys and girls. One immediately sensed a feeling of warm intimacy with Pupik. As soon as he appeared on stage an electric spark passed through the hall. "Pupik, Pupik," they all whispered. On the stage stood a young man, with a large yarmulke on his head, with a great beard and smiling eyes. "Good evening," he said with a charming smile. And a hearty applause traveled through the hall. "Excuse me, my friends," he said in a low voice. "I must ask something of you before I begin my lecture. It is against the Halacha (Jewish law) for me to speak today before a mixed audience of men and women sitting together. I therefore ask of you, that the audience please move their seats, boys on one side and girls on the other side. Please change places, otherwise it is impossible for me to begin my lecture."

And a remarkable thing happens. At first, a stillness. Nobody says a word. Then a good natured muffled laughter passes through the audience. Not a single sound of protest from the thousand young people. Many in the audience stand up, chairs move, places are changed, separated couples wink at each other. The separation is completed and the lecturer Pupik begins his talk about Teshuva. . . .

From all sides new Baali-Teshuva emerge, especially from the world of the Bohemia, the actors, the painters, avant garde celebrities. The most famous of them all, his name is Uri Zohar, has now put a yarmulke on his head, wears tzitzis, and has thrown away his whole shining career.

The number of teshuva experiences proliferated. Great numbers of Jews who were far removed from Torah were seeking to be exposed to Torah learning.

In the *P'eylim Reporter* of April 1978 appeared the following report entitled "Successful P'eylim Seminars Bring Army Officers to Torah."

> Hundreds of officers have participated in this program with unexpected results. The reactions of the officers upon completing the Seminar have been almost 100% positive. All feel that they are better Jews for the knowledge they have gained, and many decided to give their own children the benefit of a religious education which they never had.
>
> A substantial number have requested assistance to arrange more intensive courses of study and several officers have entered yeshivos for Baalei Teshuva.

In the same issue of the *P'eylim Reporter* the following report appeared.

> An indication of the remarkable success of the Reach Out project can be gained from the Annual Report for the year 5737 (1977) which shows a total of 369 new students placed in Yeshivos. From Tishrei through Tevet of the year 5738 (1978) 122 additional students were sent to Yeshivos.

The baalei teshuva movement was having a strong impact on Israeli society. Many people were changing their life-style and returning to Judaism. The *Yiddishe Vort* of January 1982 reprints an article by the well-known writer Amnon Denkner of the *Haaretz* entitled "The Real Earthquake," in which he describes the baalei teshuva movement and its far-reaching impact.

> Suddenly I look around and I have to ask myself what is happening? I feel that I am all alone!
>
> When it happens gradually, you do not feel it right away. One goes away and then another. You look for a familiar face that

suddenly vanished. And they tell you, "He went there," and they shrug their shoulders. . . .

I cannot pinpoint exactly where and when it all started. We always heard about various acquaintances who "disappeared." And suddenly they reappeared with black yarmulkes on their heads and with a new peculiar outlook. They claimed that they were happy. They hung around with us a week or two and they disappeared again. At first it was from more distant crowds, and we didn't think about it much. A temporary madness, we said, and we dismissed it with a wave of the hand. . . .

But slowly it made its way into our own crowd. You call a friend, arrange to meet him on Saturday and he wiggles his way out. It's not convenient. He has another engagement. When you begin to press him he tells you that for the last three months he has been going on Shabbos to Rechovot to some rabbi who gives lectures abut Judaism. "Are you crazy!" I holler to him. But it doesn't help. A month later you see him walking around with a black yarmulke. A week later, he is eating kosher. Two weeks later, tzitzis are hanging from his shirt, and whenever you go with him he looks to kiss a mezuzah. You sit down with him to drink a glass of coffee, and he loudly recites the blessing "shehakol." And suddenly he disappears completely. You can't find him anymore. You find out that he went to Yeshiva Ohr Samayach.

My friends leave me, one after the other, as though the earth swallowed them up.

How big this really is I felt most when I went to the wedding of my old friend, Romi, in Ohr Samayach. I came in, and I just stood there, dumbstruck. Not since I left high school did I see all together so many familiar faces. Old friends. All of them wear black yarmulkes and some of them have beards. Their clothing is a white shirt with long sleeves and dark trousers.

I look around the hall and I find many of my old friends with whom I used to hang around and go jumping at the White Gallery and many other places. One at a time, they disappeared. And suddenly I find them all here. They are all happy, dancing at the wedding.

I find a friend from my neighborhood and ask him if he is having a good time, and he answers, "Yes, yes, of course. The groom is very respected. A great Torah scholar." And this person is a friend with whom I used to run around! Now I suddenly discover that he is a "respected chasan," "a great Torah scholar."

The secular forces mounted campaigns in the media and organized committees to combat "the problem." But it was all to no avail.

The 1984 convention of the Agudas Israel of America heard a report by Uri Zohar, now Rabbi Uri Zohar, one of the leaders of the teshuva movement in Israel. Rabbi Zohar reported about the organization known as Arachim that conducts teshuva seminars. He described the amazing success of Arachim both in the impact of the seminar on the participants and the boom in the number of seminars and participants since its inception. In the year 1980, when it began, 222 people participated. After continued growth in 1981, 1982, and 1983, the number reached over 2,200 in 1984.

In 1985 *Shana B'Shana* issued the following report about the baalei teshuva yeshivot: "In the past year the crest of Baalei Teshuva students at Yeshivos rose and strengthened. About 6000 of the 53,000 students of Yeshivos in Israel are Baalei Teshuva."

The success of all these vast Torah movements—Torah elementary schools, yeshivot, kollelim, baalei teshuva, and the Torah Jews of the general population—reflected themselves in the mass outpourings of Jews in Torah activities. At the conclusion of the cycle of the Talmud of the daf yomi in 1982, celebrations were held in cities across the country. The *Yiddishe Vort* of December 1982 reported, "A quarter of a million Jews participated in the completion of the Talmud celebration of the Daf Yomi. . . ." The article went on, "20,000 packed into and outside of the auditorium in Tel-Aviv. . . . 10,000 overflowed the Binyenei Haumah in Jerusalem . . . thousands were gathered in cities all over Israel."

Torah in Israel

In 1985, after centuries of religious settlement and decades of secular-nationalist settlement, it was clear and admitted by all, by the religious thankfully and by the non-religious reluctantly, that Israel was a world Torah center.

The reluctant acceptance of this fact of Israeli society by the non-religious was illustrated by a statement of the long-time leader of secular Zionism, the zealously non-religious mayor of Jerusalem, Teddy Kollek.

In the *Jewish Press* of July 13, 1984, the following article appeared.

> Mayor Teddy Kollek urged American rabbis to stem the tide of which he called a religious extremism among orthodox youth. "Your children who are settling here are more extreme than you are," Kollek told the Rabbinical Council of America on July 10.
>
> The Mayor stressed that he always believed Orthodox youth such as the Bnaei Akiva movement represented the finest members of Israeli society and welcomed the continuing progress of Judaism in Israel.
>
> "Jerusalem is becoming a more religious city," he said. "You see from year to year more and more people walking around with kipot on their heads and tzitzit dangling at their sides. On the whole this is a good thing."

The sound of Torah was heard from hundreds of thousands of voices. Many cities in Israel were world-famous Torah centers and Jerusalem was the most celebrated of all.

The sun of Torah was rising in the east.

21

PROPHECY FULFILLED

King Solomon said in Ecclesiastes, "And the sun rises and the sun sets." The Talmud comments, "A tzaddik does not leave the world until a tzaddik like him is born. Before the sun of Eli went out, there shone the sun of Samuel."

The Talmud explains the prophecy of King Solomon to mean that world Torah leadership is always shining somewhere. Before the Torah leadership is destined to pass on, the sun of Torah leadership is lit somewhere else.

There was a time when the sun of Torah was shining in Eastern Europe. Then the time came for the setting of that sunshine. From where would the glow of Torah come?

There was a candle of Torah lit in America. Would that small candle ever become a bright sunshine? In 1939 it did not seem to be so. No one observing the social forces in America saw any hope for a world Torah center shining in America.

There was a candle of Torah lit in Israel. In 1939 it did not seem destined for that candle of Torah to become the brilliant sunshine that would be the heir to the light of the Torah of Eastern Europe.

But the Almighty knows His ways. The little candlelights in the west and the east, in America and in Israel, grew and grew and lit the world with Torah.

The sun rose before the sun set.

22

THE ANSWER

Forty years have passed since the Holocaust. History has cast its light on the dispute between Reb Chaim and Leibele.

Surely Reb Chaim spoke the truth when he said to Leibele and to the assembled, "It is foolish to believe that this is a punishment for their sins. If this was a punishment from Hashem for their sins why did all the Rabbis, the pure and holy Tzaddikim who were full of Torah and good deeds, why did they die?"

The history of the twentieth century gives us an insight into the answer. Decades have passed since the Holocaust, and effects of the Holocaust have come into view. We have seen the resurgence of Torah in the east and in the west since the Holocaust. We know that by sacrificing their lives they made it come to be.

It may therefore be that it was the will of Hashem that they gave their lives so that the Torah and the Jewish people who live by it shall live.

They died with the love of Hashem in their hearts and Ani Maamin on their lips. They were led by the holy Tzaddikim who proclaimed their readiness to give their lives for the fulfillment of the grand design of the Almighty. With their blood they gave new life to the Jewish people.

EPILOGUE

Though the first stage of redemption yet unfolds, and millions of Jews still remain under oppression in parts of the world, many more millions of Jews in other parts of the world have been freed from the yoke of oppression and persecution.

But, though oppression and persecution end with the completion of the first stage of redemption, the suffering of the Jewish people does not end. The Talmud tells us that before the final redemption the Jewish people will go through many wars. The suffering and the tragedies of war do not yet cease. The end of suffering and the coming of peace is realized only with the final redemption.

Therefore, when we behold the sacrifice of the martyrs and the purpose for which they died, we are struck with the awesome responsibility carried by those who follow them. For surely Hashem did not call upon them to give their lives for the beginning of redemption, with all the suffering that is attendant to it. They gave their lives for the total redemption that they set in process with their martyrdom. The process leading to total redemption can be hastened only by their children.

The prophet Isaiah said that in the final redemption, "The world will be filled with the knowledge of Hashem as water fills the ocean bed."

And Isaiah prophesied further, "I am Hashem, in its time I will hasten it."

The Talmud explains the seeming contradiction of the terms, "in its time" and "I will hasten it," and says, "If you do not merit it the redemption will come in its time. If you merit it, I will hasten it."

The four redemptions march along with the tempo of the rising sun of Torah. As the sun of Torah shines brighter and brighter the final redemption comes closer and closer until peace reigns and suffering is no more. The degree of commitment to Torah by the children of the Holocaust determines the pace of the process of redemption.

May it be His will, and ours, that the sunshine of Torah, which has begun to rise, continue steadily upwards until it lights the world with its brilliance. And may the people of Israel receive, in our time, His blessing of total redemption and peace.

POSTSCRIPT

The writing of this book was sparked by a conversation with Mr. Abraham Aharon Rimler while walking home from shul on a Shabbos in the early 1970s.

Mr. Rimler was born in Poland. As a young man he was trapped in the Holocaust and taken to a concentration camp. We spoke often about his life in Poland. On that Shabbos he said to me, "Don't think that the religious Jews in Poland were not having any problems with their children. More and more of them were leaving the shul and their parents' way of life to join Zionist organizations and clubs."

I was taken aback by the statement. It was a totally unexpected remark. It touched off in my mind the following chain of thought: If the holy Jews of Eastern Europe faced decline, and the rest of the Jewish world surely did too, then we can understand the history of the period that led to the Holocaust, the Holocaust itself, and results that the Almighty Himself knew would follow after the Holocaust.

From that remark was born the ideas and studies presented in this book.

A LIVING TORAH

With a tear I add this page to the book. On the thirteenth day of the Second Adar 5746, on the night before the Fast of Esther, the soul of the Rosh Yeshiva, Rabbi Moshe Feinstein, went up to the heavens, there to stay until the Almighty brings resurrection to the righteous.

I place this leaf in the book because this particular work is but one example of the boundless guidance the Rosh Yeshiva always gave to his talmidim. And also, because of the vital part he played in the triumphal progress of the Torah in the twentieth century which is recorded here in these pages.

The Torah in the twentieth century was under siege. Powerful social movements derided the Torah as being "old-fashioned," "a throwback to the Middle Ages," "fossilized," and "irrelevant to modern times." They denied that the Torah was a living spirit.

The Rosh Yeshiva joined the rabbis of his day in demonstrating the flawless nature of the Torah. And he added another dimension to Torah exposition. He applied the brilliant light of the Torah to the vital issues of the day. He gave Torah responses to modern-day problems. He presented the Torah view on such diverse and pressing issues as abortion, artificial insemination, the synagogue mechitza, and agunos. With the help of the Almighty the Rosh Yeshiva performed the miracle of convincing the world that the Torah was as new as when it was first given to Moshe Rabeinu at Mount Sinai.

A new confidence in the vitality of the Torah spread among the Jewish People. In fitting tribute, at the funeral of the Rosh Yeshiva 50,000 Jews massed in the streets of New York City to pay their respects. And when he was brought to Israel for burial, 200,000 Jews crowded the streets of Jerusalem to mourn his passing. They graphically demonstrated the vibrancy of the Torah and the role the Rosh Yeshiva played in its revitalization. He gave life to the Torah. May the memory of his life of Torah live forever.

BIBLIOGRAPHY

The in-depth study of the places and periods discussed here made it necessary to read countless books, periodicals, newspapers, organizational records and correspondence. Regretfully, this bibliography must limit itself to the listing of those publications which were studied at length and which provided a broad view of the subject under discussion. The references directly quoted are cited in the text.

Agnon, S. Y. *Ore'ach Natah Laloon.* New York: 1968.
Abramov, S. Zalman. *Perpetual Dilemma.* Rutherford, New Jersey: 1976.
Agudas Israel. *The Struggle and the Splendor.* New York: 1983.
Agudas Israel. *Yaldei Teheran Ma'ashimim.* New York: 1952.
Aronson, Gregor. *Vitebsk Amahl.* New York: 1956.
Bacalczuk-Felin, ed. *Yizkor Buch Fun Rakishak un Umgegent.* Johannesburg: 1952.
Badi, Joseph. *Religion in Israel Today.* New York: 1959.
Bardin, Shlomo. *Pioneer Youth in Palestine.* New York: 1932.
Barer, Shlomo. *The Magic Carpet.* New York: 1952.
Baron, Salo. *Social and Religious History of the Jews.* New York: 1952.
Basuk, Moshe, ed. *Sefer Hama'apilim.* Jerusalem: 1947.
Beck, Mordecai. *Learning to Learn.* Jerusalem: 1977.
Bein, Alex. *Toldot Hahityashvut Hatzionit.* Tel Aviv: 1954.
Bell, J. Bowyer. *Terror Out of Zion.* New York: 1977.
Bentwich, Norman. *Jewish Youth Comes Home.* London: 1944.
Berkman, Ted. *Sabra.* New York: 1969.
Botoshansky, Jacobo, ed. *Ratne.* Buenos Aires: 1954.
Bublick, Gedalia. *Min Hameitzar.* New York: 1923.
Bulka, Reuven P. *Dimensions of Orthodox Judaism.* New York: 1983.
Central Bureau of Statistics. *Statistical Abstract of Israel.* Jerusalem: Annual.

Cohen, Israel. *The Jews of Vilna*. Philadelphia: 1943.
Cohen, Israel. *Jewish Life in Modern Times*. New York: 1929.
Cohen, Reuven. *Hameshek Hakibutzi*. Tel Aviv: 1968.
Crossman, R. H. S. *Palestine Mission*. New York and London: 1947.
Crum, Bartley. *Behind the Silken Curtain*. New York: 1947.
Dekel, A. ed. *Binetivei Habericha*. Tel Aviv: 1959.
Don-Yihya, Eliezer. *Hadat B'Yisrael*. Jerusalem: 1975.
Pushkin, Alexander Mordecai. *Jewish Education in New York City*. New York: 1918.
Eisenstein, Miriam. *Jewish Schools in Poland 1919-1939*. New York: 1950.
Elbogen, Ismar. *A Century of Jewish Life*. Philadelphia: 1944.
Eliav, Mordecai. *Ani Ma'amin*. Jerusalem: 1969.
Elston, D. R. *No Alternative*. London: 1960.
Erez, Y. *Karpatorus*. Jerusalem: 1959.
Erez, Yehudah, ed. *Sefer Ha'aliyah Hashlishit*. Tel Aviv: 1964.
Essco Foundation. *A Study of Jewish, Arab, and British Policies*. Yale University Press: 1947.
Feigenbaum, M. J. *Bi'ala-Podluska*. Tel Aviv: 1961.
Finkelstein, Louis. *The Jews, Their History, Culture, and Religion*. New York: 1949.
Friedman, Theodore. *Jewish Life in America*. New York: 1955.
Friedner, Yekutiel. *Toldot Hadorot Ha'acharonim*. Jerusalem: 1968.
Gan Zevi, Yisrael. *Hamadrich L'Yisrael Hadatit*. Tel Aviv: 1958.
Garcia-Granados, Jorge. *The Birth of Israel*. New York: 1948.
Garfinkel, Leib and Goren, N. eds. *Yahadut Lita*. Tel Aviv: 1959.
Gartner, Lloyd P. *Jewish Education in the United States*. New York: 1969.
Gat, Ben Zion. *Hayishuv Hayehudi B'Eretz Yisrael*. Tel Aviv: 1963.
Gershuni, A. A. *Yahadut B'Russia Hasovietit*. Jerusalem: 1961.
Gilbert, Martin. *Exile and Return*. Philadelphia: 1978.
Golub, Jacob Solomon. *Jewish Immigration Into Palestine*. New York: 1937.
Grade, Chaim. *The Yeshiva*. New York: 1979.
Goldstein, Israel. *A Century of Judaism in New York*. New York: 1930.
Grayzel, Simon. *A History of the Jews*. Philadelphia: 1947.

Habas, Braha. *Choma Umigdal.* Tel Aviv: 1939.
Hapgood, Hutchins. *Spirit of the Ghetto.* New York: 1902.
Hazany, Michael Jacob. *Misedei Yaakov ad Tirat Tzvi.* Tel Aviv: 1938.
Hazany, Michael Jacob. *Hitsyashvut Hadatit al Admat Hale'am.* Jerusalem: 1951.
Heichal Shlomo. *Shana B'Shana.* Jerusalem: Annual.
Heller, Alan S. *On the Edge of Destruction.* New York: 1977.
Helmreich, William B. *The World of the Yeshiva.* New York: 1982.
Herzog, Chaim. *The Arab-Israeli Wars.* New York: 1982.
Hilberg, Raul. *The Destruction of European Jewry.* Chicago: 1961.
Hindus, Milton. *The Old East Side.* Philadelphia: 1969.
Horowitz, David. *State in the Making.* New York: 1953.
Hull, William Z. *The Fall and Rise of Israel.* Grand Rapids, Mich.: 1954.
Hyamson, A. M. *Palestine Under the Mandate.* London: 1950.
Infield, Henrik, E. *Cooperative Living in Palestine.* New York: 1948.
Jewish Agency. *Sixteen Years of Immigration to Israel.* Jerusalem: 1964.
Jewish Agency. *Sixteen Years of Immigrant Absorption.* Jerusalem: 1964.
Joseph, Dov. *The Faithful City.* New York: 1960.
Kanc, S. ed. *Sefer Bursztyn.* Jerusalem: 1960.
Kaplan, Chaim A. *Megilot Yissurim.* Tel Aviv: 1967.
Kaplinski, Baruch. *Pinkas Zshetl.* Tel Aviv: 1957.
Kimchi, Jon and David. *The Secret Roads.* New York: 1955.
Kohn, Eugene. *The Future of Judaism in America.* New Rochelle: 1934.
Lador, Yitzchak. *Hityashvutenu Ba'aretz.* Tel Aviv: 1952.
Laqueur, Walter. *A History of Zionism.* New York: 1979.
Laqueur, Walter. *The Road to Jerusalem.* London: 1968.
Lazar, Hayyim. *Af Al Pi, Sefer Aliyah B.* Tel Aviv: 1957.
Lehrman, Hal. *Israel, The Beginning and Tomorrow.* New York: 1951.
Lestschinsky, Y. *Das Sovietische Yudentum.* New York: 1941.
Levinger, Lee J. *The Jewish Student in America.* New York: 1937.
Levontin, Zalman David. *Hahityashvut B'Eretz Yisrael.* Tel Aviv: 1925.

Levontin, Zalman David. *L'Eretz Avoteinu.* Tel Aviv: 1924.
Lewin, Isaac. *Eleh Ezkerah.* New York: 1956.
Lewinsky, Y. T. *Sefer Zambrow.* Tel Aviv: 1963.
Liptzin, Sol. *Generation of Decision.* New York: 1958.
Lorch, N. *Edge of the Sword.* New York: 1961.
Maizlish, Rabbi Z. H. *Mikdeshei Hashem.* Brooklyn: 1967.
Maza, Eli Mordecai. *Ahavat Hatorah.* New York: 1943.
'Mendele Mokher Sforim. *Ale Shriften.* New York: 1910.
Mendelsohm. *The Jews of East Central Europe Between the Two World Wars.* Indiana University Press: 1983.
Mirsky, S. K. *Mosdot Hatorah B'Europa.* New York: 1958.
Morris, Yaakov. *Pioneers from the West.* Jerusalem: 1953.
Morse, A. P. *While Six Million Died.* New York: 1967.
Nachmani, Samson. *Pinkas Slutzk.* New York: 1962.
Nadav, Zevi. *Kach Hitchalnu.* Tel Aviv: 1957.
Nardi, Noah. *Education in Palestine.* New York: 1945.
Nissenbaum, Isaac. *Hadat V'Hatechiya Halomit.* Warsaw: 1920.
Nulman, Louis. *The Parent and the Jewish Day School.* Scranton: 1956.
Oshry, Efroim. *Churban Lita.* New York: 1951.
Pilch, Judah. *The Jewish Catastrophe in Europe.* New York: 1968.
Prager, Moshe. *Bitekufat Hasho'ah.* Jerusalem: 1945.
Nathan, M. *The Attitude of the Jewish Student.* New York: 1932.
Rabinowitz, Chaim Dov. *Tamtzit Divrei Yemei Yisrael.* Jerusalem: New York.
Rieger, Eliezer. *Hachinuch Haivri B'Eretz Yisrael.* Tel Aviv: 1940.
Ringelblum, Emanuel. *Notes from the Warsaw Ghetto.* New York: 1958.
Robinson, Donald. *Under Fire.* New York: 1968.
Robinson, Jacob. *And the Crooked Shell be Made Straight.* New York: 1965.
Sachar, Howard Morley. *A History of Israel.* New York: 1958.
Scharfstein, Zvi. *History of Jewish Education.* New York: 1959.
Scharfstein, Zvi. *Toldot Hachinuch B'Yisrael.* Jerusalem: 1965.
Schneiderman, Harry. *Two Generations in Perspective.* New York: 1957.
Schonfeld, Moshe. *Genocide in the Holy Land.* New York: 1980.
Schwarz, Lee W. *The Redeemers.* New York: 1953.

Shachrai, A. *Dat Umoledet, Hachareidim Bevinyan Haarez.* Tel Aviv: 1938.
Shereshevsky, Robert. *Meah Shana V'ad Esrim Medinat Yisrael.* Jerusalem: 1968.
Shtokfish, D. ed. *Sefer Frampol.* Tel Aviv: 1966.
Shtokfish, D. ed. *Sefer Wyszkow:* Tel Aviv: 1964.
Sinai, Robert and Anne eds. *Israel and the Arabs.* New York: 1972.
Soustelle, Jacques. *The Long March of Israel.* New York: 1969.
Stein, Abraham Samuel. *Pinkas Kletzk.* Tel Aviv: 1959.
Tenenblatt, M. A. ed. *Sefer Ozieran Vehaseviva.* Jerusalem:
United Palestine Appeal. *The Jewish Settlements in Palestine.* New York: 1940.
Vishniac, Roman. *Polish Jews—A Pictorial Record.* New York: 1947.
Waxman, Meyer. *History of Jewish Literature.* Cranbury, New Jersey: 1960.
World Association of Former Residents of Mlava. *Pinkas Mlava.* New York: 1950.
Yasheev, Z. ed. *Opatow.* Tel Aviv: 1966.

179.9
mz

Maza, Bernard.
With fury poured out

DATE DUE

BETH HILLEL LIBRARY
WILMETTE, ILLINOIS

WITHDRAWN